Breaking the Iron Wall

Breaking the Iron Wall

Decommodification and Immigrant Women's Labor in Canada

Habiba Zaman

LEXINGTON BOOKS

A division of
ROWMAN & LITTLEFIELD PUBLISHERS, INC.
Lanham • Boulder • New York • Toronto • Oxford

JV7284 .Z36 2006
0134110482863
Zaman, Habiba.

Breaking the iron wall :
 decommodification and
   c2006.

2008 01 03

LEXINGTON BOOKS

A division of Rowman & Littlefield Publishers, Inc.
A wholly owned subsidiary of The Rowman & Littlefield Publishing Group, Inc.
4501 Forbes Boulevard, Suite 200
Lanham, MD 20706

PO Box 317
Oxford
OX2 9RU, UK

Copyright © 2006 by Lexington Books

All rights reserved. No part of this publication may be reproduced, stored in a retrieval system, or transmitted in any form or by any means, electronic, mechanical, photocopying, recording, or otherwise, without the prior permission of the publisher.

British Library Cataloguing in Publication Information Available

Library of Congress Cataloging-in-Publication Data

Zaman, Habiba.
 Breaking the iron wall : decommodification and immigrant women's labor in Canada / Habiba Zaman.
   p. cm.
 Includes bibliographical references and index.
 ISBN-13: 978-0-7391-1235-9 (cloth : alk. paper)
 ISBN-10: 0-7391-1235-X (cloth : alk. paper)
 1. Women immigrants—Government policy—Canada. 2. Women alien labor—Canada. I. Title.
JV7284.Z36 2006
325.71082—dc22   2006010215

Printed in the United States of America

∞™ The paper used in this publication meets the minimum requirements of American National Standard for Information Sciences—Permanence of Paper for Printed Library Materials, ANSI/NISO Z39.48-1992.

To my mother, Jamila Khatun, and in memory of
my father, Abdul Hamid Khan

Contents

Preface		ix
1	Introduction	1
2	Globalization, Neo-Liberal Globalism, and Migration	21
3	Canadian Immigration in an Era of Neo-Liberalism: Trends and Impacts	39
4	The Canadian State and Immigrant Labor: Intersections of Gender, Class, and Race	61
5	Commodification of Laborers: "Defamilializing" the Privileged and "Refeudalizing" the Im/Migrants	73
6	Decommodification and Immigrant Women: Access to Social Benefits and Services	91
7	Recommodification of Labor: Results of Re-Skilling	115
8	Immigrant Women as Agents of Change: The Role of Networks and Associations	135
9	Summary and Conclusions	155
Appendix: Demographic Profiles of the Interviewees		161
Bibliography		169
Index		181
About the Author		187

Preface

The book addresses primarily the processes of commodification and the prospects of decommodification of immigrant women's labor in Canada. The book has also focused on the family/household, which has been a non- or under-commodified sector, but has increasingly shifted to a commodified sector under the restructuring of neo-liberalism. Distinguishing between commodified and decommodified sectors, the book examines various layers of commodification pertinent to immigrant women's labor. This book brings important contributions by exploring the concept of commodification and the contested but under-developed concept of decommodification pertinent to various sectors as well as immigrant women's labor.

Using a broad political economy theoretical framework and a feminist lens, this enquiry has undertaken a multi-method research including participatory collaborative research with the Philippine Women Centre in Vancouver, British Columbia, Canada. Sixty-four women from South and South-east Asia—the racialized immigrants—were interviewed for this study. These women represented neither a typical picture nor a gross generalization in terms of age, class, ethnicity, education, language, religion, and so on. Rather, they reflected the diversity of the organization of commodification of labor and the dynamics and prospects of decommodification of immigrant labor while revealing the intersections of gender, class and race. However, through various organizations, immigrant women demonstrate their agency to act and to resist oppressive forces in the workplace as well as in the wider society. The strength of this book lies in its centrality of the experiences of immigrant women in the labor market to be decommodified. This is not to suggest that only immigrant women's labor needs to be decommodified, but clarifies the focus of this book. Immigrant women are also part of the casual/flexible workforce in the larger Canadian economy, which itself offers fertile ground for other researchers.

The title *Breaking the Iron Wall* is a term used in one of the interviews, and it reflects the struggles immigrant women face to "make it" in Canada. As a metaphor, "breaking the iron wall" represents the core of the book and is illustrated throughout the book in multiple ways, including in the narration of the women interviewed.

The book is comprised of nine chapters. The first chapter lays out the background information as well as the theoretical and methodological framework of the book. The chapter illustrates some of the key concepts that will guide the readers in comprehending the significant arguments and analyses of the book. Chapter 2 advocates for the use of both macro-level and micro-level processes to understand the intersections of globalization and migration. Chapter 3 demonstrates how the "marketization of the state" is reflected in immigration policies that have shifted the demographic trend from Europe to Asia. Through tables and diagrams, this chapter illustrates various immigration trends at the beginning of the 21st century. Providing a historical overview of gendered, racialized and class-based immigration policies, chapter 4 delineates how immigrant labor has contributed to Canada's nation-building process. Examining the Live-in Caregiver Program (LCP), this chapter demonstrates how Canada has legitimized full commodification of immigrant women's labor in a previously non- or under-commodified sector while decommodifying privileged women's labor. The narrations of immigrant women in chapters 5 and 6 demonstrate how their labor stabilizes the labor market by entering into different levels of commodification. The key question raised in chapter 6 is this: How do the federal government and individual provincial governments pave the way for immigrant women's labor to be decommodified? Chapter 7 reveals immigrant women's futile efforts to decommodify their labor—efforts that ultimately lead their labor being recommodified. By examining some immigrant women's groups, chapter 8 describes how immigrant women act as agents of change, to contest immigrant women's exploitation, including racism and sexism in the workplace, and mobilize against the processes that block the decommodification of immigrant women's labor. Chapter 9, the concluding chapter, recommends an agenda for future research that could focus on how to decommodify immigrant women's labor while creating an inclusive society in Canada, where every individual irrespective of race, gender, class and nationality has access to certain social entitlements.

This book is an outcome of a SSHRC (Social Sciences and Humanities Research Council of Canada)–MCRI (Major Collaborative Research Initiative)–funded international multidisciplinary project titled *Neo-liberal Globalism and Its Challengers*, generally known as the Globalism Project, from

2000 to 2005. The research project for this book was first conceived when I received funds from Simon Fraser University's SSHRC Small Research Grant in 1999. However, the book project developed out of the Globalism Project. Earlier drafts of this work—mostly in the form of papers—were presented at globalism conferences held over the years in Mexico City (2002), Bergen (2003), and Adelaide (2005) and at national conferences in Canada such as Canadian Sociology and Anthropology Association meetings, Canadian Women's Studies Association meetings in Toronto, Halifax and Winnipeg from 2002 to 2004, and so on. Part of chapter 5 has appeared in the following publication: "Transnational Migration and the Commodification of Im/Migrant Female Labourers in Canada," *International Journal of Canadian Studies* 29 (2004).

I would like to express my gratitude to my colleague Marjorie Griffin Cohen, who recruited me as a member of the Globalism project. This international and multi-disciplinary project provided me with an enormous opportunity to enhance my knowledge pertinent to immigrants' and migrants' labor in semi-periphery countries such as Australia, Canada, Norway and Mexico although for this book I narrowed down my focus to Canada only. I am also thankful to Marjorie for her incisive comments on an earlier version of this manuscript. Special thanks go to Gordon Laxer and Satoshi Ikeda of the University of Alberta, Rhonda Sharp of the University of South Australia, Adelaide, and retired Professor Louise Sweet of the University of Manitoba, who read an earlier draft of a paper and offered invaluable comments that helped me to sharpen my focus. This book would not be possible without the support of Simon Fraser University's Dean of Arts Office for released time from teaching; thus, my sincere thanks go to John Pierce and his support staff. Acknowledgements are also due to Kathy Trulsen of Financial Services and work-study project students who have collected archival, website, published and unpublished materials, particularly Lee Anne Clarke, Shelly Fahey, Karen Singh, Heather Chase, Mohammad Kabir, Gina Tubajon, Nadia Kanani, and Joy Sioson for her time and commitment. Katie Funk of Lexington Books generously assisted me in bringing the project to its final stage. Thanks to Katie and the anonymous reviewers for useful comments on the manuscript.

My deepest appreciation goes to all the women who participated in this project despite their hectic schedules. I am deeply indebted to Cecilia Diocson for her generous support and to numerous volunteers of the Philippine Women Centre who assisted me in various ways. My sincere thanks go to two research assistants—Sanzida Zohra Habib for transcribing fourteen interviews and Rebecca Scott for compiling immigrant women's profiles as well as formatting the manuscript.

Writing is a solitary process, and going through this process is an arduous task. My children—Ayesha and Asif—provided me pleasures in this solitary process and accepted respectfully my absence in their daily lives. I thank both of them for respecting my work and for their expressed pride in the book project. I particularly thank my life-long companion Mohammad Zaman, who provided me intellectual and emotional help when I needed it most. Without his unconditional support and encouragement, this book project would not have reached fruition.

—Habiba Zaman

1

Introduction

A central concept for socialism and the critique of capitalism is commodification.... And now as we enter an era of so-called globalization more than a hundred and fifty years after Marx's death, it is the commodification of previously non- or "under-" commodified social sectors that is seen as one of the core changes of the process. (McMurty 2001: 5)

[L]*abour is changing in ways that make it a more inclusive social agent.* The main developments here have been women's massive (re)entry into the labour force and changing patterns of migration. (Panitch 2001: 369)

THE STUDY OBJECTIVES

Migrations are as old as human history. In ancient times, people chose to migrate either for survival or for better environment. With the advent of capitalism, labor migration has become in large part determined or encouraged by capital's initiative.

According to the International Organization of Migration (1995), major global factors such as colonization, industrialization, and economic liberalism have profoundly influenced international migration. In the current era of globalization, the increased circulation of capital, goods and information has in turn increased the mobility of people internationally. Recent trends indicate that Europe's standing as the dominant source of migrants has declined while Asian countries as sources of migrants have gained predominance (Counting on Diversity 1998). The deregulation and marketization of services as well as the privatization of social sectors due to neo-liberal policies have intensified the demands for laborers, especially female laborers in certain sectors, in both core and semi-periphery countries. Despite the dearth of global data on female migrants, the United Nations estimates that "As of 2000, 49 percent of all international migrants were women or girls, and the proportion of females among international migrants had reached 51 percent in more developed regions" (2005: iii). Thus, female migrants are increasingly entering the international labor market. These migrant female laborers are key components of mostly female-dominated social sectors, which, as the first opening quote indicates, are changing under neo-liberal globalism.

After the end of World War II, almost all core countries such as the US and Western Europe and some semi-periphery countries such as Canada and Australia began campaigns to obtain immigrants as well as temporary migrants because immigrant labor had become indispensable for the reconstruction of post-war national economies. Gradually, immigrant-receiving countries such as Canada began competing to recruit the "most desirable" candidates, meaning those with the best education from the sending countries and with the least racial dissimilarities to its residents. Heightened by liberalization and trade agreements between states, as well as by the development of labor import and the export policies of core, semi-periphery and periphery countries, economic globalization made labor even more mobile. In the process, immigrants' work became largely confined to low-paid, repetitive, temporary, and monotonous labor; furthermore, immigrant laborers' credentials, skills, and rights eroded. Consequently, immigrants have become commodified, their labor bought and sold for the benefit of national and global markets. This commodification of labor has become especially true for immigrant women, and the processes involved are more tangible due to these women's massive entry into the labor force.

This book focuses primarily on the processes of commodification and the prospects of decommodification of immigrant female laborers in Canada. The flow of immigrant workers into Canada since the end of World War II coincides with the demise of the colonies and the emergence of new nation-states, a subject wide in scope. This book restricts its investigation to immigration or in-migration, not emigration or out-migration. By providing empirical as well as historical evidence, this book undertakes a rigorous analysis of immigrant women's commodification and the possibility of their decommodification in Canada, a liberal welfare state. I argue that neo-liberal globalism, through deregulation, restructuring, and privatization, facilitates the commodification of immigrant women's labor in three major ways: by restricting their social mobility through numerous stipulations, by denying the credentials and skills these women have acquired in their countries of origin, and by setting up strict but ambiguous and costly procedures.

It is evident that neo-liberal globalism has been restructuring the government apparatus of Canada while destroying public sectors such as education, childcare, eldercare, housing, health, and transport in the name of efficiency. This restructuring has had far-reaching consequences for immigrant women. A study of transnational migration, globalization, and the immigration policies of Canada both reveals the processes through which immigrant women workers move toward commodification and unfolds intersections of gender, class and race. To present a comprehensive picture of commodification, this book explores the relationship between transnational migration and globalization, a relationship that sets the trajectory for immigrant women's commodification. Many semi-periphery countries[1] have been experiencing labor market shortages in certain sectors of the economy, and these shortages are mostly filled by short-term contract labor or immigrant labor. This book delineates the immigration policies of Canada as an example of a semi-peripheral country that creates an environment where immigrant women become commodified when placed in market relations.

TO WHOM DOES "IMMIGRANT" REFER?

The term "immigrant" has legal, social, class, and racial connotations. Legally, the concept of immigrant refers to those who are landed immigrants rather than citizens. While this technicality confers a certain legal status in Canada, the legal concept in everyday usage includes permanent residents, people with landed status, and so on. In addition to permanent residents, Canada has a large number of visa workers, ranging from students who have short-term work permits to seasonal farm laborers from Mexico who work for less than six months in Ontario, Quebec, Alberta, and Manitoba. For example, in 1999, Canada had 200,000 to 300,000 visa workers, who, according to the definition of the Migrant Worker Convention, were identified as "migrant workers" (Clark 2000: 1). Under Canada's Live-in Caregiver Program (LCP), domestics who migrate to Canada as temporary workers are frequently called "visa workers," "migrant workers," or "work permit holders," even though the majority of these are granted landed status after serving two to three years as domestics. The potential to acquire first permanent residency and then Canadian citizenship attracts many domestics to work as live-in caregivers. Further, any "migrant worker," "visa worker" or "work permit holder" living in Canada is legally allowed[2] to apply for permanent status, which indicates that migrant workers have prospects for gaining immigrant status eventually.

Scholars do not consistently use just one definition for immigrants. Some scholars suggest that most migrants become immigrants who still participate in the politics of their home country despite residence in host countries (Schiller and Basch 1995; Mahler 1999). Schiller and Basch in fact do not distinguish between immigrants and migrants: "(*Trans*)*migrants* are *immigrants* whose daily lives depend on multiple and constant interconnections across international borders and whose public identities are configured in relationship to more than one nation-state" (1995: 48). In contrast, Ng (1993) refers to immigrants in a way that reflects more societal perceptions rather than legal connotations; only certain groups are identified as immigrant—usually people who are visibly different (i.e., ethnically and culturally), who have accents or cannot speak English properly, and who hold a certain position in the labor market, such as a cleaning person. In this sense, the term "immigrant" carries both classist and racist notions that overshadow the legal framework. Ng's definition includes all non-English-speaking people in Canada regardless of gender, class, race, and nationalities. However, Ng's definition excludes French-speaking people.

In this book, the term "immigrant" is used comprehensively, ranging from migrant/visa workers to permanent residents (i.e., immigrants) to immigrants who have attained citizenship,[3] regardless of gender, class, and race. This book refers to English-speaking Canada only. It is worth noting that Schiller and Basch's contention is correct, that in Canada that most migrants become immigrants. Most of the interviewees quoted or described in this book are permanent residents/Canadian citizens and a few prospective immigrants who eventually become immigrants—(for example, domestic workers discussed in chapter 5).

WHY ARE GLOBALISM AND GLOBALIZATION IMPORTANT?

In the past twenty years, the globalism paradigm has been described by numerous terms: Structural Adjustment Programs, the Washington Consensus, Liberal Productivism, Neo-Liberal Globalism, and the New World Order. However it is described, globalism shows clearly the homogeneity of an ideology of governance: neo-liberal principles and policies such as reducing expenditures in public sectors, deregulating markets, privatizing public sectors, removing foreign exchange restrictions, and minimizing state intervention. Neo-liberal policies have been prescribed and implemented in some form in almost every country in the world.

Today, globalism can be described as neo-liberal globalism, an ideology that reflects the norms, institutions, and laws supporting global capital accumulation according to neo-liberal principles. States are currently oriented toward adjusting their national economies to meet globalism's imperatives, and all governments are connected to world financial markets. Globalism is clearly the dominant ideology in an integrated world economy.

Globalism is often confused with globalization. Globalization, an empirical concept, refers to the transnational flow of goods, labor, information, and communication technologies. Globalism is the ideology while globalization refers to the process. In academic discourse, transnational migration is linked frequently with the acceleration of globalization (Castles 1998; Cohen 1997; Hefti 1997; Taran 1999), and chapter 2 of this book examines this discourse. To date there has been almost no first-hand information examining neo-liberal globalism in relation to transnational migration and immigrant women workers' commodification or decommodification, as the case may be. When it exists, literature deals with core countries such as the US. However, even the limited literature recognizes that globalization has enabled transnational migrants and citizen groups to forge local, national and international links to contest globalism (Goodman 2002). Chapter 8 examines how immigrant women's groups build up links with various local as well as national and international organizations to contest commodification and barriers of decommodification as well as genderized and racialized labor in Canada.

WHAT IS "SEMI-PERIPHERY"?

The main beneficiaries of globalism and the globalization processes are the core countries, as few challengers to the status quo exist. Periphery countries such as the Philippines, India, Pakistan, and Bangladesh are powerless to contest globalism and are the main casualties of globalism and globalization. This book looks at Canada as an example of a semi-periphery country. The term "semi-periphery" has been borrowed from Wallerstein's world systems theory, but the concept is being used differently here. In world systems theory, the state, class and external forces play dynamic roles in transnational migration, and the role of domestic politics—for example, immigration policies and the welfare regime, gender and social movements—as actors of change in an era of globalization is downplayed, whereas in this book it is highlighted.

Canada has been variously described as one of the go-between nations, intermediate developing countries, semi-satellite countries, or resource-exporting economies. Each of these categories, including the term "semi-periphery" itself, carries a rich theoretical and empirical background defying easy categorization. In this book, "semi-periphery" is used to refer to a country that is Western-centered and has enjoyed more economic sovereignty than most of the "developing" countries.[4] The term "semi-periphery" is linked not only to economic divisions of the world, but also to cultural, social, and political-military divisions. Moreover, the semi-periphery creates a provocative environment from which to study both the dynamics of globalization and the resistance to globalism. Delineating the possibility of the emergence of political movements in semi-periphery countries, Chase-Dunn (1990) predicts that semi-periphery states will continuously challenge the capitalist mode of production and produce better possibilities for transformation than in core and peripheral countries. Here lies the significance and usefulness of semi-periphery states.

This enquiry refers to an economic semi-periphery measured by Gross Domestic Product (GDP) rather than to a political semi-periphery measured by military power.[5] As semi-periphery, Canada procures benefits when it interacts with periphery countries. Chapter 4 delineates the processes of these benefits. Through state-controlled immigration, Canada annually brings in a quarter of a million immigrants to supply its labor economy. Currently, most of these immigrants come from periphery countries in Asia. Chapter 3 examines Canada's current immigration policies and reveals the socio-cultural-political implications that arise under neo-liberal policies. Through its state-controlled immigration policies, Canada reproduces the hierarchy of the world economy when it addresses its labor shortage through import policies.

HOW CAN THE WELFARE STATE BE CLARIFIED?

Several scholars (Esping-Andersen 1990; Leira 1992; Michel and Mahon 2002; O'Connor, Orloff and Shaver 1999; Quadagno 1994) have used the concept of "welfare state" in their studies. However, no universal and explicit definition of the welfare state exists despite the wide use of terms such as welfare societies, welfare regimes, and welfare policies, and even analysis of a welfare state may miss significant variations among various parts—for example, "a welfare state may have a good health policy, but a poor housing policy" (Powell and Hewitt 2002: 19). Canada, like other welfare regimes, is "undergoing restructuring in response to contemporary challenges" (Mahon and Phillips 2002: 192). For example, after the 2004 general election and forging a minority government, the prime minister's declaration of increased spending for health indicates Canada's willingness to preserve its welfare policy in medicare rather than in childcare.

Esping-Andersen (1990) has classified three broad typologies of welfare state regimes: liberal, conservative and social democratic. Liberal regimes foster market provisions of services. Canada, Australia, Great Britain, and the US are liberal regimes. Variations among these countries' social policies in the domestic arena occur according to the political party in power. For example, the recent backlash in Australia against Asians, the fear by some of an "Asianization of Australia," reflects the policies of the Liberal party in power.[6]

Feminists have also analyzed the relationship between women and the welfare state and similarly have reached no consensus. Two feminist streams of thought generally emerge: one perceives the welfare state as patriarchal and consequently, oppressive (Dalla Costa and James 1975; Eisenstein 1979; Seacomb 1974) and the other perceives the welfare state as promoting potentially women-friendly policies.[7] As an example of the former, Leira (1992) finds a "patriarchal partnership" between the state and working mothers in Scandinavia and refutes the widely supported view of an egalitarian alliance between the welfare state and women there. In contrast to scholars who believe that Scandinavia has reached the peak evolution of the welfare state, Leira reveals the contradictions of the welfare state and shows that the welfare state has shifted women in Scandinavia from private to public dependence—what can be labeled as a transformation from private to public patriarchy (1992). While Leira's analysis centers on gender issues, it bypasses class and race issues. On the other hand, Quadagno's analysis centers on race and reveals that welfare policies are racialized in the US, perpetuating racial divisions in life chances and living standards: "The equal opportunity of the welfare state was replaced by a welfare state that encouraged racial isolation and the concentration of the black poor in inner cities" (1994: 197). Quadagno has eloquently pointed out how the racialized policy in the US, a liberal welfare state, perpetuates racial divisions in terms of housing, neighborhoods, and labor market. Nyberg (2002) argues that Scandinavian researchers frequently focus on the contradictory nature of the welfare state, revealing the state through its various social policies that reproduce power relationships between women and men. Similarly, Canadian researchers (Agnew 1996; Armstrong and Armstrong 1994; Calliste 1991) have shown that the discriminatory practices of the state reproduce hierarchical relationships between women and men; however, there is scant attention paid to the contradictory nature of the welfare state as it pertains to immigrant women workers. An exploration of the historical background of immigration can shed light on whether the welfare state aspires to promote equality or simply reproduces power relationships that generate genderized, class-based and racialized divisiveness. Through exploring the history of Canada's immigration, chapter 4 of this book investigates the contradictions of the welfare state when it deals with immigrants of dissimilar gender, class and race and consequently produces a gendered, class-based and racialized society.

WHY INVESTIGATE COMMODIFICATION AND DECOMMODIFICATION OF LABOR?

Many scholars (Burke 2000; Esping-Andersen 1999; McMurty 2001; Miliband 1994; Offe 1984; Polanyi 1957) have used the concepts of "commodification" and "decommodification" to explore the limitations as well as the fundamental contradictions of the welfare state. The term "commodification" is a dissected one that Marxists, neo-Marxists and feminist scholars refer to critically when they deal with labor (Armstrong and Armstrong 1994; Esping-Andersen 1990, 1999; McMurty 2001; Vosko 2000). Although widely used in the case of labor, albeit male labor, the concept of commodification is rarely used in the case of female labor, let alone immigrant female labor, especially if it is related to social reproduction—that is, childcare, eldercare and household maintenance. Use of the concept of commodification in this book has been influenced by Esping-Andersen's work (1990, 1999), which argues that women's economic role is frequently non-commodified or partially commodified (1999: 44), as well as by McMurty (2001: 5), who considers that the former non- or under-commodified sectors have been changed and shifted to commodified sectors. The concept as used in this book has also been enhanced by Burke (2000) who argues that commodification indicates an increasing reliance on the market to do things cheaper and faster through the private sector. Further, recent works (Giddings, Dingeldey and Ulbricht 2004; Nyberg 2002; Williams 2002; Williams and Windebank 2003) have solidified the portrayal of these concepts, that is, commodified and decommodified, as frequently contested but not contradictory. All of these works are illustrated in chapters 5 and 6.

Throughout this book, the analyses of immigrant women's labor—both paid and unpaid—have used a wide range of terminologies with regard to commodification. Influenced by Burke (2000), Esping-Andersen (1990, 1999) and McMurty's (2001) works, I have illustrated immigrant women's labor with numerous examples pertinent to this study. However, Burke (2000), Esping-Andersen (1990, 1999) and McMurty (2001) never mentioned immigrants, let alone immigrant women's albeit racialized women's labor. As far as I know, immigrant women's labor is neither a focal point in the literature on commodification and decommodification in Canada nor an issue in the works cited above. Rather, I find Esping-Andersen's reference to a "pre-commodified" status problematic and consequently, have not used the term in this study. The concept "pre-commodified" preconceives labor being commodified in the future and for several reasons may not apply to all immigrant women's labor in Canada. For example, for various reasons some immigrant women do not intend to join the labor force: economic privilege, aging (e.g., parents of adult immigrants), or necessity to maintain a household for the extended family. In this book, the concepts of commodification and decommodification underlie the theoretical framework within which immigrant women's paid and unpaid labor is being investigated. When comparing immigrant women's labor with Canadian-born women's labor and disadvantaged populations' labor, different layers of commodification of labor may generate some useful insight and comparison. However, this book examines only immigrant women's labor. Further, the book has focused on the family/household that was mostly a non- or under-commodified sector in the pre-welfare state, as is illustrated in chapter 5. Commodified sectors are those where state regulations are absent. In this book, commodified sectors refer to some families/households. Decommodified sectors are those where state regulations exist. Examples are schools, hospitals, and so on.

This book looks at commodification and its various layers, such as "non-commodification," "under-commodification," and "partial commodification," as they pertain to immigrant women's labor. "Commodification" applies where market relations exist. For example, first through the Canadian Domestic Scheme and later through the Live-in Caregiver Program (LCP), the family, a non- or under-commodified sector, turned into a commodified sector where services could be bought and the relationship, that is, employer and domestic worker, was contractual. Commodification is typified by the absence of family obligations and the existence of an employer-employee relationship. This contractual relationship preserves a hierarchical power relationship, which can lead to exploitative and oppressive situations due to the private nature of households, where monitoring of work conditions does not exist.

"Non-commodification" applies where market relations do not prevail; services are based on blood or marital or fictive relationships, and neither purchasing nor selling of services exists. In other words, services are based on personal relationship and mutual understanding. "Non-commodification" should not be confused or exchanged with "pre-commodification," which, as was discussed above, indicates the possibility of being commodified in the future and represents the stage before commodification.

"Under-commodification" applies where complete market relations and full contractual relations are absent; here services may be bought intermittently and employer-employee relationships conducted without the state's interference. For example, a parent can hire someone to take care of young children for a few hours without either legally binding or contractual obligations. In this case, the employer-employee relationship relies on convenience and satisfaction for both parties. A relationship between master and servant is not ruled out, but the service is not bought by entering into the market. The under-commodified sector is a blurred zone, with a boundary that is fluid and continuously changing.

"Partial commodification" applies where workers are by the nature of their labor both commodified and non-commodified. For example, after receiving immigrant status and subsequently citizenship, domestics have access to the entitlements of a welfare state such as training, education, health, and so on. However, de-skilling processes trap immigrant women's labor in commodified positions such as live-out domestics and caregivers for the elderly and make immigrant women non-commodified in their own households. This duality, being both commodified and non-commodified, places domestics in the partial commodification category. This is a fluid category because domestic workers may move from partial to full commodification if their situations change. Thus, in this book, in the case of domestic workers, the terms "commodification" and "partial commodification" are used interchangeably.

Since the 1980s, several scholars (e.g., Achtenberg and Marcuse 1983; Esping-Andersen 1985, 1990, 1999; Offe 1984) have examined the concept of decommodification as it pertains to labor and to social sectors (housing, health care, education, transport, and so on). Decommodification appears as an issue in many countries, ranging from "autonomy from paid work" in Sweden[8] to "the decommodification of low-wage labor" in the US[9] (Nyberg 2002: 63; Giddings, Dingeldey and Ulbricht 2004: 131). However, decommodification as a concept is both contested and under-developed. This concept can be utilized to explore all low-wage women's and men's labor. Further, some Canadian women, regardless of age, sexual orientation, class and dis/ability, are disadvantaged in the labor market and hence, their labor is not decommodified. In the book, the point of reference is low-wage immigrant women's labor. Exploration of the possibility of decommodification of low-wage immigrant labor, especially immigrant women's labor, is a daunting task, as relevant literature[10] does not specifically address this issue. Indeed, the concept of decommodification, as far as I know, has never been used in immigrant's labor, let alone immigrant women's labor. In this chapter, immigrant women's narrations will be used to explore the potential of decommodification of low-wage immigrant women's labor[11] in Canada. It is significant to point out that the decommodification of labor is a major issue for all disadvantaged groups in Canada, such as low-wage women and men, young Canadians, people with disabilities, single parents, aboriginal populations, and so on. Hence, the issue of decommodification of low-wage immigrant women's labor is pertinent to the larger population. However, for immigrant women, racialized, gendered and class-based immigration as well as the labor market brings a different dimension to their entry into Canada as well as to the decommodification of their labor.

The concept of decommodification was first used by Polanyi (1957) and later was refined by Offe (1984). Both Polanyi and Offe brought attention to social citizenship rights and pointed out that welfare states, independent of market participation, grant a wide range of benefits. Decommodified areas also exist in capitalist economies; following World War II, bottom-level pressures ensured that access to education, health and other social services were social rights inherent in citizenship irrespective of one's economic abilities (Miliband 1994). This "bottom-level" encompassed various community groups, trade unions, social activists and so on, who had visions of social rights and entitlements.

The concept of decommodification is a controversial issue, and no consensus exists about the degree and nature of decommodification in a welfare state. The concept of decommodification with regard to immigrant women's labor in Canada has never explored, and here lies the significance of using this contested concept in this book. This concept can be extensively used with regard to disadvantaged groups, such as lone parents' paid labor, casual/temporary workers' labor, and so on. In his works (1985, 1990, 1999), Esping-Andersen has extensively dealt with the issue of decommodification, cautioning that social democrats and conservatives both refer to decommodification, but in contexts that denote different meanings. In this book, I use the social democrats' notion of decommodification to a limited extent, that is, by exploring this concept within the context of Canada, which has a liberal and not a social democratic welfare state. In short, decommodification of labor in this book generally refers to the conferring of social benefits—employment insurance, sickness benefits, pensions, vacation and extended health care benefits. A thorough investigation of commodification and decommodification of immigrant women's labor demonstrates the nature and extent of restructuring under neo-liberal policies and reveals the welfare state's contradictory actions that eventually produce gendered, class-based and racialized labor.

HOW ARE GENDER, CLASS, AND RACE LINKED TO THE IMMIGRATION PROCESS?

This book attempts to examine sexual, racial, and class oppression from the standpoint of immigrant women and to provide insights into the intersections of gender, class and race in both public and private domains. Critical race and anti-racism scholars argue for the centrality of race as a major organizing principle of social life and point out how race is mediated through other forms of social difference, such as gender and class (Dei 1996; Leah 1995). This book is not adopting an anti-racist framework but does point out how gender, class and race (in some cases, age too) intersect in immigrant women's narrations. However, the book does not suggest that all oppressions are equal and the same. Rather it reflects what other researchers (e.g. Bishop 1994) have said—that all oppressions are to some extent interconnected and none can be eradicated in isolation. In looking at the detailed lived experiences of immigrant women, this book further reveals in chapters 5, 6 and 7 the intersections of gender, class and race oppression and exposes the forces and processes of commodification, recommodification and the prospects of decommodification of immigrant women's labor in public and private realms.

Historically, Canada's immigration policy demonstrates that the country's labor market has been gendered, class-based and racialized, a structure that has reinforced the subordination of women of color and black women within an already existing racialized and gendered labor force (Agnew 1996; Calliste 1991). Indeed, the Immigration Act of 1910 used the term "race" as a prohibitive/restrictive legal category in Section 38 (original source, Hawkins 1989: 17, cited in Jakubowski 1997: 15). In 1919, this blatant evidence of racism in the state was amended and changed to "nationality." Later on, to keep the state's racist ideology intact, the Immigration Act of 1952 changed the category "race" to "ethnic group" (Jakubowski 1997), a categorization that remains today.

In Canada, it is clear that gender, class, race and ethnicity are socially constructed and are neither fixed nor permanent entities. In the past, the Irish and Scots who moved to Eastern Canada perceived Acadians, the French settlers, as a different and inferior race; consequently, the Acadians were discriminated against and oppressed in Canada (Ng 1991). Ng (1991) rightfully points out that sexism, racism and class oppression change from time to time as productive and reproductive relations change, and members of the state participate in these relations. Chapter 4 illustrates these interconnected issues while exploring the contradictory actions of the welfare state and revealing how immigration policy in the case of domestic workers is gendered, racialized, class-based, and, indeed, ethnic-based.

STUDY METHODS

Social science researchers frequently use the terms "methodology" and "method" interchangeably although these terms may involve separate activities. Some feminists have convincingly made distinctions between these two concepts (Harding 1987; Stanley 1990). This book adopts these distinctions. On the one hand, methodology will refer to a comprehensive theoretical but informed framework, which may or may not mention any specific research method taken for the project or analysis (Stanley 1990: 26). On the other hand, methods will refer to a wide range of "techniques" or "specific sets of research practices," such as interviews, reviews of literature, surveys, statistical analysis, and ethnography (Stanley 1990: 26).

Using a broad political economy theoretical framework and a feminist lens, I have in this enquiry adopted several methods, including secondary sources (i.e., published and unpublished materials), collaborative research, participant observation, and open-ended interviewing. Reinharz (1992) refers to such combination of methods as multimethod research, which creates the opportunity to put people or texts in context and thus provides richer and more accurate interpretation.

Secondary sources in this enquiry incorporate not only trans-disciplinary published books and articles, but also government and non-government documents and statistics, unpublished papers, on-line materials, flyers, and bulletins. Secondary materials used here go beyond a review of relevant literature, generally labeled as "literature review" and referring to the examination of literature on a specific subject matter usually within a particular disciplinary framework. Examination of such a wide array of materials illustrates the fluidity of disciplinary boundaries and allows researchers to venture into new areas of knowledge.

Many researchers have advocated the intersection of academy and community in research (Culhane 2004; Pratt 1999a, 1999b; Smith 1999), an approach that I adopted for this book. This intersection took the form of a collaborative project with the Philippine Women Centre (PWC) in Vancouver, British Columbia, Canada. To forge links between the university, often called an "ivory tower" by critics, and the larger community, every semester I invite community activists and grassroots workers to speak to my classes. The PWC has provided a number of speakers over the years. My interest in the PWC's activities dates back to 1994 when in my Women's Studies evening class I met Cecilia Diocson, one of the founders of the PWC, and two other members of the PWC. These activists delivered an insightful presentation on Filipino im/migrant workers and their resistance to neo-liberal policies. Later, I approached the PWC about my ideas for collaborative research and was asked to deliver a presentation about my proposed project to the members of the collective on 17 December 1999. After receiving comments and having several phone conversations, I sent a proposal for their approval on 25 July 2000. On 20 October of that year, the proposal tentatively titled "The feminization of migration, poverty, and the de-skilling of women workers" received formal approval from the PWC.

The PWC had already successfully conducted collaborative research on other projects (McKay 1999; Pratt 1999). Indeed, the contributions of frontline activists and members of the PWC have been documented in several academic publications (McKay 1999; Pratt 1999b; Zaman and Tubajon 2001). Although this was my first collaborative project,[12] I had since 1998 built up rapport with the PWC members by attending several meetings, conferences, and workshops organized by the PWC. I continued to exchange both oral and written communications with PWC members over five years, from 1999 to 2004, which helped develop a "participatory" research framework.

As part of the collaborative project, 50 women were interviewed between January 2001 and December 2003, and all the interviews were recorded with the consent of the participants. Most of the interviews were conducted by Cecilia Diocson, although sometimes another PWC member conducted an interview to get first-hand experience and training in conducting interviews. To be acquainted with the members and participate in the process, I initially attended several interview sessions. I alone conducted one focus-group interview of five front-line activists in English at the home of one of the PWC members. Since all but five of the interviews were conducted in Tagalog, a major language in the Philippines, Cecilia frequently explained to me the issues discussed when I attended. Some of the women interviewed provided information in both Tagalog and English, a process that facilitated my comprehension of the issue. For each session, I took extensive field notes that helped me clarify the organization of immigrant women's labor. On 21 January 2001, I wrote the following reflections in my diary:

> Although most interviewees spoke Tagalog, they also used English. Occasionally, I asked questions to clarify the issues, and the interviewees elaborated on the issues in English. Sometimes, Cecilia volunteered to clarify some of my enquiries. All of us were sitting on sofas in a circle. . . . Interestingly, another group (seven to eight women in back room) which was having a meeting inside, left around 8 p.m. and used the backdoor without making any noise or sound. . . . I was amazed to see how busy the Centre was even on Sunday evening! Our meeting was scheduled from 7–10 p.m., but it lasted until 11 p.m.

All the interviews were translated, transcribed, and even edited by the members of the PWC. This process—a time-consuming and complex one—can thus claim some form of authenticity in capturing women's voices. Most of the interviewees either were members of the PWC or used the PWC's resources from time to time.[13] Visiting the PWC and using its resources possibly made the interviewees conscious of their working conditions and its consequences. Interviews for the collaborative project were generally conducted at the Centre, although some were conducted in members' houses when the Centre was too busy.

Filipinas are over-represented in the study primarily due to the collaborative nature of the project. In addition to these 50 women interviewed, I myself interviewed fourteen women between May 2002 and August 2003,[14] using the snowball technique. These women had migrated to Canada from Bangladesh, India and Burma. Out of these fourteen women, one was actively involved in the South Asian Women's Centre, one in the India Mahila Association and one in the Bangladesh Association. The sample thus included activist immigrants. Three activists out of these fourteen women were well-versed in English, had been living in Canada for more than fifteen years, and were passionate about immigrant women's issues. Interviews were mostly conducted at the interviewees' houses. Only two were conducted at my place at the interviewees' request.

To provide a human face to this methods section, I want to describe a few of the constraints involved in interviewing these fourteen immigrant women. Scheduling interviews was one of the most difficult tasks. For most of the interviews, more than one scheduling was necessary. Most of the women had flexible work hours, which meant that they had hardly any control over their work schedules. Most had paid jobs during the weekdays as well as on Saturdays, and most were the major caregivers of their families, that is, were non-commodified in the household. Illness and family obligations resulted in some last-minute cancellations. Interestingly, several women were unable to provide me with travel directions due to their limited knowledge of the roads in Greater Vancouver. In spite of their long-term stay in Canada, most of these women either did not drive cars or were new to Vancouver. In almost all cases, their husbands provided me with travel directions over the phone. Some of the men who provided me with directions were at home when I went to do the interviewing and offered me tea and snacks. Since refusing such hospitality would show lack of respect, I accepted. One of the men, a cab driver, not only welcomed me, but also narrated his immigration/life history for an hour! I listened carefully until his wife asked him to go to sleep, as he had worked the previous night. In this and all other instances, I waited to make sure that nobody was in the room except the interviewee and me before I started the interview. A few women asked for advice either for upgrading their education and training or for getting jobs. In all of these cases, I was careful not to act as a counselor, but to provide information about services and agencies that included referrals.

These fourteen detailed interviews were conducted either in English or in Bangla, the official language of Bangladesh. Interestingly, four Bangladeshi-Canadian women volunteered to use English as a medium of language because they felt more comfortable articulating their thoughts in English. These four challenge the racist myth that immigrants from Asia are reluctant to learn and speak English! All of the fourteen interviews were transcribed by a graduate research assistant in Women's Studies, and part of the Bangla transcriptions were translated by me. Despite my sincere efforts, I was unable to interview any Pakistani women. I believe that the events of 11 September 2001 in the US (also referred to as 9/11) and negative media coverage about immigrants from Pakistan deterred Pakistani women from participating in any of the taped interviews.

All of the immigrant women for this study are from South and South-east Asia. Several factors contribute to the predominance from these two regions of Asia. First, all of the women are racialized, and that drew my special attention in my exploration of the issues of commodification and decommodification of immigrant's labor. Second, as an immigrant and feminist academic woman, I am directly and indirectly involved in several South Asian and South-east Asian immigrant women's organizations in Vancouver (examined in chapter 8). Consequently, I had developed a niche for my research work and had incentive to develop this research project. Third, as a South Asian woman, my rudimentary knowledge of several languages of the region and my acquaintances with South Asian women in Canada and in South Asia proved helpful in interviewing immigrant women for this book. Fourth, my experience of immigration, of studying in Canadian universities, of raising children, and of participating in the labor market, both as a migrant and an immigrant, links me to the racialized women involved in this book. Having said this, I am not downplaying my privileged academic position that has facilitated the decommodification of my labor!

In total, 64 women, all residents of British Columbia, were interviewed. My analysis revolves around qualitative dimensions of the interviews rather than their quantitative nature. Most women were from South and South-east Asia, especially from Bangladesh, India and the Philippines. Only one each was from Malaysia, Fiji and Burma. In terms of religion, they described themselves as Christians, Hindus, Sikhs, and Muslims. These women represented neither a typical picture nor a gross generalization, but reflected the diversity of the organization of their labor and their commodification and the potentials of decommodification in several sectors of the Canadian economy. The wide range of stories they provided assisted me immensely in analyzing the various levels of commodification and the dynamics and prospects of decommodification of immigrant women's labor. The women also talked about their migration history, family lives, household chores, education, training, volunteer work, paid work, and job history. Unfortunately, due to the restricted scope for much academic writing,

I could use only partial segments of these im/migrant women's lives, the parts related to my analysis. A detailed demographic profile of the interviewees is available in the appendix.

FRAMEWORK OF THE STUDY

No comprehension of the local/national scenario is feasible without taking the global viewpoint into consideration, and vice versa. Hence, as migration and globalization are interconnected and complex processes, economic globalization that transcends the borders of the nation-states requires attention. Chapter 2 demonstrates the links between globalization and migration. Evaluating various theoretical frameworks of transnational migration, this chapter argues for the use of both macrolevel and microlevel processes to examine how transnational migration brings about wider socioeconomic disparities between semi-periphery and periphery countries. This chapter further explores how the globalized economy has created a mobile and temporal immigrant workforce in social production and reproduction, which has become increasingly feminized. Focusing on the role of national governments as important regulatory bodies in controlling the mobility of labor, this chapter reveals how transnational migration has become commodified and is leading to increasing governmental involvement and regulation. Several questions emerge: What are the implications of "transnational" as a concept, rather than "international" or "global"? Does the notion "feminization of migration" have any empirical validity? How do transnational migration and economic restructuring intersect?

Chapter 3 explores current immigration policies in Canada and their implications for peripheral countries and immigrant women. Providing a brief historical background of immigration policies, this chapter also identifies several improvements over the years. This chapter then reveals that in the name of efficiency and restructuring, governance credits market criteria for selection of immigrants in Canada, including the shifting of migrant-sending countries from Europe to Asia and the restructuring of immigrants' services and commodification. Of particular interest is how "marketization of the state" is reflected in immigration policies and what social consequences have risen from the shift of policies due to neo-liberal globalism. How has Canada as an immigrant-receiving country upheld its neo-liberal policies in selecting immigrants?

Chapter 4 provides a historical overview of the genderized and racialized immigration policies of Canada and delineates how immigrant labor has contributed to Canada's nation-building process. Focusing on the gender, class, and race dynamics of immigration, this chapter examines Canada's labor export policies, especially the links between Canada's LCP and the Philippines' Labor Export Policy (LEP). Examination of these policies has revealed an asymmetrical partnership resulting from neo-liberal globalism, ultimately transforming dependence and exploitation from a national to a global context. The example of the LCP provides concrete evidence of the Canadian state's role in legitimating commodification of immigrant women's labor while decommodifying privileged women's labor—all this despite the existence of the welfare state.

Bringing in the stories of 64 immigrant women who migrated from Asia, chapters 5 and 6 show graphically how the majority of immigrant women, after being trained as nurses, teachers, doctors, lecturers, and lawyers in their country of origin, get commodified and eventually, de-skilled. At the same time, these women solidify the Canadian labor market by entering into different levels of commodification. It is clear that Canadian democratic values and the rhetoric associated with the welfare state have failed to prevent the commodification of immigrant women's labor in a private sphere. Focusing on the domestic/private sphere, these chapters also argue that social reproduction has been transferred from mostly upper/middle-class women in Canada to women of peripheral societies because of economic restructuring under neo-liberal policies. These immigrant women's stories invite key questions: Who will perform low-paid, repetitive and monotonous jobs in the near future, when immigrant women no longer do them? Where do immigrant women stand when it comes to decommodifying women laborers? How do the federal government and individual provincial governments recognize immigrant women's educational credentials and training in their countries of origin to decommodify their labor?

Again through immigrant women's stories, chapter 7 examines the complex processes of how immigrant women's various levels of commodification of labor are recycled and solidified in the Canadian labor market. Despite their utmost efforts to upgrade their skills and become decommodified, many immigrants experience a wide array of constraints, including bureaucratic hassles, costly procedures and deregulated foreign credentials. This chapter reveals the despair in immigrant women's voices and the futile efforts to be decommodified that ultimately lead them to be recommodified.

Chapter 8 looks at some of the immigrant women's groups pertinent to the interviewees of this book and these groups' various active efforts to challenge immigrant women's subordination and exploitation, including racism and sexism in the workplace and in the wider society. These immigrant groups mobilize against various layers of commodification of immigrant women's labor and the processes that block the decommodification of immigrant women's labor. Despite their disadvantaged situation, many immigrant women actively challenge local, national and global oppressive forces.

The concluding chapter chalks out an agenda for future research that could shed light on how to decommodify immigrant women's labor and create a truly inclusive society in Canada, a society where every individual, regardless of gender, class, race and nationality, has access to basic social entitlements. This chapter suggests that a comparative study of immigrant-receiving semi-periphery countries[15] could provide an insightful analysis into variations of commodification and decommodification among immigrant workers. More specifically, and very importantly, stories of immigrant women from Africa, Latin America, and non-English-speaking Europe now living in Canada could provide a comparative but first-hand account of commodification and decommodification in several sectors—an account that is yet to be written!

NOTES

1. To meet labor shortages, current Australian immigration policies emphasize short-term contract workers rather than permanent immigrants. For example, in 1998–99, approximately 109,000 temporary migrants entered Australia to undertake specific jobs that Australians were unable to fill; this number excludes students and visitors (Australian Department of Immigration and Multicultural Affairs 2000). On the other hand, between July 1998 and June 1999, 84,143 immigrants arrived in Australia (Australian Department of Immigration and Multicultural Affairs 2000).

2. Until recently, temporary work permit holders were not allowed to apply for permanent status while staying in Canada. Except for refugees and some exceptional cases, most were forced to leave Canada to apply for immigrant status.

3. After having immigrant status and living in Canada for three years, one can apply for citizenship. Most immigrants from peripheral countries gain citizenship and hold Canadian passports. In this book, citizens are referred to those who are former immigrants, not born Canadians.

4. Among semi-periphery countries, variations exist between weak semi-periphery countries (e.g., Mexico) and strong semi-periphery (e.g., Canada and Australia). For an elaborate discussion of this issue, please see "Introduction" of *Governing under Stress: Middle Powers and the Challenge of Globalization*, edited by Marjorie Cohen and Stephen Clarkson (2004).

5. The use of the terms "economic semi-periphery" and "political semi-periphery" have been influenced by the article (1989) by Boreham et al. titled "Semi-peripheries or Particular Pathways: The Case of Australia, New Zealand and Canada as Class Formations."

6. While conducting research (January-February 2004) in Sydney, Australia, I found social activists and the Labor Party vigorously attacking the current Liberal government on this issue. For details, see Jayasuriya and Pookong (1999) and Brennan (2003).

7. In analyzing the Scandinavian experience, Leira (1992) eloquently summarizes the whole debate.

8. According to Esping-Andersen's (1990) typology, Sweden is a social democratic welfare state.

9. Both Canada and the US are liberal welfare states, according to Esping-Andersen (1990).

10. Chapters 3, 4 and 5 deal with a vast amount of literature pertinent to immigrant women.

11. Canadian-born women, especially young women, are also concentrated in low-wage labor. However, chapter 3 points out that immigrant women are significantly unemployed and if employed, are concentrated in low-paid jobs. In the labor market, immigrant women's experience also differs significantly from that of Canadian-born women.

12. Informally, I had worked with several women's and social activist groups.

13. These interviewees (e.g., from Malaysia, Fiji) used the Center's resources such as attending workshops, receiving suggestions on immigration issues, and so on, from time to time. The PWC is quite open to other disadvantaged groups/women and forms alliances to achieve specific goals.

14. I interviewed these fourteen women during my research semesters, that is, from May to August 2002 and 2003. However, the graduate student who was hired to transcribe and translate took more than the expected length of time due to her academic/familial obligations. With the open-ended questionnaire, the interviews were lengthy and took an enormous amount of time to process.

15. Australia and Canada, both semi-periphery as well as immigrant-receiving countries, are the best examples for comparison.

2

Globalization, Neo-Liberal Globalism, and Migration

The term "neo-liberalism" denotes new forms of political-economic governance premised on the extension of market relationships. (Larner 2000: 5)

Contemporary immigrants cannot be characterized as the "uprooted." Many are trans-migrants, becoming firmly rooted in their new country. . . . Migration proves to be an important transnational process that reflects and contributes to the current political configurations of the emerging global economy. (Schiller and Basch 1995: 48)

WHAT IS GLOBALIZATION?

As a modern buzzword, the term "globalization" has generated controversies and discussions for years among academics. In a general sense, it refers to social, political, and economic processes that accelerate the flow of capital, goods, services, and technologies and transcend national borders. Despite its frequent use in an array of topics ranging from migration to citizenship studies, some scholars see positive links between globalization and "international" migration in diversifying migration and increasing the roles of regional and international bodies and pacts such as the European Union, the North American Free Trade Agreement, the International Monetary Fund/World Bank and the General Agreement on Tariff and Trade in cross-border migration (Castles 1998; Pecoud and de Guchteneire 2005; Sassen 2000; Tyner 2002). Despite claims about the benefits of "international" migration, the receiving country still sets its rules and regulations to meet demands for and shortages of labor in specific sectors of the national economy.[1] In addition, the restructuring, deregulation, and privatization of neo-liberal globalism[2] further enhance demands for immigrants' cheap and competitive labor in the receiving country.

This chapter begins by analyzing some of the differences between globalization and globalism, and then demonstrates the links between globalization, neo-liberal globalism[3] and migration. The next section explores the ambiguities and significance of some of the terms that are associated with transnational migration, rather than "international" or "global" migration. Then, the following section explores how the market economy has produced and reproduced a mobile and temporal immigrant workforce that is increasingly feminized. Focusing on the role of national governments as important regulatory bodies in controlling the mobility of labor, this section also reveals how transnational migration has become commodified and is subject to increasing governmental involvement and regulation. The chapter closes by laying out the theoretical perspectives of this book as it relates to migration and immigration.

LINKS BETWEEN GLOBALIZATION, NEO-LIBERAL GLOBALISM, AND MIGRATION

Although a vast amount of literature deals with globalization rather than globalism and rarely makes distinctions between these two terms, globalism is not the same as globalization. What is the difference between globalization and globalism? Sivanandan distinguishes between them this way: "Globalization is a process, not a concept; globalism is the project. And the project is imperialism" (Sivanandan 1998/99: 6). Globalism is an ideology of governing impacted by the empirical phenomena of globalization. In other words, globalism refers to the norms, institutions, and laws that support neo-liberal principles and thus provide specific responses to globalization. On the other hand, globalization refers to multifaceted processes that permeate local, national and global economies. According to Cox (1992) and Panitch (1994), globalization is neither inevitable, nor teleological, nor irreversible, but should be understood dialectically. Migration within the context of globalization thus also needs to be investigated in a dialectical manner, that is, by exploring the links between countries sending and receiving immigrants.

Controversies have arisen in international political economy literature and international relations theory analyzing globalism and globalization. Advocates of political economy, that is, proponents of globalism, suggest that stronger national authority emerges due to globalism, whereas advocates of international relations, that is, proponents of globalization, argue that the nation-state is declining (Hoogvelt 2001). Globalism generally reflects a belief in free, efficient, and competitive markets and a belief that this ideology will benefit most people in a nation-state.

As an ideology, globalism frequently parades under "the banner of 'deregulation'" as governments restructure the welfare state and social policies (Hoogvelt 2001: 153). In other words, neo-liberalism restructures the welfare state and its policies by deregulating social sectors while at the same time emphasizing conventional family traditions. In one sense, deregulation implies a dismantling of state-sponsored forms of regulation of the domestic market, leading to a shrinking of the public sector, even a diminution of the public domain. That deregulation is considered another form of state intervention indicates how the extent and nature of state intervention has been transformed under neo-liberalism. Contradicting the proponents of globalization, deregulation reinforces rather than shrinks the authority of the state and facilitates the state's retreat from its public sectors. Kagarlitsky's discussion in "The Challenge for the Left" also asserts this point:

> During the 1980s and 1990s the scale of state intervention in economic, social and cultural life has not diminished, but on the contrary has grown. 'Deregulation' is also a form of interventionism, albeit a perverted one. Now, however, this intervention has been aimed at destroying the public sector, at reducing living standards, and at removing customs barriers. Practice shows that keeping markets open demands no less activity from governments than protectionism. (1999: 299)

One can find neo-liberalism in one of the following three distinct interpretations: policy, ideology and governmentality (Larner 2000). In reviewing neo-liberalism as policy, Larner points out that governments now focus on efficiency, international competitiveness, deregulation, and privatization rather than on inclusive social welfare systems. Although Larner's conceptualization of neo-liberalism is quite comprehensive, she asserts that focusing only on a policy framework and ignoring ideology and governmentality could undermine "the significance of contemporary transformations in governance," and she maintains that "neo-liberalism is both a political discourse about the nature of rule and a set of practices that facilitate the governing of individuals from a distance" (2000: 6).

In the case of migration, I contend that Larner's three intersected interpretations provide effective avenues for exploring neo-liberalism and its links to migration across national borders. For example, exploring migration without paying adequate attention to a nation-state's labor import policies or export policies, especially how these policies impact women in migration, is likely to be a less than useful exercise. Further, to analyse the pervasive but hidden ideology of a nation-state (i.e., as capitalist, patriarchal), it is important to examine the dynamics of immigration policies of a major receiving country like Canada. For example, current immigration policies in Canada emphasize a skilled-labor category that ultimately marginalizes women who come from peripheral countries. Without adequate attention to gender, race and class, these policies generate the commodification of immigrant labor, especially of female immigrant workers who are marginalized in numerous ways. These policies eventually perpetuate a gendered and racialized labor force where immigrant women workers become concentrated in the lower echelons of the labor market. Canada, moreover, has orchestrated effective mechanisms to facilitate labor migration and border control simultaneously for people from periphery countries.

Migration is frequently linked with globalization in academic discourse (Castles 1998; Cohen 1997; Hefti 1997; Taran 1999), yet globalization and migration are complex processes that remain inadequately understood. Some scholars have made efforts to make links between globalization and migration. In his work, Taran (1999) goes beyond individual rational choice and cost-benefit analysis and pinpoints three major components of globalization that foster migration: (1) Structural Adjustment Policies (SAP), (2) technological change, and (3) trade liberalization. According to Taran (1999), in Third World countries, the SAP of the International Monetary Fund (IMF)—a major force of globalization—requires a devaluing of national currency. This devaluing leads to a waiving of restrictions on foreign investment, stimulates exports, and drastically reduces expenditures on health, education and social services. Reduction of essential services is followed by implementation of repressive measures such as increased police and military powers. Consequently, people are forced to leave their countries of origin for economic or political reasons. The technological change associated with globalization further reorganizes work, often rendering labor redundant and reducing employment opportunities. Migration becomes a compelling choice for the many people negatively affected by technological change. On the other hand, people displaced due to environmental degradation or natural disasters are often termed "environmental migrants." These people move frequently within their own national borders, but are most likely to migrate to marginal environments because of poverty and lack of entitlement to assets needed for survival and sustenance (Taran 1999). Finally, liberalized trade favors the nation-states and fosters a sociopolitical environment that does not support the existence of trade unions, thus producing low-paid temporary workers without health and safety nets. Liberalized trade also restricts enormously labor's power to bargain with employers, fostering massive labor dislocation and eventually labor migration.

Unfortunately, Taran's analysis bypasses some groups of migrants, mostly disadvantaged groups. These groups include indigenous populations as well as people living in poverty in periphery countries, who are displaced due to the World Bank's so-called resettlement policies in the name of economic development (e.g., the construction of dams, bridges, modern highways, and so on). Further, Taran overestimates people's options for migration, a choice that applies only to those who have a certain level of educational skills, training, and wealth. However, Taran's work is noteworthy in migration literature because it illustrates the human dimension of globalization by looking at causal factors of migration. Taran's argument reveals clearly that the market economy relies heavily on low-cost migrant labor and that receiving countries' imported labor policies may foster the flow of migration under globalization.

After a careful examination of contradictions between the global market and the state, Castles (1998) states that "international migration" is a significant part of globalization and changes both receiving[4] and sending countries.[5] The state embraces the international mobility of capital, goods and commodities and restricts the international migration of people, which, Castle argues, is unlikely to succeed in an era of globalization. Castles (1998) further points out that the erosion of the state's power is likely due not only to globalization, but also to the involvement of various multi-level regional and local bodies such as the European Union and the North American Free Trade Agreement (NAFTA); however, Castles has not examined the role of these bodies pertinent to migration. Some scholars (Holton 1998; Kearney 1991) have gone further and argued that globalization has challenged the capacity and stability of the state. Kearney (1991) even argues that migration is one of the significant vehicles through which the boundaries of the state will be contested and transgressed. Migration is undoubtedly a powerful force affecting receiving countries through immigration policies that attract and recruit immigrant labor, affecting sending countries through aggressive labor export policies, and affecting organized labor through the huge profits that can be made by agents and recruiters.[6]

Connecting globalization with diasporas, Cohen (1997) predicts that an increasing wave of international migration will deterritorialize social identity and may have a profound impact on the state's hegemony over citizenship. Some scholars (Jacobson 1996; Sassen 1996) have categorically stated that globalization has lessened the state's control of immigration policies. So far, no evidence has been found that international factors and pacts have ever succeeded in influencing Canada to accept immigrant labor without internal demands and some degree of national politics. Most literature on globalization and migration that professes the declining power of the state focuses on the issue of border control and undocumented workers[7] rather than on immigration policies pertinent to migrants. Migration is still subject to the authority of the state under the banner of immigration policies and the movements of people from periphery to semi-periphery and core countries are not deregulated like trade, capital, and technology. Despite globalization and migration, Canada still has a firm grip on the flow of people into the country through immigration. In the case of immigrant labor, Canada so far shows no sign that the authority of the state is deteriorating or the state's hegemony is declining; in fact, the state in many instances commodifies immigrant workers by imposing numerous stipulations such as unequal access to jobs, training and educational opportunities and by denying credentials from country of origin.

The denials as well as the stipulations generate the commodification of immigrant women's labor in a gendered and racialized labor market and thus, create barriers to these women being decommodified.

Stalker (2001) succinctly comments on the issue of migration within the global context:

> [T]he sacred texts of globalization, from NAFTA to the establishment of the World Trade Organization, have been strangely silent on the issue of migration ... At the very least, governments need to make more realistic appraisals of their future needs of workers, and to cooperate with the sending countries to ensure that international migration is rational, regulated—and human. (132)

Stalker's comment shows that the issue of migration has gone beyond only economic reasons and that understanding the links between receiving and sending countries is crucial. For example, global economic restructuring not only causes transnational flow of capital and disrupts peripheral economies, but also constitutes an important factor in the unemployment and lack of job security that ultimately lead to transnational migration. However, attention to global restructuring has mostly focused on industries rather than on migrant labor; hence, issues of gender, race and class are often not examined closely (Piper and Ball 2001).

In sum, any analysis of the dynamics of migration must consider the complex processes of contemporary international political economy and the immigration policies that recruit immigrants. Migration may not have a profound impact on the world if one considers the percentage—migrants comprise only about 3 percent of the world population. However, migration does have a profound impact on a semi-periphery country like Canada—and vice versa. Interesting questions arise: How much does a semi-periphery country like Canada depend on immigrant labor in a market economy? To what extent does immigrant labor in a country like Canada serve the goals of deregulation, privatization and market efficiency? To what extent does immigrant labor become commodified and solidify an already gendered and racialized labor force? Are there any prospects for decommodification of labor for immigrant women?

TRANSNATIONAL MIGRATION: CAUSES AND TRENDS

The characterization of the late twentieth century by Castles and Miller (1993) as "the age of migration" is fairly recent, but for decades, scholars have used various terminologies such as transnational migration, global migration, international migration, economic migration, political migration, environmental migration, regional migration—and the list may go on (Goldring 1998; Mahler 1999; Schiller and Basch 1995; Stalker 2001). Frequently, these terminologies are used interchangeably without an exploration of their meanings and underlying assumptions. As Mahler (1999) notes, "The term *transnational* long predates its coupling with migration, and this historical fact has been at the root of much confusion with regard to the definition of *transnationalism*" (693). To counter the classic bipolar model of immigration, that is, the immigrants cut their ties to their country of origins, Mahler opts for transnational discourses and processes that influence existing power relationships and social identities.

It is clear that transnational migrants respond to either local and regional or individual conditions and maintain ties to their countries of origin in many ways. Neither the global capital nor the state system protects the interests of transnational migrants; consequently, these migrants face socioeconomic and sociopolitical insecurities as well as both physical and mental threats. In this book, transnational migration is situated within the context of the dialectical relationship between receiving (i.e., semi-periphery) and sending (i.e., periphery) countries and highlights the hierarchical power relationship between these two by investigating the commodification of female immigrants' labor. The challenges confronted by transnational migrants vary considerably across countries and regions. Indeed, the various kinds of transnational migrants[8] are constantly restrained by territorial state boundaries and the racialized immigration policies of receiving countries. Most host governments are more preoccupied with border control and national security than with migrants' well-being or rights.

Contradicting the notion of uprooted people disconnected with the geopolitical processes of the market economy, transnational migration has empowered immigrants, migrants, and political asylum-seekers, as indicated in the second quote at the start of this chapter. In theorizing transnational migration, Schiller and Basch (1995) further observe,

> *Transmigrants* are *immigrants* [authors' italics] whose daily lives depend on multiple and constant interconnections across international borders and whose public identities are configured in relationship to more than one nation-state. They are not sojourners because they settle and become incorporated in the economy and political institutions, locations and patterns of daily life of the country in which they reside. However, at the very same time, they are engaged elsewhere in the sense that they maintain connections, build institutions, conduct transactions, and influence local and national events in the countries from which they emigrated. (48)

Schiller and Basch have used the concept of immigrants rather than migrants and have not made any distinctions between immigrants and temporary migrants. However, most migrants eventually become immigrants and participate in the politics of their home country despite their residence in host countries. For example, due to transnational politics, the El Salvadoran government at one point was persuaded to provide legal assistance to political refugees in the US, so that they could seek asylum and stay in the US as immigrants who remitted $1 billion annually to the El Salvador economy (Mahler 1999). Another example: Filipino transmigrants were a major force in toppling the US-backed military dictator Ferdinand Marcos and were instrumental in bringing about political change in the Philippines (Schiller and Basch 1995). Another example: As transnational activists, Bangladeshi immigrants in Vancouver convinced UNESCO (United Nations Educational, Scientific and Cultural Organization) to recognize February 21 as International Mother Language Day.[9] These three different examples suggest that the continuous interaction of modern states and different layers of national identities are significant in immigrants' lives. National identity across borders plays a vital role in uniting people on a single issue, and immigrants generally do not forgo one national identity for another.[10] Focusing on a single issue or action performed by transnational migrants is a useful strategy to demonstrate these migrants' power (Guarnizo 2003). For example, the PWC in Vancouver in collaboration with MIGRANTE International fought successfully for the release of Sarah Balagan from the United Arab Emirates' prison (illustrated in chapter 8).

For the maintenance of transnational social fields, three major reasons have been identified by Schiller and Basch (1995): (1) the emergence of a global restructuring of capital; (2) racialized exclusion in receiving countries, which increasingly produces multi-layered insecurity for immigrants; and (3) immigrants' loyalties and social ties to both home and host societies. After 9/11, many government regulatory bodies are suspicious about dual identities and about activism that transcends national borders. To diffuse and overcome fear about immigrants who demonstrate dual loyalties, Levitt (2004) notes:

> As increasing numbers of migrants live parts of their social and economic lives across national boundaries, the question is no longer whether this is good or bad, but rather, how to ensure they are protected, represented, and that they contribute something in return. (2)

This statement acknowledges immigrants' contribution to their host economies and also documents that both core and semi-periphery countries can extract benefits from immigrants' labor. For example, the US, a core country that has been heavily populated by immigrants in the twentieth century, has become one of the wealthiest nations in the world (Stalker 2001). If one looks at growth as well as GDP, Canada and Australia, two major immigrant-receiving semi-periphery countries, have become economically powerful despite their exclusionary policies until the 1960s. (Chapter 4 highlights class-based and racialized exclusion in Canada and demonstrates how immigrant labor has contributed to the growth of the national economy.)

Transnational migration does not reflect the "borderless world" of Ohmae (1990), who predicts an inevitable trend of transnational corporations with a free flow of goods and services and migration of people. In practice, transnational migrants are not served well by a borderless or weak state. In fact, migrants rely on the state for their protection, and many eventually develop multiple national identities.[11] On this subject, in recognizing the borders of the states and national identities, Mahler (1999) points out that while transnational does indicate macrolevel processes, the existence of micro- and mesolevel (i.e., regional) processes need not be discounted. Looking at macroprocesses (i.e., immigration policies of Canada and labor export policies of sending countries) and microprocesses (i.e., processes of commodification of immigrant labor and prospects of decommodification in Canada) is essential to form a comprehensive picture of the gross wealth disparities that transnational migration and immigration policies generate between immigrants and Canadian-born citizens. As Tyner comments, "[T]ransnational migration has become increasingly commodified. Government and private institutions assume an important regulatory function in the global mobility of labor and the trend . . . is toward even greater institutional involvement" (2002: 98).

Current regulatory bodies and institutions do not serve the interests of migrant labor, but generate rules and regulations to restrict the mobility of labor. Thus, in Geneva, the United Nations formed a Global Commission on International Migration, a body of nineteen members, on 9 December 2003. One of the mandates of this commission is to examine the connection between migration and other global issues. In their research paper titled "Migration Without Borders: An Investigation Into the Free Movement of People," Pecoud and de Guchteneire (2005) argue that complete control by the state over migration has never been possible, even in the nineteenth century; in this sense, they found that the perfect power of the state was a myth. In the course of time, Pecoud and de Guchteneire (2005) argue, states have gradually achieved the ability and legitimacy to control migration. Thus, one can argue that compared with the eighteenth and nineteenth centuries, Canada in the 20th and 21st centuries has been dictating the number of immigrants in any given year and accordingly, fulfils its desired numerical goals.

Since 1965, transnational migration has grown increasingly and become more diverse and complex. According to the United Nations, "The number of international migrants has grown steadily in the past four decades to an estimated 175 million in 2000, up from an estimated 75 million in 1960" (2005: 6). However, estimating the numbers of people actually involved in transnational migration is difficult due to the absence of national data banks in many countries (Zlotnik 1999). It is clear that in order to deal with a shortage of labor, the demands of organized labor, and lack of demographic growth, some countries in the West actively facilitate the entry and settlement of immigrants. Australia and Canada are examples of countries whose national identity is historically based on European settlement, that is, the settling of the country by white settlers, which either marginalized or decimated the aboriginal population politically and culturally. Compared with most European countries, Canada and Australia—two "settler" countries—are currently experiencing substantial labor flows and are relatively open to labor migration from periphery countries. Further, both Australia and Canada have been experiencing large-scale immigration from Asia. However, in Canada and Australia the size and nature of immigration programs have become hot political issues, especially in times of economic recession, national election, or major national crisis such as 9/11. Such events seem to prompt racist and classist slurs targeting immigrants from peripheral countries, and, more specifically, racialized groups.

Since the early 1970s, labor export has been a significant mechanism by which peripheral countries have financed their development. Pointing out the gross wealth disparities between sending and receiving countries, Heyzer et al. (1994) argue that the process of labor migration must be analyzed within an historical context, and that analyses of both macrolevel and microlevel processes can facilitate understanding of this complex phenomenon. Although Heyzer's geographical focus is Asia, she includes Canada in her analytical framework because the vast majority of Filipino migrants come to Canada as domestic workers. To acquire an inside perspective on this historically "unnamed" job in the informal sector, Heyzer (1994) argues that it is crucial to gain an understanding of the interconnections between the household economy, that is, microprocess, and the national economy, that is, mesoprocess, of the receiving country. In the case of Canada, an analysis of migrant domestic workers as well as commodification and decommodification of immigrant women's labor requires looking at their migration/work history and settlement patterns, as well as their job and training experience in both country of origin and host country. Without exploring these issues, the processes and various layers of commodification and potentials of decommodification of immigrant women's labor will not be explored.

With the adoption of neo-liberal policies, many countries have been experiencing labor market shortages in certain sectors of the economy, and these shortages are generally filled by short-term contract labor or migrant labor. Historically, Europe has preferred short-term contract labor during post-war reconstruction. Preference for contract labor implies economic flexibility and deregulation because the perceived foreignness of migrant labor isolates them from local people and the lack of family/social ties with local people expedites the immigrants' removal or deportation when they are deemed unnecessary during economic upheaval. For example, since the oil boom in the 1970s, the oil-rich states of the Middle East have recruited large numbers of contract migrant workers, the vast majority from South, East and Southeast Asia. Until the economic crisis in some parts of the Asian region in 1997, the "miracle and tiger economies," namely Japan, Hong Kong, China, the

Republic of Korea, Singapore, and Taiwan in conjunction with Indonesia, Malaysia and Thailand, were major short-term migrant-receiving countries. Since 9/11, major migrant-receiving countries have imposed increasing restrictions on both immigrant and short-term contract workers, especially from certain regions of the world. More than anything else, this indicates that the authority of the state has not declined, but in fact continues to be able to make adjustments at various levels to serve its interests.

MIGRATION OF WOMEN: NUMERICAL SIGNIFICANCE AND NATURE OF JOBS

In the field of transnational migration, the migration of women in the twentieth century has been a widely discussed topic. However, the dearth of data on migrant women at both national and international levels makes it difficult to capture the complexities and dynamics of women's migration. The trends of transnational migration show that the nature, extent and objectives of women's and men's migration differ. As a result, gender, in addition to other factors, plays a key role in terms of women's participation in the host country. In terms of numbers, women comprise 49 percent of transnational migration and in developed regions, comprise as high as 51 percent (United Nations 2005). This number is staggering, but it does not indicate the category of migration and the nature of jobs women occupy once they migrate. Scholars on transnational migration (Boyle 2002; Carr and Chen 2004; Lutz 2002; Parrenas 2001; Tacoli 1999) provide insightful directions regarding these last two points. Some women migrate as independent migrants under the labor category. Most jobs for migrant women are concentrated in female-dominated occupations such as domestics, entertainers, assembly-line workers in clothing and electronics, nurses and health care workers, restaurant and hotel staff—mostly cleaning and lower echelon jobs.[12] For numerous reasons, including discriminatory practices and sexist societal perceptions in most countries, especially in Asia,[13] most women (except Filipinos) migrate as dependents of men. To some extent, migration under the dependency category determines women's perceived role in the receiving country, that is, Canada.

Migration to a foreign country for employment was predominantly male-dominated until the mid-1970s; hence, until recently, most studies of transnational migration bypassed women as migrants. One exception was Morokvasic (1984), who demonstrated that like men, women were "birds of passage" before the 1970s (cited in Kofman 1999). In Asia, in the past 30 years, transnational migration has definitely become gendered, with most female migrant workers coming from the Philippines, Indonesia and Sri Lanka. Indeed, the numbers of these migrant workers range from 60 to 80 percent—quite substantial in these countries. Most of these women are legally deployed as domestics. Migrant domestic workers from Indonesia and Sri Lanka migrate to Middle Eastern countries as well as to Malaysia, Singapore, Hong Kong, and Taiwan. However, as Asis points out, "Other countries of origin—Bangladesh, India, and Pakistan—do not allow or have very restrictive regulations concerning female emigration, which their governments consider fraught with danger" (2003: 1). Thus it is not surprising that in Canada, most immigrant women from Bangladesh, India, and Pakistan migrate as dependents of men.[14] By the mid-1980s, according to Heyzer et al., "the international [transnational] migration of women began to be visible and by the nineties it became a phenomenon that had to be addressed at multiple levels—through research, through NGO action and through policy responses from governments" (1994: 1). This migration includes women migrant workers leaving behind their families at home, women as spouses of immigrant or migrant workers currently employed in receiving countries, and women who migrate as dependents (i.e., daughters, mothers, wives and so on) of male migrants. Transnational migrants vary substantially in distribution of gender. However, in receiving countries like Australia and Canada, the proportion of female legal immigrants is particularly higher (United Nations 2005). Clearly, these traditional receiving countries have developed mechanisms to exclude undocumented or refugee women.

Unemployment and underemployment arising out of globalization have multiplied pressures on women in peripheral countries, forcing them to search for strategies to sustain household survival. One of the most embraced survival options for women in some Asian countries, especially in the Philippines, is to migrate transnationally, what Sassen (2000) has rightly labeled as "the feminization of survival" because households and whole communities rely heavily on women for their sustenance. Identifying the feminization of migration as institutionalized, Sassen asserts that women's migration does not consist only of "aggregates of individual actions": "governments too are dependent on their earnings as well as enterprises where profit making exists at the margins of the 'licit' economy" (2000: 506). Mass migration of women from the Philippines reflects both demand for their labor in the receiving country and demand for their remittances in the sending country.

How many women migrant workers are there? Although statistics on transnational migration by gender are difficult to procure, the United Nations Population Division using the 1990 general census once estimated that 57 million women are living outside their country of origin, a number representing approximately 48 percent of all migrants (OECD 2000). In 2000, this percentage represented 49 percent of all migrants, and the estimated number of female migrants was 85,080,716 (United Nations 2005: 10). However, it is important to remember that current statistics suffer from various methodological inadequacies and sociocultural biases (Zaman 1996) and may well be providing both inaccurate information on and underestimation of female migrants.

Despite the limitations of current statistical data, 49 percent of transnational women migrants represent a huge number of women laborers who are economically mobile and contribute to their countries by sending remittances. For example, a study of Haitian remittances from New York City to Haiti points out that "women sent larger amounts of money than men did, with women who 'headed households' sending the greatest amount" (Schiller and Basch 1995: 54). Increasingly, women as autonomous agents migrate to support their dependents and families—what Parrenas (2001) has termed as "mothering from a distance" in the case of Filipinos. This migration of women has been made possible through continuous high demand in core and some semi-periphery countries for domestic and childcare workers and the need for workers in low-paid occupations such as the clothing and garment industry, sweatshops, eldercare, health care, and entertainment. Governments of sending countries find it difficult either to halt or to impose an embargo on migrant labor because these countries have high unemployment rates and need the benefit of remittances for their stagnant economies. In fact, to promote labor export, various government agencies in periphery countries have set up a national level government office. Examples are the Center for Overseas Employment of the Department of Manpower in Indonesia, the Philippines Overseas Employment Administration, the Sri Lanka Bureau of Foreign Employment, the Korean Overseas Development Office, the Bangladesh Bureau of Manpower Employment and Training, and the Overseas Employment Administration Office of the Thai Department of Labor.

Women migrants often become more reliable sources of foreign exchange than men because labor-importing countries have persistent demand for women workers. For example, about 1.5 million Asian women work abroad in "typically female" high-demand jobs ranging from domestic workers to "entertainers" (quite frequently a euphemism for sex workers) (UNESCO 1998). To support and sustain their families back home, domestics as well as caregivers migrate from Asia, Africa, Latin America, and Eastern Europe. This trend reflects not only the feminization of migration, but reveals that the labor market in a domestic economy with regard to care work has been shifted from a national to an international context. Thus, the increasing Asian women workers' transnational migration and concentration in female-dominated, low-wage jobs poignantly reveal how racialized, gendered and class-based labor has become in the global economy.

Sending countries, especially those in Asia, have played a proactive role in advancing migration flows. As mentioned above, Bangladesh, Indonesia, Korea, the Philippines, Sri Lanka, and Thailand all have government offices and departments to facilitate labor exports. Further, in the past three decades, the development of "an immigration industry" in Asia has significantly promoted both legal and illegal migration of women. Asian women migrants are heavily concentrated in women-dominated occupations such as domestic helpers, restaurant and hotel workers (including cleaners, clerks, and assistants), assembly line workers in labor-intensive manufacturing, and entertainers. These jobs not only belong to the lowest echelons of the occupational hierarchy, but also are perceived of as "feminine," suitable for women who are considered as docile, caring, diligent, and passionate—very much a racialized and gendered labor force. These jobs also involve the flexible work hours and lack of securities that meet the requirements of global capitalism and consequently, make women's labor commodified and deter them from becoming decommodified. Interestingly, in order to get these jobs, most migrant women (e.g., doctors, nurses and teachers in the Philippines) understate their educational qualifications and training. Moreover, these jobs are quite individualized and often isolated, factors that hinder the development of a social network and the exchange of information essential for survival in a foreign environment.[15] The result? Eventually, the skills of many of these trained, educated migrant women become eroded and despite their continuous efforts to be re-skilled, their labor becomes commodified again. However, various immigrant women's groups contest the local, national and global forces responsible for commodification (examined in chapter 8).

The feminization of migration thus not only refers to quantity or numerical significance, but also indicates social perceptions and features inherent in specific kinds of jobs for which immigrant women are considered suitable because of their perceived femininity and racialization of labor. This also indicates a global labor market where gendered, class-based and racialized divisions are generated. Social perceptions have further commodified these women's labor by creating inhospitable work environments where social entitlements related to work do not exist. The concentration of women migrant workers in the lower strata of occupations has transformed the global migrant market to one that is sex-segregated and has created a transnational racialized division of labor. Sassen (2000) sums up this situation: "[W]e are witnessing the return of the so-called 'serving classes' in globalized cities around the world, composed of immigrant and migrant women" (510). This statement implies that the differences between immigrant and migrant women's labor are irrelevant when one considers the nature and conditions of work in the global economy—and its subsequent consequences, that is, being commodified without opportunities for becoming decommodified.

Demonstrating the significance of the study of migrant women workers, Gulati (1997) points out how governments in Asia perceive women as "wives" and "mothers" being cared for by male "breadwinners"; consequently, women's employment and unemployment, let alone migration and various layers of commodification, are not considered major concerns. I contend that because of the quantitative dimension as well as the nature of the jobs women occupy and the discriminatory practices women migrant workers face, it is essential to focus on women and the commodification and decommodification of their labor in migration studies and at the same time explore the racialized and class-based nature of migration. In my view, gender, class and race are the fundamental intersecting principles organizing the current global and national labor market.

THEORIES OF IMMIGRATION AND THE THEORETICAL FRAMEWORK OF THE STUDY

Currently, there is no single, coherent theory that explains transnational migration and immigration adequately. Although a variety of theories have been developed and used from time to time, these remain fragmented due to disciplinary boundaries. To explore immigration and migration processes and their aftermath, a single discipline or a single theoretical framework is not sufficient. An array of theoretical approaches needs to be considered to understand the context, processes and various perspectives in the field.

Theoretical approaches in migration literature (Boyd 1984; Castles and Miller 1993; Massey et al. 1993; Ohmae 1990; Schiller and Basch 1995) cover a wide range of assumptions, concepts and perspectives. In the 1960s and '70s, "push-pull" forces and social/family/kin networks were the predominant explanations used in migration studies to account for the composition, flow, integration, and settlement of migrant populations (Boyd 1984). In referring to the acceleration of migration in the 1970s and 1980s, Boyd (1984) countered widely used existing explanatory frameworks and urged the development of alternative theories to explore the complicated dynamics related to migration. In the decades since then, several theoretical frameworks have been developed and used to investigate current processes of transnational migration as well as immigration policies. For example, Massey et al. (1993) and Meyers (2000) have extensively examined the major theoretical approaches used in migration and immigration studies. These are neoclassical economics: macro and micro theory, the new economics of migration, dual labor market theory, Marxism and Neo-Marxism, world systems theory, network theory, national identity approach, institutional theory, the theory of cumulative causation, and systems theory. The assumptions, hypothesis and propositions originating in each theoretical perspective are not contradictory; nonetheless, they generate different implications for the analysis of transnational migration and make it evident that theoretical frameworks on immigration are not well developed.

Immigration, a domestic issue, is now an interdisciplinary subject needed for its analysis of theories of comparative politics rather than for its explanation of how international relations contribute to one's understanding of immigration (Meyers 2000). To reveal the role of migration in shaping national identity and to reveal the complex dynamics of migration in immigrant women's lives, this book will employ a combination of the political economy approach and the national identity approach. A brief overview of the political economy approach and the national identity approach is presented below as part of laying out the book's theoretical framework.

The Political Economy Approach

The political economy approach generally argues that migration facilitates the growth of capitalism as capitalists procure profit by keeping wages of migrant laborers down. In other words, migration serves the privileged class and keeps a reserve army, that is, migrant labor, intact. To rectify what Meyers (2000) calls "the crises of capitalism," migrant labor serves two important purposes: first, it is productive and less costly; and second, it is expendable during periods of recession. The political economy approach thus presents these characteristics: (1) importing labor is a structural feature of capitalism; and (2) governance regulates and deregulates immigration depending on the performance of the market economy (Meyers 2000). Although Meyers' view is directed to temporary contract or migrant labor, even permanent-status migrants' labor in Canada is cheap and expendable, as will be seen in chapters 5 and 6. The political economy approach helps to explore the ways in which national governance through regulation and deregulation has expanded in the field of immigrant labor. However, one of the major limitations of the political economy approach is that it overlooks discrimination against immigrants based on gender and race.

The National Identity Approach

Utilizing a historical approach and downplaying external factors, the national identity approach focuses on variations in citizenship and immigration policies between receiving and sending countries based on their different perceptions of national identity. The national identity approach explains that immigration policies are influenced by the history and politics of the society as well as by the perception of national identity. As Meyers comments, this approach explains why "some countries favor permanent immigration, while others prefer temporary labor migration" (2000: 1255). For example, Australia and Canada prefer more permanent immigration than many European countries, and the national identity approach delineates the causes of these differences. Indeed, the national identity approach shows that sex, class, race, ethnicity, and religion frequently influence immigration policies, and that immigration policies may ultimately affect the demographic composition of countries. The national identity approach further allows for the mobilization of immigrant workers to contest and challenge local, national and global predatory forces. However, one of the major limitations of the national identity approach is its ambiguity over the definition of national identity.

The integration of these two approaches—the political economy approach and the national identity approach—explores historical, global, local, and national processes in transnational migration. Integrating these approaches, chapter 3 examines the immigration policies of Canada, which currently focuses more on the skilled category of immigrant to meet its labor market needs, and explores the dynamics of immigration in women's lives. The national identity approach demonstrates how the multi-ethnic identity of migrants will shape Canada's directions in the future. Using a feminist analysis, chapters 3 and 4 demonstrate how the labor market in Canada is gendered, class-based and racialized.

NOTES

1. This refers only to documented migrant workers and excludes undocumented migrants. In this book, my point of analysis pertains only to documented immigrant and migrant workers.

2. In an introduction to the journal *Citizenship Studies*, Brodie (2004) points out that neo-liberal globalism emphasizes economic growth and market forces and enforces a diverse range of privatization, restructuring public sectors by deregulation. Brodie examines citizenship and globalization, both contested and transgressed issues, beyond the nation state. In contrast to Brodie, I will use and examine neo-liberal globalism within the context of the nation state and its domestic issues, more specifically, immigration policies and their impact on various layers of commodification of immigrant labor, especially female immigrants.

3. I have used the terms "neo-liberal globalism" and "globalism" interchangeably.

4. A migrant-receiving country goes through a change of national identity—for example, from an Anglo-Saxon society to a diverse ethnic population. The two best examples are Australia and Canada.

5. A migrant-sending country loses its skilled labor—what critics identify as a "brain drain." Most of these migrants eventually settle permanently in the immigrant-receiving country.

6. I am not underestimating the organized groups of international smugglers and snakeheads who facilitate the migration of people transnationally. Based on the documentation of international human smuggling worldwide, one may argue that the sovereignty and power of the state has declined due to migration caused by globalization. This book focuses on immigration policies and their effectiveness or ineffectiveness with regard to commodification and decommodification of immigrant labor, but does not address issues around border control.

7. Contrary to popular beliefs, undocumented migrants are generally people who enter a country with legal documents, but overstay once their visas or work-permits expire. I am not totally ruling out people who cross borders without proper documentation. However, their numbers are negligible in Canada, especially after the increase in customs and border enforcement between Canada and the US after 9/11.

8. Transnational migrants (sometimes called transmigrants) include immigrants, migrant workers, guest workers, students, undocumented workers, refugees, women who are trafficked, and so on.

9. February 21 is the Language Martyrs Day in Bangladesh. In 1952, several university students were killed by the police during a demonstration to establish *Bangla* (Bengali) as one of the state languages of Pakistan. Bangladesh (the former East Pakistan) was a part of Pakistan at that time and became independent through armed struggles in 1971.

10. Identity is a fluid category, and an immigrant's identity relies on the sociopolitical and economic context and geographical space. Under normal circumstances (i.e., absence of physical

or psychological or other threat), an immigrant carries dual identities and is not willing to abandon either.

11. The Filipino community around the world successfully organized protests and demonstrations pressuring the government in the Philippines to protect its citizens when two domestics—one in Singapore and one in the United Arab Emirates—were sentenced to death. In the latter case, the Philippine government was successful in releasing the person.

12. In this category, I have not included sex workers or trafficked women and girls, who are beyond the scope of this book.

13. For the past few years, most immigrants in Canada come from Asian countries. The country of origin (including ancestry) of all the women I interviewed was Asia. Consequently, Asia dominates in my citation and analysis.

14. All but one of the fourteen interviewees (from Bangladesh, India and Burma) in my study migrated to Canada under the dependent/family category.

15. Exceptions exist. For example, of all migrant and immigrant communities, the Filipino community is the most organized in terms of advancing its labor rights and providing opportunities for developing a social network.

3

Canadian Immigration in an Era of Neo-Liberalism

Trends and Impacts

> The top five source countries of immigrants remained unchanged from the first quarter of this year.... Fifty-nine percent of these new immigrants were female, a fact that is largely attributable to immigrants who qualify for permanent residence as part of the Live-in Caregiver Program. (Citizenship and Immigration Canada 2004c: 1–2)

> B.C. gets the lowest mark in the country for its immigrant language services. ... B.C. is also the only province that stops providing fully funded ESL (English as a second language) classes once students achieve rudimentary English skills. (*Vancouver Sun* 2005: A1)

CANADIAN IMMIGRATION PLAN

Immigration has been vital to Canada's socioeconomic development since the beginning of Canada's nation-building process in the nineteenth and twentieth centuries. Over fourteen million people have immigrated to Canada since 1867. These immigrants, as well as their descendants, have contributed to Canada's socioeconomic development and have defined the country's identity (Citizenship and Immigration Canada 1999). In order to be competitive in what Citizenship and Immigration refers to as a "knowledge based" and "service oriented" world economy and for its continued economic growth, Canada presently focuses more on recruiting skilled immigrants (1999). This focus on "skills" differs significantly from the Canadian government's previous emphasis on "family category" and from its historical use of "unskilled" labor from Asia, which will be examined in chapter 4.[1]

The growth of immigration in Canada is inextricably linked to the history of colonization and subjugation of the First Nations people in Canada. Over the past 40 years, the shift from "unskilled" to "family category" to "skilled category" indicates new directions in Canada's immigration policy: First, the immigration policy based on the earlier racial preference has been shifted to focus on skills of the applicant irrespective of national origins. In addition to the economic need for skilled workers, this shift from racial preference to emphasis on skills and educational qualifications of immigrants happened due to protests and campaigns by the racialized population as well as increasing pressures from the international community, including the Commonwealth countries. Second, the liberalization of immigration policies fostered the arrival of large numbers of racialized women, including children and wives of racialized men who were already living in Canada, as well as domestic workers and nurses from the Caribbean and the Philippines. Third, the changed immigration legislation facilitated the entry of racialized people, specifically people from Asia, in greater numbers compared with the European population. Fourth, the 1976 Act emphasized unlimited family reunifications. Consequently, a vast number of racialized immigrants gained entry through the family class—something that would not easily happen through the independent class categories in the 1970s and 1980s.

Since Canada lacks both a steady natural population growth that provides an abundance of labor and a younger population that provides a cheap labor pool, immigration is essential to maintain a viable and competitive labor force for Canada's economy. This need is clearly reflected in Canada's Annual Immigration Plan. According to the Immigration Plan, for the year 2000, the target range was between 200,000 to 225,000; for 2001, the target numbers reflected the same plan and proposed an increase of 210,000 to 235,000 for the year 2002 (Citizenship and Immigration Canada 2001). The three-year consecutive plans also indicate that Canada has its own set plans about numbers and about who will be admitted to Canada.[2] These numbers also include Convention refugees. The following table clearly reveals Canada's planned and actual immigrant intake.

Table 3.1 illustrates a number of points argued in chapter 1. For example, globalization and global agreements and pacts have in fact not succeeded in stimulating a free flow of people as they have capital and goods. While these agreements and pacts have enhanced the movements of the skilled workers across nations where skilled labor is in intense demand, receiving countries like Canada have established effective regulatory systems that successfully control and manipulate the flow of immigrants.

This chapter investigates current immigration trends of Canada in this era of neo-globalism and the implications of these trends for immigrants from Asia. By examining the recent patterns of immigrants, the chapter reveals the shifting from emphasis on "family class" to the "skilled category" of immigrants, where the majority of women enter Canada as "dependents."

Table 3.1. Planned and Actual Immigrant and Refugee Landings by Category in Canada, 2002

Immigration Category	Family	Skilled Worker	Business	Other	Total Immigrants	Refugees	Total Immigrants and Refugees
Planned Landings Range	56,000–62,000	115,800–125,300	12,000–13,000	2,000–2,800	187,000–204,600	23,000–30,400	210,000–235,000
Actual Landings	65,277	123,357	11,041	2,145	203,947	25,111	229,058

Note: "Other" category includes live-in caregivers, post-determination refugee claimants, deferred removal orders, and retirees. Refugee category includes dependents who live abroad of refugees landed in Canada.

Source: "Facts and Figures 2002: Immigration Overview"—Citizenship and Immigration Canada: 4.

Investigating the job-market differentials between Canadian-born laborers and immigrants, the chapter then reveals the inadequate job and language training, the absence of accreditation, and the government's declining support to settlement that ultimately deter immigrant women's labor from being decommodified. These factors combine to produce immigrants, especially racialized women, who are vulnerable to all sorts of marginalization. In addition, these factors combine to foster the growth of different layers of commodification.

The first section of this chapter discusses briefly the major tenets of Canadian immigration policies, which have shifted focus from Europe to Asia. To show the top ten source countries of immigrants in the beginning of the 21st century, the chapter provides immigration charts for three consecutive years, from 2000–2002. The next section briefly describes how immigrants are categorized and examines the causes and the consequences of the shifting from family class to skilled category. The third section examines gender variation in the skilled category in terms of immigration numbers, education, and age. In other words, the skilled category is gendered, as only 25 percent of women migrate under this category. Exploring how Canadian immigration reproduces immigrant women's secondary status and different layers of commodification when they enter Canada, the next section analyzes how access to job markets differs between immigrant men and women and how unemployment rates vary between immigrant men and women as a result. The final section briefly examines programs and accreditation, including language and job training, provided for immigrants. These programs ultimately foster the commodification of immigrants' labor and eliminate or greatly reduce any possibilities for decommodification in the future. A more detailed examination of immigrants' accreditation and barriers to decommodification will be laid out in chapter 7 through the narrations of immigrant women.

RECENT IMMIGRANTS TO CANADA: COUNTRIES OF ORIGIN AND TOP SOURCES

Immigrants to Canada originate in an array of countries. These immigrants' countries of origin shape the ethnic composition of Canada and contribute to its national identity. In the last decade of the 20th century and the beginning of the 21st century, there has been a significant shift in Canada's primary-source countries. In 1990, Hong Kong and Poland were the two primary-source countries, accounting for about 20 percent of Canada's immigrants; in 2000, China and India were the two top source countries, accounting for about 30 percent of immigrants (R.B. Global 2004). In fact, China and India were the two top source countries for five consecutive years, that is, 1998 to 2002. The following three figures of annual immigration clearly indicate this trend.

Figure 3.1. Immigration to Canada by Top Ten Source Countries, 2000

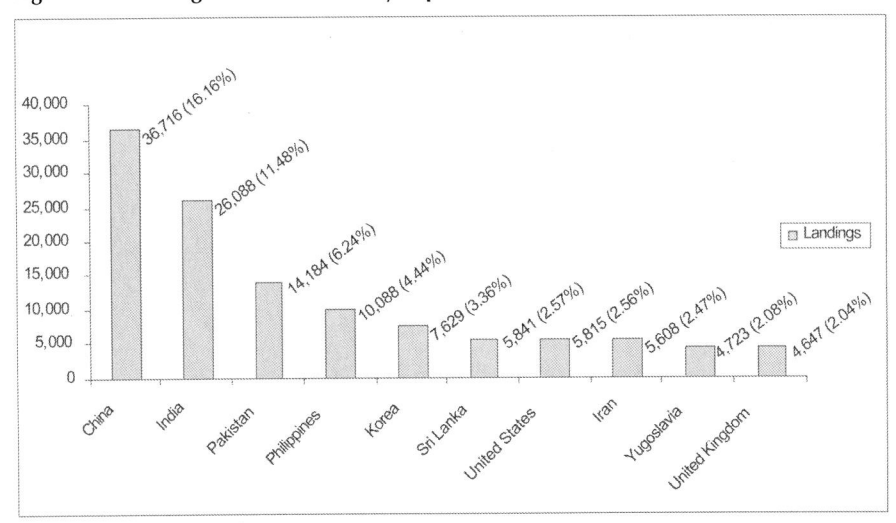

Country	Landings
China	36,716 (16.16%)
India	26,088 (11.48%)
Pakistan	14,184 (6.24%)
Philippines	10,088 (4.44%)
Korea	7,629 (3.36%)
Sri Lanka	5,841 (2.57%)
United States	5,815 (2.56%)
Iran	5,608 (2.47%)
Yugoslavia	4,723 (2.08%)
United Kingdom	4,647 (2.04%)

Note: Korea refers to the Republic of Korea and China refers to the People's Republic of China. Totals include principal applicants and dependents.

Source: "Facts and Figures 2002: Immigration Overview"—Citizenship and Immigration Canada: 8.

Figure 3.2. Immigration to Canada by Top Ten Source Countries, 2001

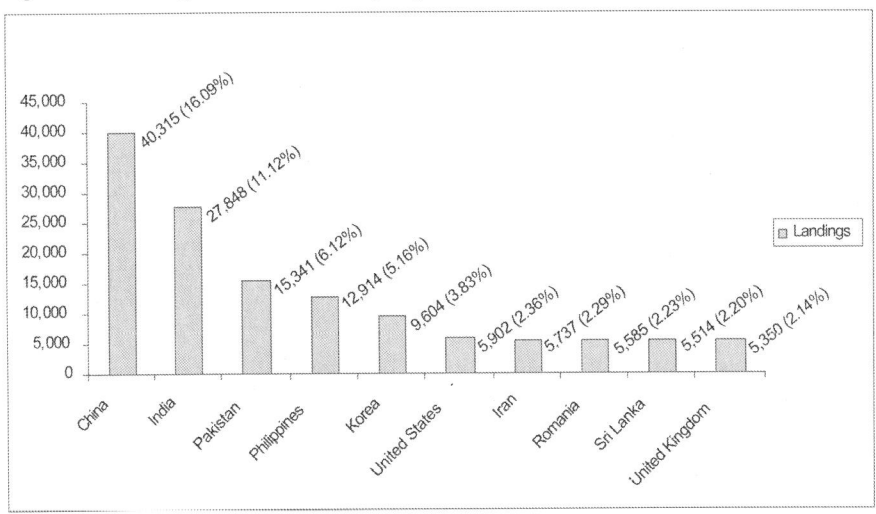

Country	Landings
China	40,315 (16.09%)
India	27,848 (11.12%)
Pakistan	15,341 (6.12%)
Philippines	12,914 (5.16%)
Korea	9,604 (3.83%)
United States	5,902 (2.36%)
Iran	5,737 (2.29%)
Romania	5,585 (2.23%)
Sri Lanka	5,514 (2.20%)
United Kingdom	5,350 (2.14%)

Note: Korea refers to the Republic of Korea and China refers to the People's Republic of China. Totals include principal applicants and dependents.

Source: "Facts and Figures 2002: Immigration Overview"—Citizenship and Immigration Canada: 8.

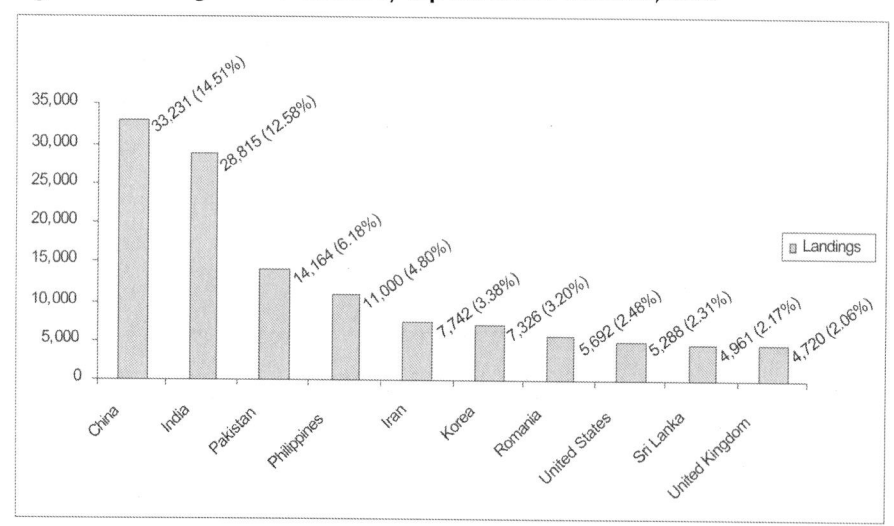

Figure 3.3. Immigration to Canada by Top Ten Source Countries, 2002

China: 33,231 (14.51%)
India: 28,815 (12.58%)
Pakistan: 14,164 (6.18%)
Philippines: 11,000 (4.80%)
Iran: 7,742 (3.38%)
Korea: 7,326 (3.20%)
Romania: 5,692 (2.48%)
United States: 5,288 (2.31%)
Sri Lanka: 4,961 (2.17%)
United Kingdom: 4,720 (2.06%)

Note: Korea refers to the Republic of Korea and China refers to the People's Republic of China. Totals include principal applicants and dependents.
Source: "Facts and Figures 2002: Immigration Overview"—Citizenship and Immigration Canada: 8.

The above figures demonstrate that seven (China, India, Pakistan, Philippines, Korea, Sri Lanka, and Iran) of the top ten source countries are in Asia and almost 50 percent of recent immigrants originate in Asia. As Halli and Driedger comment, this is clearly a marked variation from Canada's previous pattern of immigration: "In 1951 nine of the top ten source countries were European; six of these nine were northern European. Immigrants from the tenth country, the United States, were largely originally of European stock as well" (1999: 4). The current shift, that is, from Europe to Asia, happened mostly due to changes in Canada's immigration policy.[3] For example, in addition to removing the racist content of its immigration policy in 1962, Canada introduced a non-discriminatory points system in 1967. The introduction of a points system made a dramatic change in the evaluating of applicants' entry criteria. Applicants for immigration were assessed not on their country of origin, but on their potential to contribute to the Canadian economy (Akbari 1999). Since 1967, a number of Immigrant Acts have been passed that eliminated open discrimination based on racial grounds. The points system and non-discriminatory acts shifted the countries of origin toward the countries of Asia. The following three-year annual figure clearly indicates that from 2000–2002, more than 50 percent of current immigrants in Canada came from Asia and the Pacific.

The introduction of the 1967 Immigration Act and its new selection criteria clearly changed dramatically the demographic composition of Canada's immigrants. As Halli and Driedger state,

In 1976, six of the top ten countries of origin were non-European, and by 1984, six years after the new Immigration Act [1978] had been proclaimed, two Asian countries—Vietnam and Hong Kong—ranked first and second, Britain had dropped to fifth place, and seven of the ten leading countries of origin were in the Third World. This trend has continued into the nineties, when Britain dropped to ninth place. By 1993, the seven top donor countries were Asian and they were sending visible minorities. (1999: 4)

Although Canada's immigration policy has received mixed reactions from different groups of people (Samuel 1990), the 2001 census identified Canada as one of the most diverse nations in the world. Changes through the immigration policy have created a multiracial and multicultural Canadian society. Anderson (2003) describes Canada as a "kaleidoscope" of cultures, languages, and nationalities reflecting more than 200 diverse ethnic groups—a mix second only to Australia's.

This shift of source countries from Europe to Asia has happened for several reasons: First, English-speaking Europeans have enough jobs in Europe due to the formation of the European Union and other pacts and the labor markets' relatively better performance in Europe. Second, China's neo-liberal economic policies have allowed the Chinese population to emigrate to Canada on a large scale: "The liberalization of emigration policy in the People's Republic of China (PRC) in the mid-1990s to allow the departure of highly-skilled workers meant that, by the late 1990s, Canada no longer relied on family members to fill quotas" (DeVoretz 2003: 6). This reason alone

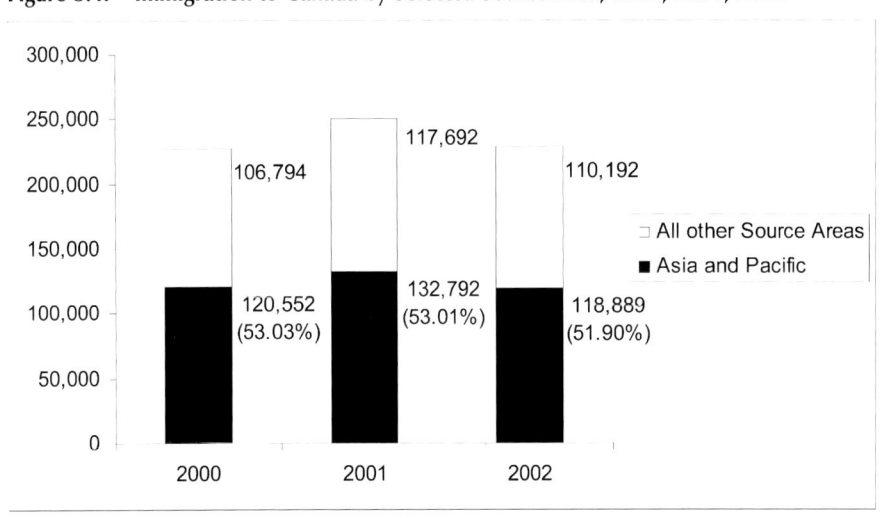

Figure 3.4. Immigration to Canada by Selected Source Area, 2000, 2001, 2002

Note: Totals include principal applicants and dependents.

Source: "Facts and Figures 2002: Immigration Overview"—Citizenship and Immigration Canada: 8.

reveals the significance of the source country in meeting the labor requirements of Canada. Third, as the next section will show, the recent shift from "family class" to "skilled category" in immigration also contributed to boosting the number of immigrants from Asia. In several key sectors of the economy, Canada lacks enough skilled workers, which countries in Asia supply. Fourth, compared with European countries, the population growth of Asia as well as its liberalized economies, especially in China and India, has generated a steady supply of "skilled" labor. Finally, the aggressive labor export policies of Asian countries such as the Philippines have produced a continuous labor supply to receiving countries such as Canada.

In 2003, China was again the primary-source country, followed by India, Pakistan and the Philippines. In fact, in 2003, an increase of 9 percent was found for China and the Philippines. Interestingly, during the same period, permanent residents from India declined by 15 percent and from Pakistan by 13 percent (Citizenship and Immigration Canada 2004b). In the case of India, this decline may have happened for a number of plausible reasons. Due to the booming of Information Technology and the relocation of multinational companies to cities such as Bangalore, Delhi and Hyderabad, commonly identified as "Silicon Valley," some "skilled" migrants may prefer to stay in India and others may find better opportunities than those in Canada (for details, see DeVoretz 2003; Dryburgh and Hamel 2004). In addition, many immigrants from India used to enter Canada under the family category, which is in decline due to the focus on skilled immigrants. In the case of Pakistan, 9/11 and Canada's current security measures may have deterred prospective immigrants from entering Canada.[4]

FROM "FAMILY CLASS" TO "SKILLED" CATEGORY: VIABILITY OF THE SKILLED CATEGORY

Immigrants are selected either to reunite families or on the basis of possible economic contribution to Canada. To fulfill its international humanitarian commitment, Canada also accepts a certain number of refugees annually. Most immigrants to Canada apply under four major categories[5]: family, skilled workers,[6] business, and refugees. Skilled workers are frequently termed "economic migrants," and current admission into Canada based on skilled category (including applicants and their dependents) is more than half of Canada's total intake. Table 3.2 that follows demonstrates the entry of immigrants and their categories.

From 2000–2002, more than 50 percent of immigrants entered Canada under the skilled category, a significant departure from the previous trend that heavily weighed the family category.[7] Table 3.2 demonstrates that the federal government meets the target numbers set in the Annual Immigration Plan that has been mentioned earlier, and its target numbers are never exceeded.

Table 3.2. Immigration to Canada by Category by Year, 2000, 2001, 2002

Immigration Category	2000	2001	2002
Family	*60,566*	*66,711*	*65,277*
Spouse	35,262	37,727	35,469
Parents and Grandparents	17,758	21,300	22,502
Total Family % of Total Immigrants and Refugees	26.64%	26.63%	28.49%
Economic	*136,210*	*155,622*	*138,506*
Skilled Workers	118,510	137,135	123,357
Total Skilled Workers % of Total Immigrants and Refugees	52.13%	54.75%	53.85%
Refugees	*30,064*	*27,905*	*25,111*
Total Refugees % of Total Immigrants and Refugees	13.22%	11.14%	10.96%
Total Immigrants and Refugees	*227,300*	*250,443*	*229,058*

Note: "Refugees" include Kosovo refugees who arrived as part of a special movement, as well as dependents living abroad of refugees landed in Canada.

Source: "Facts and Figures 2002: Immigration Overview"— Citizenship and Immigration Canada: 5.

It is thus evident that despite various global forces, Canada has a firm grip over its yearly intake of immigrants. DeVoretz supports this point:

[O]ver 230,000 entered during the boom period of 1973 while only 84,000 were admitted during the 1984 recession. By 1992–93, arrivals had again surged to 254,000. It appears that, in the aggregate, a "tap on, tap off" immigration policy was feasible and that Canadian demand—not the supply—ultimately dictated yearly intakes. (2003: 3)

Since the publication of the 1997 immigration legislative review report, *Not Just Numbers*, the Liberal government has charted new directions for immigration policy that ultimately facilitate the entry of immigrants who will contribute to Canada's economic prosperity.[8] The selection criteria emphasize "skills" that include education, proficiency in at least one of the two official languages (English and French), and self-sufficiency (meaning that an immigrant has enough funds for his or her initial settlement in Canada). The requirements of the skilled category consequently have discriminatory effects on women—more specifically, women from non-English-speaking countries such as Asia. The immigration officers' discretionary power and the devaluing of women's credentials from their countries of origin place women in a precarious situation, especially women from Asia, where women already have a secondary position.[9] Despite good qualifications in their countries of origin, many immigrant women are simply classified as "dependents." This dependent status fosters the growth of various layers of commodification of immigrant women's labor and compromises their having access to benefits and entitlements and their becoming decommodified in a liberal welfare state like Canada.

Immigration of skilled workers played a crucial role in the 1960s when Canada attempted to transform its economy from resource-based to urban/industrial-based (Stein 2003). The shortage of skilled workers and the growing expansion of an urban/industrial-based economy persuaded the federal government to change its immigration policy first in 1962 to nondiscriminatory and in 1967 a points system (Stein 2003). It was thus not the altruistic or benevolent nature of the federal government that transformed the immigration policy from racist to non-discriminatory, but Canada's desperate need for skilled labor for the manufacturing and service sectors of the economy that influenced the government to adopt universal criteria[10] for admission. Family class predominated for about three decades after the introduction of the 1967 Immigration Act. The family-class category made women, especially racialized women, dependents, and this has had long-term adverse impact on women. First, women as dependents were ineligible for various entitlements that immigrant men as principal applicants enjoyed—for example, free language training courses, social assistance and so on. Second, this very dependent status facilitated immigrant women's labor being commodified and hindered them from being decommodified in the labor market. Third, immigrant women's labor, especially racialized women's labor, gets concentrated in different layers of commodification without prospects for being decommodified, as is illustrated in chapter 4. Currently, the increasing shift to "skilled" category has made the family class the least preferred choice: "[T]he Department of Citizenship and Immigration would first process available independent-class immigrants and then, at year's end, fill the annual quota by processing those in the more plentiful family class" (DeVoretz 2003: 4). This reveals Canada's strong preference for the skilled category in processing, with the family class perceived as an abundant source of supply but of the lowest priority.[11]

In December 2002, apparently in order to assess prospective "skilled" category immigrants more rigorously, the new Immigration and Refugee Protection Act increased the points system from 70 to 75. According to DeVoretz, this increase of points was introduced as a response to "the declining economic performance of Canada's highly skilled immigrants in the 1990s" (DeVoretz 2003: 7). If that is so, then racialized women have the least economic performance and the least chance to be decommodified. This increase of qualified points also indicates that racialized women have the least chance to enter Canada under the skilled category. It is evident that according to Canada's immigrant policy, when immigrants' performance is lower than that of the Canadian-born population, immigrants themselves bear the sole responsibility. This kind of interpretation overlooks several inter-related factors. First, new immigrants look for jobs on their own, and it takes time to find these "skill"-related jobs. Second, the lack of recognition of immigrants' skills and their adjustment period to a new country require more time than the policy makers expect. Third, this interpretation overlooks the barriers to decommodification created by the state and underestimates various forms of commodification.

In a highly competitive global economy, Canada is competing with core countries such as the US and semi-periphery countries such as Australia to recruit "skilled" workers. Recent studies (Dryburgh and Hamel 2004; DeVoretz 2003) further suggest that those who enter Canada as skilled workers are more likely to emigrate. As DeVoretz comments,

> [P]olitical institutions in Canada have actually hastened the strategic onward of highly-skilled immigrants. A Canadian passport, for example, allows erstwhile immigrants to enter the US under a Temporary Non-Immigrant (TN) NAFTA visa. But regardless of all the possible permutations for onward mobility in a world of dual citizenships and multiple passports, the point remains that those who come to Canada in the future will not necessarily stay. (2003: 9)

Trade agreements, pacts such as NAFTA, and dual national identities may have accelerated the emigration of skilled and business-class immigrants to Canada. However, recent events suggest that even these immigrants do not provide enough workers for the Canadian labor market. In 2004, painting a gloomy picture of a shortage of skilled workers, Denis Coderre, then Immigration Minister, lowered the passing grade for skilled immigrants from 75 to 67 (*The Globe and Mail* 2004). This lowering indicates clearly that the entry points set in 2002 were too high and created barriers to meeting Canada's Annual Immigration Plan. The supply of immigrants under the skilled category is not infinite; the fierce competition in the global economy and Canada's complex immigration procedure continue to produce a shortage of skilled laborers for Canada's national economy.[12] To keep skilled immigrant workers in the country, the government undoubtedly needs to develop a regulatory system that will establish universal criteria in conjunction with professional bodies and associations to recognize immigrants' educational qualifications and job/training experience in their countries of origin. If a regulatory system is established, the process will pave the way for immigrant workers, especially racialized women, to be decommodified, although this single step is certainly not enough for racialized women. The regulatory system requires incorporating an anti-racist and anti-sexist framework to address racism and sexism embedded in the labor market.

WOMEN AS "DEPENDENTS": INTERSECTION OF GENDER AND CLASS

As table 3.3 shows, out of the total number of immigrants from 2000 to 2002, men and women up to 44 years old have almost equal representation in terms of age.

Table 3.3. Immigration to Canada by Selected Ages and Gender, 2000, 2001, 2002

	2000 Male Total	%	2000 Female Total	%	2001 Male Total	%	2001 Female Total	%	2002 Male Total	%	2002 Female Total	%
0–14 Years	26,176	23.31	24,966	21.71	29,091	23.54	28,159	22.19	26,315	23.33	24,650	21.20
15–24 Years	14,072	12.53	18,617	16.19	15,040	12.17	19,276	15.19	13,665	12.11	17,939	15.43
25–44 Years	58,177	51.80	56,764	49.35	63,427	51.33	62,646	49.36	56,804	50.35	56,684	48.75
Total, all ages	112,313		115,022		123,558		126,916		112,811		116,278	

Note: Totals include principal applicants and dependents.

Source: "Facts and Figures 2002: Immigration Overview"—Citizenship and Immigration Canada: 10.

This equal representation indicates that Immigration Canada seeks gender balance in recruitment. One result of this acceptance of almost 50 percent female immigrants is that women as reproducers have roles in Canada despite their entry as "dependents."

Although in all categories the majority of women immigrants enter as dependents, gender is distributed highly unequally across skill levels. During the period 2000–2002, 75 percent of "skilled" workers were males, and 25 percent females (Citizenship and Immigration Canada 2002: 93). This gender differentiation in the skilled category further reflects that most women under the skilled category are entering Canada as dependents. Indeed, in the period 2000–2002, 62 percent of the dependents in the skilled category were women, and 38 percent men; this percentage includes both female and male children (Citizenship and Immigration Canada 2002: 92). Analysis of gender distribution reveals that a disproportionately increasing number of men has been selected for the skilled category. In terms of the gender distribution of immigrants destined for the labor market, immigrant men are the dominant group now, at the beginning of the 21st century: "The number of professional-level female immigrants has declined relative to male professional, from above 40 percent in the early 1990s to just 27% in 2000. . . . At the skilled and technical level, the proportion of women has been fluctuating between 30 percent and 40 percent, with a slightly decreasing trend in recent years, but no clear general pattern" (Citizenship and Immigration Canada 2004a: 5). Citizenship and Immigrant's reluctance to a general pattern is clear, although the quotation reflects that most racialized women, specially women from Asia, enter as dependents, also that the process of recognition of professional immigrant women's credentials is questionable. Entry of racialized women as dependents thus perpetuates women's roles as reproducers and makes their labor commodified as soon as they enter the labor market, with few prospects of decommodification of their labor.

Under the family category, women historically enter as dependents, and this trend still persists. Although women enter as dependents under the family class, women usually have almost the same or more education than men do in the family class. Table 3.4 that follows illustrates that from 2000–2002, the percentage of women with a bachelor's degree or master's degree was higher than the percentage of men, but more men than women had doctorates.

Compared with the skilled category,[13] it is clear that women who enter as immigrants under the family class category have good qualifications—in fact, qualifications on par with the men.

The non-discriminatory act of 1962 and the subsequent immigration acts generally tend to bring into Canada immigrants from high socioeconomic background. For example, the Immigration Act of 1976 introduced the business-class category that included entrepreneurs, investors, and self-employed persons whose selection was based on their ability to create jobs for themselves and others in Canada. This business-class category has been

Table 3.4. Family Class by Selected Level of Education and Gender, 2000, 2001, and 2002

	2000 Male Total	%	2000 Female Total	%	2001 Male Total	%	2001 Female Total	%	2002 Male Total	%	2002 Female Total	%
Bachelor's Degree	2,940	18.13	5,438	21.09	3,337	18.61	6,253	22.60	3,582	20.37	6,197	23.37
Master's Degree	618	3.81	1,219	4.73	713	3.98	1,327	4.80	788	4.48	1,458	5.50
Doctorate	157	0.97	138	0.54	216	1.20	170	0.61	199	1.13	169	0.64
Total, all education levels	16,212		25,787		17,936		27,663		17,583		26,515	

Note: Totals include principal applicants only, aged 15 or older.

Source: "Facts and Figures 2002: Immigration Overview"—Citizenship and Immigration Canada: 48.

continued despite the government's increasing focus on skills. Even the current emphasis on skills selects for a high socioeconomic category from the sending countries. The high cost of application, other subsequent expenses, and the landed immigration fee (i.e., $975 per immigrant) ensure that only upper-class people from sending countries enter Canada. It appears that the discriminatory race-based act before 1962 has been replaced by a class-based act, with upper-class people from Asia as the preferred group. Yet, even when women enter Canada as part of a preferred group, gender differentiation in terms of accepting women's skills and credentials creates a situation where women enter as "secondary," "dependent," and "unequal," no matter what their qualifications. This secondary status has made racialized immigrant women's labor secondary and thus commodified in the labor market, with remote chance of becoming decommodified. Dependent status creates unequal status as soon as racialized women enter the labor market.

IMMIGRANT WOMEN AND THE LABOR MARKET: A BRIEF OVERVIEW

Since the 1990s, the skilled category has become the largest immigrant group, and as already mentioned, gender is unevenly distributed across the skill category. Immigrants are increasingly entering Canada with more credentials and higher skills (i.e., education and training in countries of origin), as reflected by the higher numbers of trained engineers and scientists (Citizenship and Immigration Canada 2004 Spring). Immigrants to Canada, historically, have demonstrated better performance in the labor market even though their initial earnings were lower than those of Canadian-born workers. However, the increasing recruitment of immigrants based on "skills" has not enhanced immigrants' labor market participation. In contrast, the nature and pattern of their jobs and the entitlements pertinent to their jobs have deteriorated, and nearly one of three immigrants works in sales and services. In the last decade, immigrants are less likely to be employed, and their education and credentials do not assist them in finding the jobs they anticipated. In the labor market, a significant difference exists between the Canadian-born population and immigrants, with immigrant women performing the least well when compared with immigrant men and Canadian-born women. Badets and Howatson-Leo comment: "For Canadian-born women, employment rates climbed from 52 percent for those with less than high school to 86 percent for the university educated. In contrast, the employment rate of recent immigrant women with a university degree was just 58 percent" (1999: 18). This indicates that immigrant women with a university degree have an employment rate almost equivalent to a Canadian-born high-school dropout.

Like Canadian women who are high-school dropouts, immigrant women have no prospects of being decommodified. Badets and Howatson-Leo's findings are based on the 1996 census, yet this trend continues today. Thompson (2002) has summarized three principal characteristics of immigrants' labor market performance: (1) higher unemployment rates; (2) higher incidence of poverty among immigrants; (3) lower earnings. For example, in Toronto in 1981, 45 percent of people living in high-poverty neighborhoods were immigrants [read racialized population], and twenty years later, that is, in 2001, the percentage of immigrants had increased to 65 percent in these neighborhoods (*Toronto Star* 2005 April 8).

As mentioned above, in the labor market, immigrant women perform the least compared with immigrant men and Canadian-born women and men. For instance, in the 1996 census, the rate of unemployment among immigrant women was 20 percent, whereas the rate of unemployment among Canadian-born women was 8.6 percent (Thompson 2002: 10). Compared with the 1986 census, the unemployment rate among immigrant women in 1996 had increased by 5 percent whereas the unemployment rate among Canadian-born women had declined by 2 percent (Thompson 2002: 10). This declining rate of immigrant women's performance in the labor market has been analyzed in numerous ways by both policy makers and academics. Two major streams of thought are found: (1) free trade agreements, technological change, language ability, the labor market in the 1990s, and lack of networks are factors that contribute to the poor performance of immigrant women in the labor market[14]; (2) racism, sexism and classism contribute to immigrant women's low participation in the economy.[15] Both these streams of thought are aware of the non-recognition of immigrant women's credentials, which include degrees, training, and job experience in their countries of origin and also job experience in other countries (for example, Hong Kong). However, these streams of thought never explore various layers of commodification of immigrants' labor, let alone racialized women and the decommodification of their labor. If one examines these two major streams of thought, it becomes clear that the issue of immigrant women's declining performance in the labor market has not received much in-depth analysis and that what analysis there is has not benefited from immigrant women's narrations. Indeed, the prospect of decommodification of immigrant women's labor is never an issue in immigration literature. Literature dealing with immigrants, albeit racialized women's labor, is more concerned with the percentage of immigrants rather than their entitlements and various layers of commodification and decommodification. Chapters 6 and 7 later in this book analyse this issue further, demonstrating through immigrant women's narrations their multiple layers of commodification and the systemic and structural barriers to their labor being decommodified.

IMMIGRANTS' SETTLEMENT AND INTEGRATION: PROGRAMS AND ACCREDITATION

Canada's three major cities—Vancouver (British Columbia), Toronto (Ontario) and Montreal (Quebec)—absorbed 73 percent of the immigrants who arrived between 1991 and 2001, according to a Statistics Canada study (Greenway 2004). The study further mentions that just twenty years earlier, that is, in the 1970s, 58 percent of immigrants lived in these three large metropolitan centers. The increase to 73 percent by 2001 is a sharp one, creating pressures on immigrant services as well as on city services. As the Statistics Canada study found, recent immigrants are more likely to need public transport, immigrant-support services and English-language classes as well as housing.

Beyond the three major cities, other immigrants settled in large cities in Ontario, Alberta, Manitoba, and Quebec (for example, Ottawa, Hamilton, Kitchener, Windsor, London, Calgary, Edmonton, Winnipeg, Gatineau). Between 1981 and 1996, 2.1 million immigrants entered overall, and more recent immigrants than Canadian-born persons are of prime working age, according to Citizenship and Immigration Canada:

> Almost one-half of recent immigrants (48 percent) are 25 to 44 years of age, and 14 percent are children under 15. Of Canada's Canadian-born population, those at ages from 25 to 44 make up one third (32 percent) and children one quarter (24 percent). There are relatively fewer persons of 45 and over among recent immigrants. (Citizenship and Immigration Canada 2001: xii)

The 1996 census clearly indicates that immigration is the greatest source of a young and active labor force in Canada. For the past several years, the focus on the "skilled" category, which contributed 55 percent of the total intake of immigrants in 2004,[16] continuously renews this labor force. The question arises: How do the federal and provincial governments provide services to this vast, active and "skilled" immigrant labor force so that the immigrants involved can settle and integrate? To be integrated, immigrants also require having access to job-related entitlements and benefits. In other words, decommodification of labor in the liberal welfare state is one of the pre-conditions of integration and settlement.

Of the provinces, Ontario is the largest immigrant-receiving province, and British Columbia the second largest. Clearly, Canada's most popular immigrant destinations are Ontario and British Columbia—the arrival of immigrants increased in these two provinces at 20 percent of the national rate (Citizenship and Immigration Canada 2004 Spring). Since 1981, three quarters of Vancouver's immigrants have come from Asia and the Pacific, and 16 percent of immigrants from Asia have selected Vancouver as their residence (Citizenship and Immigration Canada 2001b). Of the recent Filipino immigrants, 62 percent are women, a considerably higher percentage of women than from any other group (Citizenship and Immigration Canada 2001b). In 2003, most immigrants from the Philippines settled outside of Toronto, Vancouver and Montreal (Citizenship and Immigration Canada 2004 Fall). The federal government currently is working to persuade immigrants to settle outside the major cities, and the settlement pattern of Filipino migrants seems to reflect that effort. However, the increasing number of female Filipino migrants and their settlement outside major cities may be as likely related to the high demand for live-in caregivers and for "mail-order brides" outside of the three mega-cities. (Several interviewees for this book live outside of Greater Vancouver, and many of the interviewees were live-in caregivers.)

Both the federal government and provincial governments play significant roles in terms of immigrants' entry, settlement and integration. Of all the provinces and territories, Quebec has had the right since 1978 to select its own "skilled" and business-class immigrants, as a result of a separate agreement Quebec made with the federal government. As Quebec has the lowest number of childbirths in Canada, it is likely that Quebec would accept any prospective immigrant who would fill either its demographic or its economic needs. Due to the current shortage of "skilled" labor across the country, other provinces have also made special arrangements with the federal government. For example, in March 2002, a provincial nominee program was introduced in Alberta (*Calgary Herald* 2005). Under this agreement, in response to demands from employers, Alberta is allowed to recruit a certain number of skilled workers to be fast-tracked for immigration. Half the jobs are in businesses with fewer than 50 people, and three-quarters of the jobs are outside Calgary and Edmonton. Clearly, the shortage of labor extends beyond major cities. It may also be true that Canadian-born workers and immigrants under the family category are reluctant to move to smaller places.

The federal government's funding for new immigrants' settlement services varies from province to province; in addition, the number of new immigrants in a province does not determine the amount of funding. For instance, while 57 percent of new immigrants settled in Ontario in 2004, the province received 34 percent of federal support for settlement and language training services (*Toronto Star* 2005 April). It is worthwhile to mention here that community-based agencies, not the provincial government, provide support and services to new immigrants, and these agencies receive financial support from both the federal government and individual provincial governments. However, in recent years, continuous restructuring of both the federal and the provincial governments has slashed funds to these agencies.

Under neo-liberal policies, funding for language programs and vocational programs has been restructured and reduced, resulting in the restriction of immigrants' access to services. For example, to implement cost-free immigrant settlement services—another neo-liberal strategy—the federal government now charges $975 as a landing fee, a move that forces immigrants to bear the costs for their own settlement and services. In 2003, when 54 percent of 221,352 new Canadian immigrants settled in Ontario, that province received $800 per immigrant from the federal government (*The Windsor Star* 2005). This kind of transfer of payment per immigrant in Ontario, which received more that 50 percent of new immigrants yearly, indicates clearly that Canada has adopted a market-driven, "cost-effective," neo-liberal strategy. Further, the federal government does not transfer to Ontario the full amount ($975) charged to immigrants, keeping $175 per immigrant for immigration services. With agencies receiving inadequate funds, immigrants are not receiving adequate services for language or job training and as a result cannot utilize their credentials and skills, participate in the labor force, or integrate successfully in Canada. Consequently, when immigrants, especially racialized women, enter the labor market, their labor is commodified and likely to stay that way for their entire lives.

Despite being the second highest receiving province, British Columbia (BC) lags behind the rest of the provinces when it comes to language training. In the category of settlement and host services, BC received 57 percent, which is equal to Alberta and Manitoba (*The Vancouver Sun* 2005).[17] Immigrants in Vancouver have to wait three to six months for ESL classes once their English skills are assessed, and assessment happens after a waiting period averaging nine weeks. The restructuring of the current provincial government has eliminated several government-funded ESL classes and withdrawn funds from fully subsidized ESL classes. In other words, BC stops funding ESL classes once students acquire the rudimentary English skills that are needed for "unskilled," low-paid jobs. These jobs make racialized women commodified in the labor market with slim chance of being decommodified. Lack of English language training in BC could lead to higher unemployment rates among racialized women than in Ontario, which provides more extensive language training. This precarious situation takes away immigrant women's choice about being commodified and forces them to be non-commodified in the household. For racialized women, being commodified in the labor market is itself a gigantic achievement, let alone decommodification of their labor.

Whatever category they enter under, immigrants generally face numerous constraints once they enter Canada, such as obtaining work experience, finding regulatory agencies to assess their credentials, and, most important, finding jobs in their own fields. As Ontario receives more than 50 percent of new immigrants, the *Toronto Star*, a provincial newspaper, regularly discusses settlement policies and issues of accreditation. As the *Toronto Star* has noted, "the country loses $4 billion to $6 billion each year because we fail to recognize the skills and credentials immigrants bring to Canada" (2005 April). It is difficult to assess the financial loss to Canada precisely, because estimates vary across researchers and policy planners.

Citing the research of Jeffrey Reitz, the *Toronto Star* (2005 February) points out that the underutilization of immigrants' skills costs the country $2 billion annually in "lost output." One can easily point out that lack of accreditation of immigrants' credentials and skills is an immense problem across Canada and requires addressing at both federal and provincial levels. The efforts of various agencies, licensing bodies, and professional associations remain disjointed, as *The Toronto Star* finds:

> The politician who's officially responsible for integrating foreign-trained professionals into the workforce is Hedy Fry, parliamentary secretary to the immigration minister. But the Vancouver MP says the issue is too complex and crosses too many jurisdictional boundaries to be rolled into a single action plan. . . . The best choice would be Prime Minister Paul Martin. He could pull the issue out of the bureaucratic morass. He could speed things up. He could send an unequivocal message: Canada needs a 21st-century immigrant settlement policy and he is committed to delivering it. (2005 February)[18]

In April 2005, a national newspaper, *The Globe and Mail,* reported the federal government's plan to approve immigrants' job credentials:

> The government unveiled its internationally trained workers initiative yesterday—a multipronged, $269-million strategy to help newcomers enter the Canadian job market and obtain recognition for their foreign credentials. (April 26, A11)

More than a dozen Liberal MPs echoed this announcement in Vancouver and Toronto—both places with major concentrations of immigrants. This promise of the Liberal party, a minority government, may be an election attempt to attract the votes of immigrants. However, at an immigrant settlement and language-training center in Toronto, the Immigration Minister Joe Volpe recognized accreditation as a long-overdue issue and talked about the need to build an infrastructure and networks for integrating immigrants. The recognition of international credentials is currently a widely discussed issue in Canada, and both federal and provincial governments are being forced to find ways to tap immigrants' human capital. Although the federal government and several agencies provide lip service to accreditation and recognition of credentials, decommodification of labor is never an agenda for immigrants, let alone for racialized immigrant women. The issue of accreditation is a complex problem that cuts across several jurisdictions, regulated professions and regulatory bodies. Through women's narrations, chapter 7 will shed some light on this multi-faceted issue. It is clear that unless Canada immediately adopts policies to recognize international credentials, many skilled immigrants, including racialized immigrants, will emigrate to be decommodified, and the infinite labor supply of skilled immigrant workers will be threatened.

NOTES

1. From the late eighteenth century to the late 1940s, i.e., in the pre-welfare state, Canada intermittently brought "unskilled" migrant laborers from Asia who had been commodified throughout their lives.

2. Canada as a receiving country regulates the entry of immigrants in numerous ways. To acquire an informed perspective about the processes, see the NFB film *Who Gets In* (1988). The film not only explains the discretionary powers of the immigration officer, but also poignantly illustrates the classist and racist implications of the regulatory system.

3. In addition to non-discriminatory immigration policies, several factors played key roles in this shift from Europe to Asia, which I have illustrated in the last part of this section. I believe that the non-discriminatory policy did not originate out of altruism, but out of Canada's desperate need for labor as the supply of European immigrants diminished.

4. This view is based on the current global political situation and various media reports. As I mentioned earlier, despite my utmost efforts, I was unable to interview a single Pakistani-Canadian woman. My personal interaction with the community at large has convinced me that the strict security measures prevented Pakistanis from migrating to Canada.

5. To avoid ambiguities and technicalities, I use broad categories pertinent to my analysis.

6. Skilled workers generally come under the independent category that also includes entrepreneurs, investors and the self-employed. For more information, see Citizenship and Immigration Canada's web page: http://cicnet.ci.gc.ca/english/immigr.

7. Since the non-discriminatory immigration legislation in 1962, 1967, and 1976, family reunification remained a significant principle under which most women migrated. Indeed, the number of immigrants under the family category was substantially higher than either the skilled or the economic category (Boyd 1990; Habib 2003).

8. Based on several consultation processes, the New Immigration and Refugee Act was passed in 2002. For details, see Habib 2003.

9. My goal is not to undermine women's agency in Asia. Most countries in Asia proclaim equal rights under their Constitutions; however, few Asian countries put this constitutional right into practice. Consequently, many women hold secondary positions in Asian society. Their subordinate status is evident in the nature of their jobs and in non-recognition of their educational qualifications and credentials.

10. DeVoretz (2003) identified this non-discriminatory universal criteria as "color blind."

11. For an informed perspective on women's contributions, see Marylin Waring's book *If Women Counted* (1988). It provides a perspective that cross-cuts national economies.

12. To meet the shortage of skilled workers, some provinces have negotiated with the federal government to introduce a new immigration program generally called the provincial nominee program.

13. As mentioned earlier, 75 percent of men enter under the "skilled" category. Based on this percentage, it is not exaggerating to say that women have fewer credentials on immigration applications than men under this category.

14. In general, policy makers, government officials, data analysts, liberal social scientists, and politicians generate this stream of thought.

15. Left-oriented scholars, activists, feminists, and anti-racist scholars make these arguments.

16. Citizenship and Immigration Canada (2004) reported this percentage through its news release, *The Monitor*.

17. The *Vancouver Sun*'s report was based on a study done by Chris Friesen, director of settlement services for the Immigrant Services Society of British Columbia.

18. Carol Goar is the author of this report for the *Toronto Star*. As a member of a research network titled Research for Immigration and Integration in the Metropolis (RIIM), I received this piece. Special thanks go to Linda Sheldon, a member of RIIM, who regularly circulates current materials regarding settlement, language training and accreditation difficulties. This chapter has received enormous benefits from the RIIM network's circulation of materials.

4

The Canadian State and Immigrant Labor
Intersections of Gender, Class, and Race

[Immigration] policy directions suggest Canada is opening its doors to individuals with human capital, those people who are highly skilled, well-educated, and perceived as self-sufficient. Simultaneously, state power is being used to enact tougher border control through the adoption of stricter selection criteria for those deemed less desirable, especially members of the family class and refugees, erroneously constructed as "dependent" non-contributors. . . . As a whole, the area of immigration reveals a powerful way in which the nation-state continues to exercise power in the contemporary era of globalization, which is certainly not "shrinking" as a result of neo-liberalism. (Abu-Laban and Gabriel 2002: 167)

WHO GETS IN?

There is a two-tier system in Canadian immigration—one for those who are considered "marketable," "skilled," and "independent" and another for those who are considered "dependent," "visa workers,"[1] and "unskilled." The latter category, called family/dependent class or domestics (i.e., "unskilled"), includes mostly women and children whose labor is assumed to be non-marketable, non-productive, and thus not an asset in the Canadian economy. The discriminatory practices embedded in immigration produce social relationships that serve the interests of what Burke (2000) calls "the market model." This discourse about who is "marketable," "skilled," or "independent" provides an ideological basis for commodifying immigrant women's labor and simultaneously justifies these women's exploitation and exclusion, depending upon the nature and the extent of the restructuring of the state.

Commodification of immigrant women's labor happens as a result of various factors. First, the education and skills gained in immigrant women's countries of origin are not recognized either by employers or by professional associations. Accreditation processes allot more points to education and training received in the Western- and English-speaking world and thus place immigrants from Asia, especially women, in a disadvantaged situation in the labor market. Second, the "dependent" status generates an environment where immigrant women are expected to contribute their unpaid labor (i.e., childcare, household maintenance and so on) to the family. Third, the nonrecognition of credentials de-skills women, reconstructs their labor as "unskilled," "low-paid," and "flexible," and ultimately obstructs them from claiming social benefits and entitlements in their paid work. These combined factors make immigrant women's labor commodified in the labor market and remove any possibilities of decommodification.

In this chapter, I argue that despite its democratic traditions and welfare policies, the Canadian state produces structural and systemic barriers for immigrants, and that these barriers have far-reaching gender, class and race implications in terms of commodification and decommodification of labor. I have already examined the concept of "the welfare state"[2] (in chapter 1). To provide a historical perspective and outline the implications of immigration policies, this chapter briefly examines major discriminatory acts, such as the Chinese Exclusion Act and Head Tax and the Continuous Voyage Act, and analyses their adverse impacts on immigrant women from Asia. The chapter then reveals how the state reinforces immigrant women's subordinate and secondary position in the labor market because of their gender, class and race. By examining Domestic Schemes and subsequent policies, including the current LCP, the chapter further demonstrates how the state has created a reserve army of labor while transferring the state's public childcare services to the private sector. In the process, the state has become "leaner and meaner" and kept control over immigration and indeed, over future immigrants. Moreover, this chapter argues that Canada's LCP and the Philippines' LEP are born out of neo-liberal globalism and that the process has gradually commodified immigrant women's labor. The LCP has further created a commodified sector, that is, family, which was previously under- or non-commodified. Through examining immigrant women's location in Canadian society, this chapter reveals the welfare state's contradictions, conflicts and tensions born out of neo-liberalism and the restructuring of the state over time and also explores the participation of the welfare state in the commodification of immigrant women's labor.

CANADA'S IMMIGRATION ACTS: A HISTORY OF DISCRIMINATION

Canada's growth and development as a nation-state are inextricably linked to immigration. In developing its nation-building immigration strategies,

Canada adopted several discriminatory policies based on gender, class and race. The 1962 Immigration Act introduced the current non-discriminatory points system,[3] which was discussed in chapter 3. During the early years of its nation-building process, Canada actively sought white immigrants, mostly from Britain and the US. Later on, Italians, Finns, Ukrainians, and other Europeans were encouraged to settle in Canada (Henry et al. 1995). Despite these new arrivals, more laborers were needed for the construction of the Canadian Pacific Railway as well as in mining and steel industries. Consequently, in 1880, thousands of Chinese male workers were admitted to Canada. Even though Japanese and East Indians were categorized as "undesirables" and "prohibited classes," they too were recruited as disposable contract labor (Knowles 1996). For various reasons—for example, the hostility of the local population, economic recession, lack of demand for laborers—Canada legislated numerous discriminatory acts to restrict immigrants, especially those from Asia. Canada was quick to utilize laborers from Asia to fill national shortages of labor, yet slow to provide these laborers with basic entitlements and benefits.

These discriminatory policies received due attention in various studies of immigration. Some scholars have argued that the Canadian state through its immigration policies perpetuates gender inequality, racism, and social class inequality (Arat-Koc 1999/2000; Calliste 1996a; Ng 1992; Thobani 1998). Others also have suggested that these discriminatory acts had numerous gender, class and race implications (Agnew 1996a; Das Gupta 1994; Driedger 1996; Jakubowski 1997). For example, thousands of Chinese male laborers were admitted to Canada in the second half of the nineteenth century for the construction of the Canadian Pacific Railway. Once the railroad, a vital link in Canada's unification, was completed in November 1885, Chinese labor was deemed unnecessary and hence disposable (Ungerleider 1992). To restrict and regulate Chinese immigration into Canada in 1885, the state passed the Chinese Immigration Act, which placed a $50 head tax on every Chinese arrived (Ungerleider 1992). The head tax increased in 1903 to $500. Then, in 1923, the state passed the Chinese Immigration Act terminating the entry of Chinese except merchants and students. Consequently, from 1923 to 1947, fewer than 50 Chinese entered Canada (Ungerleider 1992). While the head tax restricted the immigration of Chinese men, it also effectively prohibited Chinese women and the wives of immigrant male laborers from migrating, since women were perceived as "unproductive" and "economic liabilities" unable to repay the head tax (Adilman 1984). These policies had numerous long-term effects upon Chinese women—many were physically isolated from their husbands and male relatives for years. After the amendment of the Chinese Immigration Act in 1947, these women were allowed to reunite with their husbands and male relatives, but many were no longer able to connect themselves to these kin (Chinese Women's Collective 1992).[4]

Similarly, the Immigration Act of 1908 controlled the entry of immigrants from India and Sri Lanka (Taylor 1991). The number of South Asian immigrants had jumped from 45 in 1904–1905 to 2,623 in 1907–1908, and this legislation was passed to stop this trend (Das Gupta 1994). In addition to legislation, the state persuaded one steamship company, which provided "continuous journey"[5] from India, not to issue tickets to Canada. The number of South Asian immigrants dropped drastically; in 1909, there were only six immigrants from South Asia (Ungerleider 1992). Until 1920, this legislation successfully prohibited South Asian women and children from entering Canada (Agnew 1996; Das Gupta 1994). One legacy of the Act is that it has politicized many South Asian immigrants living in British Columbia (Das Gupta 1994). South Asian immigrant organizations such as the South Asian Network for Secularism and Democracy (SANSAD),[6] the South Asian Women's Centre (SAWC),[7] and the India *Mahila* Association (IMA)[8] continue to carry out political activism pertinent to immigrant women from South Asia. Through women's narrations, chapter 8 explores the multifaceted roles of both the IMA and the SAWC.

REPRODUCTION OF IMMIGRANT WOMEN'S COMMODIFIED AND SUBORDINATE POSITION IN THE LABOR MARKET: THE ROLE OF THE STATE

Despite its intention to shift from discriminatory to non-discriminatory immigration policies in the late 1960s, the Canadian state through the points system continues to reinforce the idea of immigrant women as "legally dependent," with a need to be "sponsored." Further, many of these women's position as "secondary" in the socioeconomic-political structure of their countries of origin blocks them from the "skilled," "primary" and "independent" immigrant category. The prevailing neo-liberal ideology, professing belief in self-reliance, limits the obligations of the state, and restricts the entitlements of immigrant women who are in this category of "secondary" status and thus encloses them in commodified sectors. In what has been described as "inequalities of citizenship" (Arat-Koc 1999/2000), these immigrant women as "dependents" are not entitled to receive much government-sponsored or subsidized job training and upgrading, language-training programs, or the allowance for attending such programs (Boyd 1986 and 1990; Ng 1992).[9] Thus, it is no wonder immigrant women's labor has been commodified throughout their entire lives, and has faced barriers to becoming decommodified. Boyd (1990) has extensively documented how gender, race and country of origin of immigrant women produce triple negative effects in the labor market. Boyd (1990) recommends educational upgrading and job-training programs for immigrant women and simultaneously urges the state to adopt affirmative-action policies to eradicate discriminatory hiring practices. While these actions are necessary, Boyd's recommendations underestimate the role of the state in producing and maintaining the situation that ultimately places immigrant women in a commodified position. Affirmative action in Canada is a hotly debated issue; even Canadian-born women, let alone immigrant women, are not protected by affirmative action despite their disadvantaged position in various sectors of the economy. It should be noted here that the labor of many Canadian-born women is also commodified due to their concentration in flexible, low-paid and casual work. Gender is clearly one of the organizing principles in the labor market when it comes to commodification of labor.

Based on the state's assumptions about their contributions to the economy, independent-class immigrants are considered more "deserving" of certain kinds of rights and are given access to them (Arat-Koc 1999/2000). On the other hand, family-class immigrants are assumed to be non-contributors to the economy despite their significant contributions to their families, their communities and the labor market. Differential sets of rights and entitlements for the family-class category relegate individuals, more specifically women, to a precarious situation in the labor market. Their domestic responsibilities, their lack of accreditation, and their limited access to programs for upgrading force family-class immigrant women to perform low-paid, "unskilled" jobs. In these jobs, immigrant women can be exploited, and their opportunities for upward mobility are restricted. These factors relegate immigrant women's labor to non-commodified and commodified sectors.

Due to the state's categorization of "dependents" and its limiting of immigrant women's entitlements, many immigrant women find it difficult to upgrade their job skills and educational qualifications. Moreover, the absence of regulated agencies to evaluate these women's qualifications relegates them to a sex-segregated, racialized and class-based labor market. As a result, immigrant women are more frequently concentrated either in low-wage jobs or in the invisible economy that reproduces their secondary and subordinate position in commodified sectors and in society. In other words, they have few prospects for being decommodified. Statistics Canada (2003) confirms this situation:

> Immigrant men fare better than immigrant women in the labor market, partly because of their circumstances in coming to Canada. Men are more likely than women to be admitted as economic class principal applicants. People in this category are expected to be able to find work and contribute to the economy once they've settled in their new homeland. In contrast, female immigrants are more likely to come to Canada on the basis of a family class application (i.e., by virtue of being related to an economic-class immigrant) or for reasons of family reunification. (Catalogue no. 71-222: 85)

Statistics Canada's statement provides unequivocal support to the principal argument of this book that the nature of Canada's immigration policy produces women who are "dependent" and "less economic," and that this structural subordination perpetuates women's commodified and marginalized situation in the labor market. For instance, during the period 1980–2000, Canadian-born women's earnings rose 19 percent while female immigrants' rose only 13 percent. The unemployment data further reveal the gap between immigrant women and Canadian-born women. In 2002, 8.6 percent of Canadian-born women were unemployed, while 20.2 percent of immigrant women were unemployed (Thompson 2002: 10). This wide gap is not due to the migration of less "skilled" women, but to an inadequate government system that deters this group from having their credentials and education properly evaluated. For example, in 2000, of the immigrant women employed in full-time jobs, 38 percent had a university degree, and of Canadian-born women employed in full-time jobs, 22 percent had a degree (Statistics Canada 2003). This figure does not indicate the nature of the jobs or the pay scale, but reflects that a full-time position for an immigrant woman likely requires a university degree. Smith and Jackson describe the situation well:

> [The] 2001 Canadian Social Welfare Policy Conference indicated that immigrants traditionally "caught up" to average Canadian earnings within 10 to 14 years of their arrival in Canada, but this has changed since the mid-1980s, particularly for immigrants from Asia and Africa. Orstein reports that, even when educational levels are the same, racialized groups are under-represented in managerial, professional and high-income occupations, and they are over-represented in low-end occupations and low-paying jobs. Again, this is particularly the case for specific racial groups, notably Blacks and South Asians. (2002: 3)

The above quotation eloquently points out that racialized groups are represented significantly in low-wage occupations and thus commodified with little chance to be decommodified. Among racialized groups, women have the least opportunities to be decommodified due to their sex and class. Although the immigration policy in Canada has been shifted dramatically from a racist to a non-discriminatory system, and now allows a huge proportion of racialized people's entry from Asia and Africa, the gendered, racialized and class-based labor market has not been dismantled. The result is that the labor of racialized groups, especially of racialized women, will continue to be commodified without the least chance of being decommodified.

"Married" women from Asia are categorized as "family class" or "dependent" irrespective of their educational and work experience, while their husbands are automatically assigned independent status. As mentioned in chapter 3, seven of the ten top sending countries are in Asia. In the current skilled, independent category of immigrants migrating to Canada, 75 percent are males and 25 percent are females, indicating that the majority of Asian immigrant women (except from the Philippines) are migrating to Canada as "dependents" under the independent category. During the sponsorship period, immigration law prevents immigrant women who migrate under the family class category from having access to some family benefits, social welfare and other forms of state assistance. The only exception is a break in the sponsorship agreement, which can happen only in the case of divorce or separation or proof of violence. These women contribute to taxes when they participate in the labor force. The welfare state's underlying principle is that as taxpayers, these immigrant women are entitled to access programs funded by the state; however, this principle is not applied to these women (Thobani 1998). The provisions in the immigration policy complement other forms of gender and racial inequalities inherent in Canada, producing multiple disadvantages and a captive situation for immigrant women in the labor market as well as in the broader society (Ng 1992). Through immigrant women's voices, this precarious situation as well as the commodification of immigrant women's labor will be further illustrated in chapters 5, 6 and 7.

THE DOMESTIC SCHEME: AN EXAMPLE OF SUSTAINED CLASS AND RACIAL INEQUALITY

Historically, Canada has relied on outside sources for its domestic labor because many Canadian-born women irrespective of race or class have declined to perform this isolated and privatized work. Between the 1890s and the 1920s, most domestic workers who migrated to Canada as immigrants and permanent residents were of British and Scottish ancestry and were required to live in service for six months (Bakan and Stasiulis 1994; Grandea 1996). To meet the demands for domestics, recruitment expanded from white English-speaking to white, East European, non-English-speaking refugees during World War II (for details, see Bakan and Stasiulis 1994). Officially, the first Domestic Scheme, which recruited about 100 women from Guadeloupe, was introduced in 1910–1911 (Calliste 1991: 141). In the 1950s, the second Domestic Scheme was introduced, coinciding with the first full-scale recruitment of Caribbean domestics to work under a one-year contract in return for migrating as permanent residents (Calliste 1991; Jakubowski 1997; Silvera 1989). Unlike domestics from Europe, Black domestics from Caribbean countries—mostly from Jamaica and Barbados—faced stipulations on their acquiring permanent residence, including being tested for venereal disease or being returned to their countries of origin if considered unsuited for the job (for details, see Bakan and Stasiulis 1994: 13; Grandea 1996). Highly educated and trained in their countries of origin, most of the women from Caribbean countries found the working conditions in Canada unacceptable and quit their jobs after fulfilling the one-year contractual obligation (Arat-Koc 1990).

Due to the continuing high demand for domestic workers, in 1973 the Canadian government restructured the Second Domestic Scheme and introduced the Temporary Employment Authorization Program.[10] Unlike previous schemes, this scheme did not entitle domestics to enter Canada as permanent residents, but allowed them to work on temporary visas requiring each domestic to work for a particular employer for a specific period. Should the conditions of the work require change, the domestic worker was legally obliged to report to the Employment and Immigration Commission (Silvera 1989; Jakubowski 1997). Domestics under the temporary visa program were also prohibited from quitting a job without leaving the country (Grandea 1996). In short, this system created a disposable labor pool, mostly from the Caribbean, and created an inhospitable work environment for domestics. Through such federal government regulations, immigrant domestic labor became subject to the stipulations of full-fledged contractual relationships. These relationships in the domestic sphere are called "defamilialization," meaning that childcare, eldercare, and household maintenance are performed through market provision (Esping-Andersen 1999). Defamilialization liberates privileged Canadian women from childcare, eldercare, and household maintenance and helps them participate in the paid labor market. Defamilialization is one of the prerequisites of decommodification and thus, defamilialized women, that is, the employers of the domestics, have far better chances to be decommodified.

During the 1960s and 1970s, a large number of Canadian women entered the labor market, creating heavy demand for more domestics as government-sponsored and -supervised childcare centers were minimal. In 1981, under a revised policy entitled the Foreign Domestic Movement program (FDM),[11] domestics were allowed to apply for landed immigration status if they met certain conditions, such as doing live-in domestic service for two years, being proficient in either English or French, and having specific job skills. (Bakan and Stasiulis 1994; Grandea 1996; Jakubowski 1997). In 1992, the federal government replaced the FDM with the Live-in Caregiver Program (LCP). The LCP included a number of conditions, such as having a Grade 12 education, being able to speak English or French, and performing live-in service. Within their first three years of residence in Canada, domestic workers are now eligible to apply for landed immigrant status provided they have completed two years of live-in domestic service. The LCP is an improvement on the past Domestic Schemes and the Temporary Authorization Program and happened as a result of the advocacy and active roles of several activist and women's organizations as well as domestic workers' associations. Several studies (Arat-Koc 1989; Calliste 1991; Grandea 1996; Macklin 1992 and 1994; Pratt 1999a) indicate that many of these domestic workers live in undesirable conditions and constitute a captive labor force in Canada. Gorz correctly points out, "The professionalization of domestic tasks is . . . the very antithesis of a liberation. It relieves a privileged minority of all or part of their work-for-themselves and makes that work the sole source of livelihood for a new class of underpaid servants, who are forced to take on other peoples' domestic tasks alongside their own" (1989: 156). My research with the PWC reveals clearly that almost all domestic workers apply for landed status once they fulfill the requirements, that is, completion of two years of live-in domestic service, and receive their immigrant status when they submit applications to the immigration office.[12] Receiving immigrant status after working as domestics for at least two years is one of the great attractions for Filipinas, albeit women from periphery countries. As the domestic workers are an integral part of the Canadian Yearly Immigration Plan, the LCP is the best possible avenue for racialized women to get away from unemployment/underemployment and acquire the immigration status that is almost impossible for them in the Independent and Business Categories. Despite their precarious work conditions and concentration in commodified sectors, there exists no dearth of immigrant domestic workers to Canada from periphery countries, especially from the Philippines. Once landed status is granted, some domestic laborers work as live-out domestics in the private sphere as well as performing their own household responsibilities, which are both invisible and unaccounted for. This combination of "defamilialization" and "familialization" make these women's labor both "commodified" and "non-commodified," and such intersections of the "commodified" and "non-commodified" produce a sector that is partially commodified. This issue is further discussed in chapter 5.

CANADA'S LCP AND THE PHILIPPINES' LEP— SHIFTING SOCIAL REPRODUCTION FROM THE SEMI-PERIPHERY TO THE PERIPHERY

In the mid-twentieth century, domestic work as "the single largest category of employment" in the North declined; indeed, some assumed that this occupation would eventually be obsolete (Hondagneu-Sotelo 1994). However, since then, the Domestic Scheme of the pre-welfare state has been extended in numerous ways due to several factors. First, the provincial governments'[13] continuous slashing of support for childcare and eldercare has accelerated the demand for alternative options. Second, the hiring of one live-in domestic is less costly[14] than sending two or three children to daycare, especially in large cities in BC and Ontario where there is a major concentration of domestic workers as well as immigrants. Third, for full-time, dual-earner couples[15] in upper- or upper-middle class families, hiring a live-in domestic is less expensive and more efficient than placing children in daycare. In addition to taking care of children, almost all domestics do some household chores including cleaning washrooms, cooking, driving children to an array of activities, and even snow shoveling. Chapter 5 will describe the wide range of domestics' duties in more detail.

Researchers have found that identities of domestic workers in Canada are quite "raced," classed and gendered (Anderson 2000; Bakan and Stasiulis 1995; England and Stiell 1997). Many domestic workers in Canada come from

Asia, where the increasing trend is to migrate to either core or semi-periphery countries in order to sustain and support families back home (Anderson 2000; Heyzer 1994). Thus, the live-in caregiver issue is tied up not only with class and poverty issues, but also with gender, race and nationality. The links between women's migration and the transfer of social reproduction from mostly white upper- and middle-class women of a semi-periphery country like Canada to women of periphery countries have been explored in a number of studies (Arat-Koc 1989; Bakan and Stasiulis 1995; Cohen 1987; Macklin 1992). Anderson observes: "It is important to emphasize that social reproduction is not confined to the family. It refers also to the perpetuation of modes of production and social reproduction with their associated relations such as those of class, 'race,' gender and generation" (2000: 13).

Today, employers' perceptions of gender, race and nationality continue to influence country of origin of domestic applicants (Bakan and Stasiulis 1995; Tacoli 1999). In Canada, the hiring of caregivers for Canadians has shifted to Filipino, Tagalog-speaking women. Social reproduction has been transferred from privileged women in a semi-periphery country to migrant women in a periphery country. This relocation of social reproduction reflects the structural exploitation and subordination of some women in the Philippines by some privileged women in Canada. Filipino women's migration under the LCP in Canada is inextricably linked to the Philippines' LEP. It is estimated that nearly 2,000 overseas contract workers leave the Philippines daily. This number does not include the workers who leave the country without contracts or work permits (Bronson and Rousseau 1995: 9) and reflects not only the globalization of labor markets, but also the transforming of dependence and exploitation from a national to a global context.

From the 1900s to the 1940s, labor migration was a part of the Philippines' economy under American colonial rule—the US brought male farmers to work on plantations in Hawaii, to pick vegetables and fruits in California, and to work in fish canneries in Alaska (Grandea 1996). In the 1950s, Filipino professionals, including doctors and nurses, began to move to the US for better paying jobs. In the mid-1970s, when military dictator President Marcos introduced the LEP, the pattern of migration changed. The LEP had two objectives: (1) to generate remittances from abroad in order to balance the country's chronic deficit and pay off international debt, especially to the International Monetary Fund (IMF), and (2) to export workers as a way of solving the Philippines' huge unemployment problem. Almost 40 years later, the LEP remains, although it has been somewhat restructured. In general, the LEP affirms the state's neo-liberal policies by deregulating and opening up borders to a free flow not only of capital and goods, but also of laborers. For example, Marcos' successor, the Ramos government, elevated the status of this so-called development policy by renaming it "Philippines 2000" and labeling each migrant as the "Modern Filipino Hero." In 1996, the Philippines received $7 billion in remittance and estimated that each migrant supported an average of seven Filipinos back home (Wichterich 2000). In 2005, the level of remittance is expected to exceed $12 billion. In addition to providing remittances, migration boosts the domestic economy as thousands of would-be migrants pay millions of dollars to various agencies ranging from training centers and health clinics to migrant agents and organizations.

Official statistics from the late 1990s suggest that 3.5 million Filipinos work abroad, with unofficial sources suggesting the number is closer to 7 million; both sources agree that 60 percent of the migrant workers are women (Wichterich 2000). This number reveals a vicious feature of transnational migration—the feminization of Filipino labor exports. Compared with any countries of South-east Asia and South Asia, the Philippines' neo-liberal policies export female labor aggressively, procuring more remittances from female labor than from any other sectors in the economy. Consequently, Filipinas' labor has become commodified in the global labor market, and Canada through the LCP extracts benefits out of the Philippines' LEP. The commodification, decommodification, and eventual recommodification of many of these immigrant laborers are the subject of the next three chapters.

NOTES

1. The category "visa workers" indicates that the jobs are temporary and the workers will leave once the permit expires. Domestic workers under the LCP are considered visa workers, and they hold temporary work permits. However, almost all of them get immigration status, as I will illustrate in the later part of the book.

2. This concept, "welfare state," entered the popular lexicon during and after World War II. However, several welfare policies in Canada and Australia were introduced before World War II (Garton and McCallum 1996: 118). Dumenil and Levy (2002) argue that the establishment of the welfare state after World War II modified the treatment of labor and wage relations. The term "welfare state" remains problematic in its use and interpretation.

3. The points may vary from year to year, but the basic tenet of immigration policy, that it is non-discriminatory, remains intact.

4. The Chinese Women's Collective (1992) narrates Chinese women's dislocation, suffering, and despair, which produced scars on family lives across generations.

5. "Continuous journey" refers to traveling directly from the country of origin and possessing $200 per person upon landing in Canada (Agnew 1996; Das Gupta 1994).

6. The South Asian Network for Secularism and Democracy (SANSAD) is a left-oriented group comprised of mostly immigrant academics, researchers and social activists, and the majority are men. Recently, when Starbucks fired two immigrant women workers who had pierced noses, SANSAD mobilized public support against the company's violation of the women's human rights.

7. The South Asian Women's Center in BC organized demonstrations and protests when a physician in Seattle targeted South Asian, that is, racialized women, for the abortion of female fetuses. Chapter 8 also discusses this issue.

8. The India *Mahila* Association organized demonstrations and protests against the brutal killing of a teenage South Asian immigrant woman, Reena Virk, in Victoria, BC, and ensuing racist, gendered and classist media coverage. The protests received national coverage. The case is closed now.

9. The laws regarding language, training and job programs change from time to time. Some basic programs are non-discriminatory. For example, current rudimentary ESL government programs in BC, which I mentioned in chapter 3, are non-discriminatory. Most immigrant women from former English-speaking colonies, such as India, Bangladesh and the Philippines, are accustomed to that level of English and hence, these ESL programs are useless for these women. This insightful comment was made by one of the interviewees. Generally, when immigrant women upgrade their skills (i.e., language, job), they have to pay hefty fees, which most families cannot afford. When these families can afford upgrading, men get priority, which eventually places immigrant women in "secondary" positions even within their own families.

10. This and consequent legislation was passed long after the establishment of the welfare state. This reveals one of the examples of how neo-liberal policies defeat one of the basic tenets of the welfare state, that is, equal opportunity for all irrespective of gender, class and race.

11. In response to the increasing demand from upper- and upper-middle-class households for domestic workers, the then Immigration Minister Lloyd Axworthy took the initiative to create the Foreign Domestic Movement program (Cyr 2004).

12. My understanding is that this immigration procedure is easy-going. Domestic workers I talked with never complained about the bureaucratic procedures. Some even mentioned that immigration officers provided useful tips for speeding up processing the application. It is clear that the federal government unequivocally accepts domestic workers as future immigrants.

13. Childcare is a provincial government's arena, and the policies of the provincial governments vary according to the party in power. For example, the NDP (a left-leaning) government in Manitoba has progressive policies for childcare and eldercare, whereas in BC, the current Liberal government, since coming to power in 2001, has slashed the budget.

14. For a child more than two years old, the average cost for daycare is from $700 to $900 monthly, which includes supervision for an eight- to nine-hour weekday only. In British Columbia, to get a space for a child less than two years old in a licensed public daycare is a nightmare, and the cost may be as high as $1,000. Childcare for an average family of two children costs approximately $1,500 to $2,000 a month. Most domestic workers average a take-home salary of $600 to $800, excluding accommodation and food. The next chapter will present the narrations of domestic workers, which will vividly demonstrate the range of services and the working hours.

15. In 2000, the *Globe and Mail* (September 16, A3) published a report titled "Bureaucratic Sea Stands Nannies," which points out that parents must prove to the Immigration Department that they both work. This statement indicates that the increase of dual-career couples with younger children may have accelerated demands for domestic workers. After meeting all the bureaucratic procedures, according to this report, the waiting period to get a domestic worker is about a year.

5

Commodification of Laborers
"Defamilializing" the Privileged and "Refeudalizing" the Im/Migrants

As commodities, workers are replaceable, easily redundant, and atomized. (Esping-Andersen 1990: 37)

[G]lobalization has enhanced not diminished the significance of the national state, as a site of regulation. The positions of migrant women are dependent not only on whether they are regular or irregular migrants, but also on the specific regulatory framework for entering a country. (Williams and Balaz 2004: 1817)

This chapter focuses on the socioeconomic relationships between employers and immigrant employees in a private but commodified social sector in British Columbia (BC), Canada. The BC provincial government's labor regulations lag behind those of most other provinces, and the federal government's controlled immigration rules make immigrant workers vulnerable when they are in commodified but unregulated sectors. As chapter 4 shows, the federal government, through the Live-in Caregiver Program (LCP), endorses a two-tier immigration system. Those who are well educated, "skilled," or privileged in wealth (i.e., entrepreneurs) are welcomed to Canada as independent immigrants and enjoy social rights and entitlements immediately.[1] Immigrants who lack these qualifications enter Canada as an underprivileged class. In the short run, the LCP transforms domestics into low-paid "housewives" and "surrogate parents." In the end, the LCP creates barriers for decommodification of labor by putting up bureaucratic hurdles that erode immigrants' original skills and educational credentials. This very process enhances the commodification of immigrant women's labor and reduces the likelihood that their labor will be decommodified in the future.

To examine the consequences of commodification, this chapter takes a closer look at the meaning of commodification and some of the ways it is used by various scholars. Next, the chapter demonstrates the meaning of erosion of skills, linking it to the commodified but invisible private sector, that is, the family/household, where lack of government regulations exist. Through women's narrations, the chapter then describes the multifaceted dimensions of commodification and the socioeconomic relations between domestics and their employers. In the process, the chapter also reveals the different layers of bureaucratic control mechanisms maintained by the federal and provincial governments. Finally, this chapter argues that the LCP has freed many non-commodified and under-commodified privileged women in Canada from household and reproductive work—what Esping-Andersen identifies as "defamilialization." At the same time, the LCP has forced many women from the Philippines into an exploitative employer-employee relationship in a commodified sector. This relationship is comparable to contractual relations of the feudal system, and one may identify the process as "re-feudalizing" immigrant women workers in a welfare state in the 21st century.

WHAT IS COMMODIFICATION?

The concept of commodification refers to a situation where workers are treated as things that can be bought and sold and must rely on the sale of their labor power for economic survival. Based on this concept, Esping-Andersen's *The Three Worlds of Welfare Capitalism* (1990) charts out a typology of welfare-state regimes: conservative, liberal, and social democratic. Canada, Australia, and the US belong to the liberal category and Sweden belongs to the social democratic. Of these typologies, social democratic regimes are the most worker-friendly and the most decommodifying, that is, they produce the most autonomy from paid work (Nyberg 2002). The concept of decommodification will be defined and illustrated with examples in the following chapter (chapter 6).

As mentioned in the introduction to this book, I refer to the concept of social rights the way social democrats do. Social democrats argue that reliance on the market fails to provide social rights to citizens and thus breeds inequality and social injustice. Social democrats also favor state regulation in both commodified and decommodified sectors, as well as strong state control. In this book, the concept of commodification is applied to immigrants' labor as well as to social sectors.

Despite its extensive use, Esping-Andersen's detailed discussion of welfare regimes overlooks the role of the welfare state in perpetuating and maintaining a market-driven scheme that extends to a non- or under-commodified Canadian sector: the family/household. Thus, commodification also refers to structural changes in the state, such as shifting childcare from public to private sectors. This shift happens when the government restructures daycare by either reducing or not increasing workers and spaces. Consequently, parents either rely on private/family-run daycare or hire a domestic worker at home, and both actions eventually transform the household from a non- or under-commodified to a commodified sector. Irrespective of class and citizenship status, this gradual shift from public to private has had adverse impacts upon the population, especially on immigrant women and on the non-/under-commodified sector—in this case, the family/household.

The concept of commodification is used in this book within the context of the Canadian welfare state, which has been celebrated since its establishment after World War II. The Canadian welfare state provides numerous provisions to workers,[2] such as unemployment insurance, the right to form unions and so on. However, as Offe (1984: 151) has commented, "the welfare state has made the exploitation of labour more complicated and less predictable"; herein lie the contradictions of the welfare state. This contradictory nature of the welfare state is evident in Canada if one examines the LCP, which reproduces power relationships between immigrant women and mostly Canadian-born privileged women in a commodified sector, that is, the household.

Contemporary scholars have used the concept of commodification to explore a number of issues pertinent to labor. Drawing on Esping-Andersen's concept of commodification of labor, Giddings, Dingeldey and Ulbricht (2004) attempt to explore various types of commodification of "lone mothers' labor" in the US and Germany and how these variations affect lone mothers' participation in the labor market. Using the concepts of commodification and decommodification, Nyberg (2002) investigates whether women in Sweden, independent of men, can maintain independent households that include children. Influenced by Esping-Andersen's theoretical framework, Nyberg (2002) and Giddings, Dingeldey and Ulbricht (2004) analyze women's labor in general while delineating the differences between women and men. Differences among women, for example, between immigrant and native-born, within the context of the commodification of labor are absent in both works. In examining health care and migration, Held (2002) and Williams and Balaz (2004) use the concept of commodification without referring to Esping-Andersen's work and thus bypass the meaning of the concept. Despite their limitations, all of these studies apply the concept of commodification to female labor and are therefore pertinent to feminist analyses.

Using a feminist lens, Vosko (2000) substantiates the historical connections between racialization and forms of labor exploitation in Canada by means of political legal compulsion. Vosko explores the gendered character of prevailing employment trends and traces the rise and decline of the standard employment relationship that provides social entitlements. Vosko has made a historical attempt to investigate the emergence of a precarious feminized employment relationship. The nature of flexible but feminized work, what

Vosko (2000) identifies as "temporary work," is an expanding category in current economic restructuring, where the workers represent an array of diversity from computer programmers, clerical workers, domestics to assemblers. However, the voices of these "temporary" workers, let alone voices of immigrant women, are absent throughout the text, and her investigation is historical (from 1897 to 1997) where the cutting period is 1997.

In analyzing neo-liberalism, scholars have examined commodification of sectors in a number of ways. According to Burke (2000), commodification indicates "an increasing reliance on the market" for the financing or delivery of services. This aspect of commodification is true for Canada, where both federal and provincial governments increasingly rely on the global market for a constant supply of domestics to the household—previously non- or under-commodified—especially from the Philippines, for childcare and eldercare financed by private employers. The absence of private bonds and obligations in the household has further created an unregulated, neglected area where laborers are mostly at the mercy of their employers. Without a regulatory framework, domestics' work in a private household—a commodified sector—leads to the commodification of the domestic's labor and has great potential for the exploitation of that labor. This commodification of labor in a private sector has far-reaching implications including deprivation of social entitlements such as extended health care, vacation and Employment Insurance (EI).

Commodification is increasingly devaluing the Canadian national standard of various social sectors and fundamentally restructuring the welfare state (Burke 2000). Childcare, eldercare, health care, and education all have been restructured and deregulated significantly in the name of efficiency, under the assumption that the government can do things better if a market-driven strategy is adopted. The federal government is increasingly relying on the provincial governments to provide these services, yet has made no provision for monitoring or for maintaining a national standard.[3] With increasing deregulation and privatization, childcare and especially eldercare have been increasingly transferred from decommodified sectors, that is, government-regulated daycare, or institutional residential care, to commodified sectors, that is, private homes, individual/family care.

DIFFERENT LEVELS OF COMMODIFICATION

As mentioned earlier, this chapter explores the often-invisible social relationships between employers and domestics in the commodified but private sector by analysing the narrations of women who came to Canada from the Philippines under the LCP. As commodities, domestics enter into an exploitative socioeconomic relationship in an under- and non-commodified sector that transforms them into captives of their employers. In the twentieth century, before the introduction of the Domestic Scheme and most recently the LCP, all households in Canada were either non- or under-commodified; that is, domestic helpers were recruited privately and temporarily without any government sanctions. With the formal introduction of the first Domestic Scheme in the twentieth century, a few households in Canada were commodified. The second Domestic Scheme in the 1950s slowly transformed more households into commodified sectors. The Temporary Employment Authorization Program of 1973 formally authorized the commodification of more households. Later on, in 1992, the commodification of households was solidified by the LCP.

Neo-liberalism is constantly changing previously non- or under-commodified social sectors (McMurty 2001). Through the LCP, the Canadian state has transformed household/family, previously a non- or under-commodified sector, into a commodified social sector. However, not all households make this transformation; only some privileged upper-class and middle-class households enjoy the benefits. Some privileged families, for ideological or privacy reasons, may refrain from hiring domestics and those households are still non- or under-commodified. Rather, these families may opt either for government-regulated daycare or for private arrangements. These kinds of alternate arrangements have not been investigated and are beyond the scope of this book.

Questions thus emerge: how does immigrant women's labor become commodified in a welfare state like Canada? Do differences exist in immigrant women's labor when the various levels of commodification, that is, partial commodification, full commodification, non-commodification, and under-commodification, are applied? In addition, what are the implications of commodified household/family sectors in a welfare state like Canada?

FULL OR PARTIAL COMMODIFICATION: "HOUSEWIFIZATION" AND EROSION OF SKILLS

In contrast to the first half of the twentieth century, current migrant caregivers/domestics usually come from middle-class backgrounds in Asia, especially from the Philippines. The only exception is the Caribbean Domestic Scheme under which Black domestics who were highly educated and trained migrated from Caribbean countries—mostly from Jamaica and Barbados (Calliste 1991; Jakubowski 1997; Silvera 1989). *The Centre Update* (1996) reports that as of 1996, 50,000 Filipinas entered Canada as domestic workers under the LCP and that 6,000 Filipinas worked in Vancouver as domestic workers in 1995. Vancouver received 824 Filipino domestic workers in 1996, 607 in 1997, and 875 in 1998 under the LCP (The City of Vancouver, Canadian Heritage and MOSAIC 2000). Working-class people in most Asian countries can rarely afford the high economic—let alone psychological—costs involved in migrating. In terms of educational background and training, most caregivers and domestics who emigrate to Canada hold university degrees and have been trained in such professions as teaching, nursing, law, and computer operations (Anderson 2000; Wichterich 2000). Further, most can speak English, as the transnational job market demands it. However, low wages, lengthy work hours, immigration rules, and numerous forms of abuse and harassment in the commodified sector, that is, private homes, result in the erosion of skills of the vast majority of these domestic workers (Wichterich 2000). Mies (1986) describes this alienating, monotonous, and invisible process as "housewifization," and Gorz describes the process as "the transferring of what was traditionally regarded as 'housewife's work' to an economically and socially marginalized mass of people" (1989: 156). This process of "housewifization" and erosion of skills shuts out decommodification of labor for immigrant women in a welfare state. The fostering of equality in the welfare state requires allowing all immigrant women, including domestics, to have chances to be decommodified.

Domestics who enter the international labor market as commodities could be decommodified one day, but instead become partly or fully commodified due to immigration stipulations and the erosion of skills. After working as domestics for years and finally gaining permanent status, most domestics establish their own households either through sponsoring families or through new relationships. Despite having permanent status, most domestics perform daily activities in the non-commodified sector, that is, their own households, while still pursuing domestic work in private households, that is, commodified sectors, because they no longer have the credentials/Canadian training to pursue other kinds of paid work. Thus, a combination of commodification and non-commodification makes domestics partly commodified and can trap them in jobs where they are vulnerable. The following narration is an example:

> I finally received my landed visa last August 2000. My children arrived last December 2000 [24-year-old son and 19-year-old daughter].... I am going to work with another employer as a live-in still. I want to be a live-out.... Of course it is hard, especially since my kids are just new here. Sometimes I ask my employer if they'll allow me to go home once in a while to my family since I only work from 7 until 5 [7 a.m. to 5 p.m.]. They want me to live-in in case they have to leave the house early. It's only 30 minutes from my workplace to our apartment.

The above narrator's husband had died before she migrated to Canada as a domestic; consequently, she left her children in the Philippines with her relatives. The narrator's precarious situation forced her to accept an offer that did not suit her situation. This narration clearly indicates that a migrant worker can find herself trapped in the commodified sector where 24/7 is the norm rather than the exception and where government labor codes do not apply. It is highly unlikely that many Canadian-born women or white

English-speaking immigrant women consider being able to live out as an issue while doing a job search!

EROSION OF SKILLS AND ITS MULTIFACETED DIMENSIONS

This section looks at what erosion of skills means, how commodification fosters social inequality, and who does childcare and eldercare in the commodified private sector. Each of these issues is illustrated by narrations from immigrant women.

Erosion of Skills: What Does It Mean?

Erosion of skills, commonly termed as de-skilling, refers to the systematic and structural processes involved in eliminating educational and professional skills, whether by force, by constructing barriers, or by imposing government regulations/deregulations.[4] For example, with high unemployment, political uncertainties, and a debt crisis in the Philippines, when Filipino women are forced to leave to seek employment in Canada, they often forego their original educational qualifications and training and never have the opportunity to upgrade their skills or acquire new ones.

Despite strong democratic traditions in Canada, immigration rules impose numerous restrictions on migrant workers, ultimately deterring the upgrading of domestic workers' skills. To upgrade their skills, migrant contract workers are required to get student authorization forms every time they take a course. Furthermore, the fee for a student visa is currently CDN $125. A migrant worker who aspires to take several courses over a long period and from a wide range of institutions for upgrading may end up paying this amount several times over—on top of course fees. In other words, workers are not free to upgrade their skills without going through immigration procedures—a time-consuming, costly process. Furthermore, the domestic worker may have to ask the employer, who has hired the domestic to work on weekdays, for a weekday off to visit the nearest immigration office. By complicating upgrading skills through such immigration rules, governance creates barriers to decommodification and fosters the growth of re-commodification[5] or partial commodification.

Commodification Fosters Growing Social Inequality

The following quotes from Filipino women working in Canada illustrate the commodification process and its consequences:

> I did not think that we would be de-skilled here in Canada. I didn't know that I couldn't practice my profession. I thought the time would come when I could practice my profession. Now I am very confused about whether I'll be staying

here for good or not. I haven't decided yet. I haven't done any upgrading. I have not applied for an open visa [immigration status].

My expectations of getting out of being a maid and finding ways to at least get accreditation and a better job were not truly fulfilled. Now that I have enough comprehension, I understand that the LCP is nothing but an extremely organized agency to lure or attract migrants and immigrants as a big business, particularly well-trained, well-educated, potentially skilled workers from the Third World.

The above quotations reflect the frustrations of domestics who migrated to Canada under the LCP and eventually became trapped in a commodified private sector. Both[6] quotations indicate a common pattern: Assuming that they would receive credit for their experience and qualifications one day and become decommodified, both women accepted jobs and sacrificed their original credentials.

The interviews show that the unregulated, domesticated, and alienating structure of the LCP forces women to work in a hidden commodified sector and frequently places them in an abusive working situation. As McMurty rightly points out, "It is not commodity production per se that is for Marx a necessary evil, but the development of an entire social structure which is predicated on this type of exchange which is exploitative. Once the commodity is conceived in this negative way . . . the entire problem comes into a different light and spaces for resistance shine forth" (2001: 17). However, few women file formal complaints because workers require references from their employers in order to get another job. Most of all, there exists strong pressure to complete the 24-month-long program that is required in order to be able to file an application for permanent residency, that is, achieve immigration status and hope to be decommodified.

The following narrations from three different women show the suffering of many domestic workers and point out the hidden inequities inside the Canadian labor standard:

> I was working more than eight hours a day. My day off was only two days in a month. . . . She [the employer] has two children; one is 7 years old and one is newly born. I washed their clothes every day using my hands because there are some of their delicate clothes that need to be washed by hand. There are also some of her clothes that could have been washed in the washing machine, plus the clothes of the newborn baby. I have to hand-wash them too because she said it's not good to wash them in the washing machine. . . . I started at 7 a.m. [and worked] until 9 p.m. So, I was working fourteen hours a day.

> I did the cleaning, cooking, ironing, hand-washing some of their clothes, cleaning the garage, shovelling the snow, and cleaning all the time. I had a lot of work. . . . They have two children: 20 years old and 15 years old. I have to prepare meals for them. They have seven washrooms and I have to clean them every day. . . . Even though I work long hours, my salary was still $1,000 net. My

employer was saying that I had enough rest because they're not always at home. . . . And, I really have to do everything like clean the washrooms every day. I don't have enough rest. Imagine that—seven washrooms I have to clean every day! Sometimes I don't have enough time to eat.

Sometimes I was working ten hours a day. Sometimes I also had overtime but they still paid my overtime rate at $5 an hour. And I'm sure that $5 wasn't enough because the house was so big! Plus I have to cook, clean, wash the clothes and one thing—when I arrived there my employer had only three kids but when I was already three months working there she told me that she was pregnant with their fourth child. I was the only one who looked after her fourth child. I asked her to at least raise my salary, but she said I wasn't that busy, that sometimes I had nothing to do. But she didn't realize that I was always the one who looked after her baby.

Undoubtedly, the LCP perpetuates commodification of labor that ties a domestic worker to a private home free from the provincial government's labor regulations. Earning less than minimum wage even after completing the two-year live-in requirement traps many domestic workers in low-paying jobs. The savings they could use for upgrading often go to the Philippines to support families and pay off debts incurred during the costly migration process.

Although the range of exploitation in a private commodified sector, that is, the household, is diverse, immigration processes enslave Filipino women workers and eventually transform them into partial commodification in the labor market. One woman sarcastically compared the employers' maltreatment of domestics to the use of robots: "Whenever they [employers] want you [domestic workers] to move, they just click on, and if they want you to stop, they just click off" (2001). Workers' narrations also clearly point out that upper-/middle-class lifestyles in Canada have been changing, with high expectations for cleanliness, more preference for hand-washing clothes, and an increasing number of privileged women choosing to pursue a career path and free themselves from housework by exploiting women living in poverty in Canada. Gorz summarizes the situation: "They [domestics] do what their clients [employers] would not have been able to do for themselves. Their labor enables their clients to save time and improve their quality of life" (1989: 138). If one looks at this quotation within the context of domestic-employer contractual relationships, it indicates that the employers, mostly Canadian-born privileged women, have far better chances of being decommodified while defamilializing themselves.

Eldercare in the Commodified Sector: Who Does It?

Many migrant workers find that their contracts do not outline in exact terms what is meant by "flexible work hours" or "extra chores," such as caring for the elderly and the infirm in a commodified private sector. The excessive physical demands of such work can erode workers' original professional skills and self-esteem, as these excerpts from two interviews show:

> I'm taking care of a man who is 58 years old with muscular dystrophy. He's in a wheelchair. I give him a bath, prepare his food, give him his medication, drive him to the doctor or wherever he wants to go and clean the house. . . . He cannot go to the bathroom by himself, so they wake me up. . . . [T]hey wake me up because I have to clean his bum and his clothes. . . . He does not have control of his bowels. . . . [I]n my contract it is written that my working hours are flexible, like not straight hours—three hours in the morning, three hours in the evening or three hours in the afternoon.

> It was the . . . [top-ranking government official] who interviewed me and when he learned that I am a nurse, then he asked me if I know how to put on the sling and know how to put the dislocation back and I said I am not sure. But when I first tried, when the shoulder came out, I was able to put it back. That's when they began to trust me. Before they had home support, but they stopped the service. . . . [T]he mother [81 years old] was living alone in that big house but then . . . in October 1995, the [top-ranking government official] was diagnosed with cancer, so he . . . moved back here in Vancouver. So, I also had to look after [him]. . . . She [mother] never went to any social gatherings because by five o'clock she was already drunk.

The hiring of both the above women to take care of the elderly or the infirm in a commodified private sector, that is, the household, was due to the nursing experience, educational training and credentials they had acquired in the Philippines, even though these qualifications are not accredited in the labor market of Canada. Under the LCP, both women were forced to stay in live-in situations, caring for the elderly or the infirm, performing flexible but uncharted work hours, and taking on extra workloads—for example, caring for two persons instead of the one contracted for. The LCP, which was originally legislated to meet the childcare needs of the dual-career couple, has been extended to eldercare, and the boundaries between childcare and eldercare have been ignored. As though one kind of care is the same as another, eldercare has intruded into the arena of childcare—a gross violation of the LCP. In the name of care, the household as a commodified sector has been extended from childcare to household chores to eldercare to care for people who are ill or who have disabilities.

The current demographic trend of Canada is an increasingly aging population, indicating that the number of commodified households will accelerate. The demand for caregivers for the elderly and the infirm at home will continue to intensify as the population in Canada ages and the social safety net erodes under neo-liberal globalism. This intensification will affect all provinces, but especially BC and Ontario, which hire the most immigrant workers. For example, the current BC Liberal government's plans to shut down many residential care facilities and transfer seniors into assisted living units can only accelerate the demand for caregivers for elders in the households. The closure of government-supported residential care facilities suggests that there will be a dramatic shift of eldercare from decommodified to commodified sectors. Thus, governance both credits market criteria for services and at the same time devalues non-market criteria; in essence, in the name of efficiency, governance endorses commodification. Burke describes such commodification of health as "a process that is much more vigorous, explicit and purposeful than is implied by the phrases 'privatization by default' or 'passive privatization'" (2000: 182).

As the need for caregivers intensifies due to restructuring—from decommodified to commodified sectors—and privatization of health care, it will obviously be profitable to exploit highly trained, educated, migrant professionals as low-paid caregivers. The following quotation demonstrates the experiences of four im/migrant workers:

> I trained as a nurse in the Philippines and I worked in a hospital for seven years. I have a lot of experience working as a nurse in the Philippines, but I came here under the LCP. It's very frustrating.
>
> In the Philippines I finished my Bachelor of Science in Nursing and I'm a registered nurse in the Philippines... I came to Canada in 1994 as a live-in caregiver. ... I don't particularly like it, because I really want to pursue my career. I feel bad when I hear the news about Canada's nursing crisis. I feel deceived. Why did Canada ask me to come here as a domestic worker and then not hire me as a nurse? I feel discriminated against.
>
> I felt hopeless because they [Registered Nurses of British Columbia] told me that I have to go back to school to get the proper registration. I said with my salary how would I be able to go? I had to save for my landing fee [currently $975].
>
> [I]n my workplace... there are four of us who are nurses from the Philippines. But they said they don't want to pursue nursing because their minds are "going downhill."

As the last narration above especially shows, by limiting migrant women workers' skills to the role of caregivers, the LCP not only denies the educational qualifications of nurses and other professionals, but also effectively erodes their skills and consequently, commodifies their labor in the private sector, that is, the household. This structural devaluation of credentials, skills and training traps immigrant women workers in commodified sectors. There these women eventually lose self-esteem and confidence and their labor is commodified with little chance of being decommodified.

Range of Childcare Tasks

Childcare in the commodified private sector incorporates all kinds of "no-name" activities, as the following narrations from two interviews illustrate:

> When I arrived here, they asked me to get a driver's license. For me it was a bonus to know how to drive, but I didn't realize that they would take advantage of it. Right after I passed, they bought a car for me. It was so stressful because I had to drive the kids to school and after school to their extra-curricular activities and even their doctor's appointment. Their doctor was in Surrey, their dentist was in Richmond, they have their ballet in Richmond, in Granville Island, and I had to drive them to the zoo! I still had to clean the house, cook and iron. I was doing my ironing during the night because I didn't have time during the day.

> In the morning, I have to clean the whole house. They also have two dogs that sleep with the couple.... I stopped eating with them because even the two dogs have their own plates and are eating together at the table! ... So, I told them that I couldn't eat with them because I have asthma.... I also have to fix their [dogs'] bedrooms and their [dogs'] place because they lived in the basement. So I have to clean the whole house: from the first level to the third.

The first narration illustrates that getting a driver's license does not necessarily provide benefits or upgrading for a domestic worker. In fact, the employer receives most of the advantages of the worker's upgrading because she can now drive children to all kinds of activities. In effect, the domestic is forced to act as a "surrogate parent," even taking children to an appointment with the doctor. The second narration indicates that the job of a caregiver can also include caring for and feeding animals. The original objective of the LCP to create what Arat-Koc (1990) calls "privatized solutions" for childcare is obviously defeated if one closely scrutinizes these two different narrations. As Arat-Koc so aptly commented, "The state plays an active role in structuring and controlling not only the volume but also the conditions of these workers" (1990: 97). The active role of the state reinforces domestic workers' commodified status while denying decommodification of labor in the future.

BUREAUCRACY OF THE PERMANENT RESIDENCY PERMIT

To get permanent residency, that is, immigration status, some workers stay in the private but commodified sector for several years. For these workers, persistent demands on their services, lack of respect by employers for schedules, and lack of labor regulations are the norms. This intensity of degree of commodification does not generally occur in the public sector and even if it happens, co-workers fight back against the employer's unjust action. The following story demonstrates such an employer-employee relationship in a household. This narration shows the multiple tasks a worker performed for a couple and her precarious situation in the home that was also her workplace for five years. The story also indicates that even after achieving permanent status, a migrant worker still has the potential to be commodified in the household for years ahead:

> When I first arrived they only had one child, and then they had another child. ... I had to do all the work like cleaning the house, looking after the children, their appointments and activities, driving to school and buying the groceries. ... My employers would just come home and eat. ... Usually I don't go out of the house from Monday to Thursday, so in the evenings I'm downstairs [in her own room]. Sometimes they would ask me to watch the kids in the evenings. They said they were just sleeping anyway. I would agree and they became used to it. One Thursday I had somewhere to go. ... At 5:30 pm the husband called saying he wouldn't be coming because he had something to do [the wife was out of town]. ... I told him that he should tell me ahead of time. ... I did not speak to him for almost three days. On the third day he said to me, "If you're not going to talk to me, then you better just pack up your things and leave!" So, I said, "Fine!" ... He knew he wasn't respecting my rights and his solution was to fire me.

Such unreasonable demands are sources of stress for many domestic workers. The result is all too often depression and loss of assertiveness in addition to erosion of rights and skills—all conditions that eventually solidify partial commodification.

Indeed, many domestics find that they have few rights. For example, many domestics report that although they pay $350 a month for board and food in BC, they rarely have any voice in selecting the food they eat. The following narration explains the sub-standard accommodation and food some domestics are forced to tolerate:

> It [the accommodation] was awful. They [the employers] called it a basement suite. ... It was unfinished. My closet didn't have a door. There was only a foot distance between my bed and the bathroom. ... [M]y employer was not that rich. ... [O]ne can of mushroom soup, with two packages of noodles and water, and that was the whole family's [two adults and three children] dinner. ... I would usually buy extra food for myself because it wasn't enough. ... After five months, I was forced to find another employer because they can't afford to pay me anymore.

Gindin (2001) aptly points out that the greatest victory of neo-liberalism has been "the lowering of expectations" and the above narration is a case in point. Despite lack of proper food and suitable accommodation, the domestic did not quit the job until she was forced to. Hiring a domestic worker is often more affordable and cost-effective than placing children in a government regulated/public daycare.

Clearly not all employers can afford to hire domestics for the contract period, and the state fails to clarify labor standards and practices in private households. Lack of monitoring as well as lack of enforcement puts many domestics in sub-standard commodified sectors. In BC, the government's failure to monitor labor conditions, that is, length of work hours, nature of activities, wages, accommodation, food, and holidays, creates an inhospitable commodified sector for many Filipino domestics.

Deregulation and Underground Agents

Certainly, lack of effective monitoring by governments has produced a proliferation of underground agents who control, manipulate and commodify immigrant domestics' labor in numerous ways. The following narrations of three women indicate the nature and extent of commodification under the welfare state's de-regulation:

> I arrived in Canada in 1994 as a domestic worker under the LCP program.... They [agents] brought us [two domestics] to their house. For two weeks, we were working in their house without any pay and the agent told us that that's a part of our training.... The agent's arrangement was if one was arriving the other one should go, so we were like chains.

> [W]e were the ones cleaning their [agents'] house. When I arrived, my friend was already employed but her employer was not satisfied with her, so the agent brought her back to their house.

> We listened to him [the agent's friend, an insurance broker] since we heard many stories of domestic workers who died abroad and whose bodies could not be brought home to the Philippines. So we thought it was a good thing and were convinced to finally buy the insurance.... We paid $47 insurance [medical], all our own expenses, plus we were obliged to send money to the Philippines.

These three women's narrations point out that an underground agent system has emerged because neither the federal government nor the provincial governments enforce labor regulations in the commodified/private sector. In the above case, the immigration system failed to scrutinize the validity of the employers. Consequently, these domestics, after arrival in Canada, found themselves serving agents—unauthorized people—without pay and relying on these agents' good will. Lack of a government monitoring system in BC created a situation where these workers were both financially and psychologically commodified. Financial commodification refers to the usual employer-employee relationship, whereas psychological commodification refers to a feudal relationship that perpetuates emotional reliance on employers. The situation described above runs completely counter to the LCP guidelines and grossly violates workers' rights and entitlements in the hidden and unregulated structure of the commodified workplace.

Lack of Regulation Breeds Environments for Perpetual Commodification

The BC provincial government has failed to monitor labor conditions in the private commodified household, that is, length of work hours, nature of activities, wages, accommodation, food, and holidays. This lack of monitoring creates an inhospitable environment that perpetuates commodification of labor for many immigrant women. The following narrations from three women are just a few examples of what such workers face:

> My sister and I were working together at my first job. I didn't have any problems because my sister was helping me.... I was paid, but my sister wasn't.

> They had three children, one set of twins. My work included bringing the kids to school.... We rode the bus.... They lived on Marine Drive. We had to ride two buses between there and Metrotown [a transit stop] two times a day.... The twins were girls, four years old and the youngest one was three. They were very active and naughty.... I only worked with them for five months and then I was released. I was unemployed for a long time because I used my employer as my reference, but they did not give me a good reference.... They usually woke me up at 5 o'clock in the morning ... they would leave the house at 6 am and then they'd come back at six in the evening.

> Their [children's] ages were two years old and a six-month-old baby.... [T]he baby would sleep with me.... My work duties were cleaning, cooking, looking after the children. Sometimes, I was carrying the baby around with me!

To make the situation tolerable, the first woman received help from her sister, who worked without salary. The second domestic worker literally put in many extra miles to perform her job, which included riding two buses twice a day to take younger children to school. In all, this woman regularly worked for at least thirteen hours without any extra payment. The third worker's story clearly shows again that many domestics indeed perform a parental role, which can only be comparable to the role of a surrogate parent.

"DEFAMILIALIZING" THE PRIVILEGED AND "REFEUDALIZING" THE DOMESTICS

The arrangement between the LCP and the Canadian government has freed many non-commodified or under-commodified, upper-/middle-class, educated women in Canada from housework, that is, cleaning, cooking, washing, ironing clothes, and so on, and reproductive work, that is, childcare and care of the elderly or infirm. Esping-Andersen (1999) describes this process as "defamilialization":

> A de-familializing regime is one that seeks to unburden the household and diminish individuals' welfare dependence on kinship. The concept of de-familialization parallels the concept of de-commodification; in fact, for women de-familialization is generally a precondition for their capacity to "commodify themselves." Hence, de-familization would indicate the degree to which social policy (or perhaps markets) render women autonomous to become "commodified." (51)

In contrast, the arrangement between the LCP and the Canadian government has meant that the labor of many women from the Philippines is commodified, and the women are forced to live in the precarious and unregulated commodified sector. In this way, the employer-employee relationship is feudalized and commodified in the private sector, that is, the household. Consequently, domestic workers' commodification is recycled, enclosing them in a racialized, gendered and class-based labor market. This very process defeats the notion of equal opportunity irrespective of gender, race and class in a welfare state. After attaining the "immigrant" status that facilitates domestics' access to citizens' entitlements in Canada, the majority of domestic workers continue to work as caregivers for the elderly or as live-out domestics or in minimum wage, flexible-hours jobs that Vosko (2000) identifies as temporary work. These workers are commodified once they lose their original credentials and begin performing services involved with childcare and eldercare. Through the LCP, the federal government reinforces social inequality by keeping domestic workers, albeit one group of citizens, in the lower strata, that is, in the commodified/private sector, and restricting them from moving out of this strata. Reliance on this labor pool to solve the domestic care crisis in Canada both erodes the basic principle of the welfare state, that is, equal opportunity for all irrespective of gender, race and class, and prolongs social inequality between immigrants and Canadian-born people.

The narratives in this chapter clearly show that the Canadian welfare state has created structural and systemic barriers for immigrants who migrate to Canada as domestic workers under the LCP and become commodified in the private sphere. Consequently, after achieving permanent status, these domestic workers are partially or fully commodified as they, in addition to their family obligations, undertake jobs from childcare to eldercare—what some activists label as "from stroller to wheelchair." The situation some immigrants find themselves in prevents them from reuniting with family members, a situation that can breed alienation, dislocation and violence. Parrenas (2001) identifies this as "mothering from a distance." The

National Film Board's film *When Strangers Unite* (1999) illustrates the adverse impacts of segregation of family members upon domestic workers, which may be comparable to the impacts of the head tax earlier in Canada's history (for details, see The Women's Book Committee 1992). As Eda, a young teen and daughter of a caregiver from Vancouver commented, "I have a mother but I do not know her" (*The Philippine Times* 2000: 14).[7] On the other hand, like the "continuous journey" provision described earlier in this book, the situations arising from the LCP have fostered the establishment and growth of the Philippine Women Centre in Vancouver (that chapter 8 examines). These Filipino immigrants have not only continuously challenged the LCP and the gendered and racialized nature of the labor market, but also demanded that the federal government review the program and address its problems, especially its live-in requirement and the status of temporary workers in commodified sectors.[8]

NOTES

1. Chapter 3 describes this situation and argues that the majority of women immigrants enter Canada as "secondary," "dependent," and "unequal."
2. I use the concept of workers in a general sense. The analysis in this chapter shows that variations exist between Canadian-born and im/migrant women workers. I am also aware that differences and discriminations exist between Canadian-born men and women workers.
3. In chapter 3, it was mentioned that BC, the second-largest immigrant-receiving province, gets a failing grade (in a study reported by Chris Friesen in the *Vancouver Sun*, 2005) in providing English language services to its immigrant population. This is one example of how the federal government, due to its lack of a regulatory system, fails to maintain a national standard for serving immigrants.
4. The Philippine Women Centre (1997) in its own study titled "Trapped: 'Holding on to the Knife's Edge,'" identified the impacts of de-skilling as economic violence and identified its various forms.
5. The concept of re-commodification will be illustrated and examined in chapter 7.
6. The first interview, held in 1996, was conducted by the Philippine Women Centre for its own internal research, and I use this quote with the PWC's permission.
7. In Winnipeg, Filipino Canadian women met with the then Immigration Minister, and one young woman made this statement (*The Philippine Times* 2000).
8. On August 29, 2000, delegates—mostly of Filipino ancestry—of the national consultative forum in Winnipeg met with the then Immigration Minister to demand that the LCP be scrapped. The Minister stated: "I value the program and I'm not going to do anything to jeopardize it" ("Scrap the LCP," *The Philippine Times* 5, no. 9 (2000): 14.

6

Decommodification and Immigrant Women
Access to Social Benefits and Services

[T]he decommodification of labor cannot arise from ideology, nor can it await the revolution. Collective social services, unemployment and sickness compensation, employment security, and general income maintenance must be established. (Esping-Andersen 1985: 30–31)

No mere declaration of rights can suffice: institutions are required to make the rights effective. (Polanyi 1957: 256)

This chapter first traces the origin, meaning, and application of the concept of decommodification in the welfare state, then briefly discusses various interpretations generated by conservatives and social democrats. Elaborating on the possibility of decommodification of low-wage immigrant women's labor in Canada, the next section reveals a number of factors pertinent to federal and provincial governments' regulation and deregulation, which are responsible for erecting barriers to decommodification of low-wage immigrant women's labor. These factors range from the federal government's limited settlement services (English[1] language courses and access to housing); lack of government-funded support for immigrant women's job search; inadequate labor regulations by the BC provincial government, and limited government-funded, affordable daycare. Finally, the chapter argues that immigrant women's concentration in low-wage labor has deprived them of many benefits, such as extended health care, Employment Insurance (EI), sick leave, vacation, retirement savings, and so on, and ultimately results in material insecurity throughout their lives. The deprivation of social benefits pertinent to jobs hinders immigrant women from becoming decommodified in Canada.

DECOMMODIFICATION: ORIGIN, MEANING, AND APPLICATION IN THE WELFARE STATE

The controversial issue of decommodification was first introduced by Polanyi (1957) and later expanded by Offe (1984) and Esping-Andersen (1985, 1990, 1999). Broadly, the concept of decommodification indicates that the welfare state grants benefits and entitlements, as well as social rights, irrespective of participation in the labor market. The concept of decommodification has thus countered to some extent the limitations of commodification of labor by referring to social rights irrespective of gender, class and race. Scholars such as Esping-Andersen (1985, 1990, 1999), Miliband (1994), and Offe (1984) have explored the concept of decommodification within the context of the welfare state. Consequently, the concept may not be applicable where welfare policies do not prevail.

Social rights can be effective only where institutions have legal sanctions and enforcements (Polanyi 1957). Polanyi argued that a declaration of rights is not sufficient, although he urged that all citizens' rights be incorporated within the Bill of Rights. Incorporation of rights in an Act certainly provides ammunition for individuals to challenge deprivation and violation of rights in a court of law. Polanyi's advocacy of social rights was unrestricted and inclusive, but implied state regulation: "The list should be headed by the right of the individual to a job under approved conditions, irrespective of his or her political or religious views, or of color and race" (1957: 256). Under Polanyi's vision, individuals who "legally"[2] resided in a state were thus entitled to social rights, including the right of employment, and these rights required regulating and enforcing by the state. However, in supporting social rights enforced by the welfare state's regulatory framework, Polanyi underestimated resistant forces inside and outside the state, including neo-liberal policies and global forces.

When the welfare state monopolizes social policies, contradictions between the welfare state and capitalism may arise (Offe 1984). Pointing out the contradictions between commodified markets and decommodified social sectors, Offe found that welfare-state policies might eventually paralyze the capitalist economy. Offe thus proposed that decommodified sectors—for instance, hospitals and schools—be expanded and transformed into autonomous organizations for the production and distribution of use values. Offe pointed out the limitations of the welfare state while refuting the conventional understanding of the welfare state as a service provider. However, Offe also overestimated the development and growth of decommodified sectors. In the name of restructuring, for example, the current BC provincial government is revamping the decommodified health care sector and allowing private clinics. It is clear that BC's health sector is gradually moving away from decommodification.

In writing the foreword of Offe's book *Contradictions of the Welfare State*, Keane[3] argued that Offe's thesis was "generic" and overlooked the significance of social inequality embedded in welfare-state policies—the welfare state certainly frames discrimination when it comes to "social security provisions for citizens" (1984). For example, the welfare state clearly distinguishes between "employment insurance" and "welfare assistance" and makes limited provisions for citizens whom it constitutes the "undeserving poor." Keane further commented: "Second-class citizenship and 'poverty traps,' in other words, have always been an endemic feature of the post-war extension of 'citizenship rights'" (1984: 17). As discussed earlier, many immigrant women, because of their status as "dependents" and "family class," enter Canada as "second-class citizens." Their "familial obligations"[4] and lack of Canadian degrees and job experience keep these women concentrated in low-paid jobs that restrict them from becoming decommodified. As a result, low-wage immigrant women are denied access to social security provisions such as Employment Insurance, extended medical and dental benefits, sick leave, childcare, vacation, retirement savings—and the list goes on.

The issue of decommodification has been extensively dealt with in Esping-Andersen's works (1985, 1990, 1999). He cautions scholars not to confuse the concept of decommodification with the full elimination of labor as a commodity: "Rather, the concept refers to the degree to which individuals, or families, can uphold a socially acceptable standard of living independently of market participation" (Esping-Andersen 1990: 37). Examples of the best decommodifying welfare states currently are Scandinavian countries, which Esping-Andersen identifies as social democratic. One of the best possible features of the social democratic welfare state is the combination of welfare and work. Esping-Andersen's comparison of decommodification with de-proletarization deserves special attention in a welfare state. The process of de-proletarization occurs only when work becomes a "choice" rather than a "necessity." In the case of low-wage women's labor, the term "choice" is used in a limited manner (Esping-Andersen 1999). For example, sick leave and Employment Insurance provide women with a choice not to go to work. It is evident from the research assembled here that the majority of immigrant women enter the labor market[5] and hold part-time, flexible, "unskilled," low-paid jobs out of sheer necessity, and that this situation precludes most of these women from having access to the decommodification of their labor. It should be noted that while the term "unskilled" in the labor market does exist, in fact, any job requires some skills. The categories of "skilled" and "unskilled" generate a division of labor that eventually favors employers and paves the way to create a gendered and racialized labor market.

To examine the concept of decommodification, Esping-Andersen (1990) focuses on social rights and the social policy of the welfare state. Social rights, according to Esping-Andersen, have the capacity for decommodification and allow people to live independently irrespective of their participation in the market forces; hence, social rights diminish citizens' status as "commodities" (1990: 3). This concept of social rights will be used in this chapter within the context of decommodification of low-wage immigrant women's labor. Esping-Andersen (1990) further argues that decommodification is a process that in numerous ways provides a certain level of welfare and security for the individual. Security, in this book, refers to material security, for example, job-related benefits, access to housing and so on. Immigrant women's narrations in the following section illustrate that Canada has failed to provide immigrant women with a certain level of welfare and security. Rather, due to its increasing neo-liberal policies, the state has inadvertently developed a system where the individual immigrant woman is herself responsible for establishing personal/family welfare and material security.

INTERPRETATIONS BY CONSERVATIVES AND SOCIAL DEMOCRATS

In using the concept of decommodification, social democrats and conservatives differ not only on who should have access to decommodification, but also on how these people should gain access. Decommodified areas already exist in capitalist economies; following World War II, decommodified areas ensured access to health, education and other services (Miliband 1994). Conservatives urged reducing the area of decommodification, maintaining strict criteria for eligibility to access the services, and privatizing the services. Social democrats, on the other hand, argued for minimizing the inequality between class divisions and urged a rewritten contract between the state and disadvantaged groups, including women.

Both conservatives and social democrats use similar concepts but with different underlying assumptions. For example, for conservatives, "pro-family" refers to the male bread-winner model; for social democrats, "pro-family" means to create a balance between work and family obligations, with the state providing services for care, that is, childcare and eldercare. This latter balance has taken place in the Nordic countries since the late 1960s, originating with the social movement that took place in Sweden in 1960.[6] In general, then, decommodification has the potential to reduce risks for disadvantaged groups such as women, single parents, "unskilled" individuals, immigrant women, people with disabilities, seniors, and so on. Esping-Andersen comments, "the policy shift came not so much from the commanding heights of the labor movement as from a massive popular campaign led by women's organizations" (1999: 45).

The nature and degree of decommodification vary according to the commitment of the welfare state. For example, although the US and Germany are both liberal welfare states, significant differences exist between them. For example, as mentioned in the previous chapter, in comparing lone mothers in the US and in Germany, researchers have found that while in both countries the labor force participation among lone mothers has increased, the contexts are different:

> While labor force participation in Germany offered independence from welfare payments as well as future access to decommodification of labor, the workfare programs in the US required lone mothers receiving temporary welfare assistance to move off welfare rolls into precarious, low-wage employment, with limited opportunities to secure basic needs for their families. (Giddings, Dingeldey, and Ulbricht 2004: 137)

The above study points out that due to their low wages, lone mothers in the US have few opportunities to escape from poverty or to have access to decommodification of their labor in the future. In Germany, the decommodification of labor upon retirement provides lone parents with incentives to participate in the labor market voluntarily. Similarly, state-initiated social rights in Canada would alleviate low-wage immigrant women's material insecurity, and low-wage immigrant women's access to the decommodification of labor will not hinder their increasing participation in the Canadian labor market.

BARRIERS TO DECOMMODIFICATION: MULTIFACETED DIMENSIONS

This section's narrations by immigrant women illustrate the barriers that prevent access by low-wage or non-wage immigrant women to decommodification of labor. Most of the narrators are women from South Asia,[7] and only a few sought help from government agencies with any successful results.

Lack of Canadian Job Experience

In searching for jobs, most immigrants, including immigrant women, face a frequent and challenging question: "Do you have Canadian experience?" In 1986, Das Gupta argued that many South Asian women had never participated in the labor market in their countries of origin:

> Most South Asian immigrant women had not worked for pay prior to coming to Canada. Their primary roles were as wives, mothers, or daughters. As such, they often helped with the family farm or small business. Most are from petty bourgeois families from urban and rural areas. In such cases, it is sometimes a disgrace to send women to work. . . . After immigration, many women are forced to work out of sheer necessity. (68)

In contrast to Das Gupta's argument, my research indicates that the majority of immigrant women in Canada worked for pay in their countries of origin. Women who had never worked for pay were newly wed or had been completing their education before migration or were living in remote areas where suitable jobs were unavailable. Whatever their work and educational experience, however, the immigrant women interviewed faced similar constraints, as the following examples show.

Abha, who had just completed her master's degree in social work from the University of Delhi, a prestigious university in India, got married when she was preparing herself for the Indian Civil Service (ICS) competitive exam. She then migrated to Canada. Her "lack of Canadian experience" shattered her job prospects and hence, her chances for decommodification of labor:

> I did apply for jobs, but because of a lack of Canadian experience or because I was not educated in Canada or because I was an outsider [South Asian]. . . . I was not able to break that *iron wall* [the author's emphasis] from the beginning and it was very tough, very frustrating. . . . [T]here was a government organization that was created to help immigrants. I sent my resume to them. . . . They would forward it to wherever they thought appropriate. But nothing ever happened. . . . I was beginning to think of studying, but I became pregnant. And then I became very ill.

Abha explored many different ways, including seeking help from a government agency, to get a job in her field. However, she was never successful. Abha aspired to be a top civil servant in India, but she was never given the opportunity of entering the Canadian labor market, despite her fluency in English,[8] her M.Sc. (Master of Science) degree from the University of Delhi, and education in an English school in India. To make matters worse, her difficult pregnancy forced her to stay at home and sacrifice her dream of upgrading.

As a sponsored immigrant, Iqbal Jahan, along with her three children and husband, migrated to Canada in 1974 and lived in the North for many years. In South Asia, she had never worked for pay, and her husband had a well-paid job in a town. Her first job in Canada was in the library of an elementary school her children attended. To gain Canadian experience as well as job experience, she volunteered at the school for about two years. This eventually helped her acquire two jobs—as a crosswalk guard and a library worker, both part-time, low-paid jobs. Iqbal Jahan describes how she acquired these jobs:

> My four children [fourth was born in Canada] used to go to the same elementary school close to our home. . . . I started to do volunteering at the school library; during recess time, I supervised children. In addition, I used to volunteer as a crossing-guard to help children cross the road safely. You have to apply to the City Hall to get this job.

To gain Canadian experience, Iqbal Jahan volunteered for a long period in two different sectors while adjusting her schedules and work with her four children. Later on, when her children were grown up, Iqbal Jahan quit these jobs and took a job in a hospital where she worked as a nurse's aide. She took part-time jobs out of sheer financial necessity because one income, that is, her husband's, was insufficient to support the needs of her family as her children grew up. Iqbal Jahan's desperate financial need as well as her familial obligations kept her in low-wage jobs, consequently commodified, throughout her life, and she never had access to decommodification of her labor.

In contrast to Abha and to Iqbal Jahan, Rita Chowdhury, who came as a spouse of an independent immigrant, got a job immediately without Canadian experience. Rita comments, "[O]n the eighth day of residing in Canada we [includes Rita's husband] went for an interview and we were lucky. We were selected and we started the job" (August 2002). Actually, it was not Rita's luck, but her qualifications and job experience in London, England, that landed her the job:

> I lived in different countries in my life. I lived in India. My primary and secondary school I did in New Delhi. . . . Then I went to London. I studied there a few years and worked there as well. . . . I resided there about ten years.

Rita's qualifications and experience surpassed the employer's demand for Canadian experience. However, the job, which was with a telemarketing company, lasted only a few months because the company shut down its business. Rita's job was far below her qualifications, but getting a job right away after migration provided her immense satisfaction. Many immigrants like Rita accept job offers well below their qualifications just to acquire Canadian experience, although they rarely decommodify in the end.

Interestingly, none of the women I interviewed sought social assistance or assistance from the Canada Employment and Immigration Centre (CEIC), at least at the initial stage of their job search. This contradicts Vosko's findings:

> Several temporary help workers who recently immigrated to Canada also reported that when they first arrived and applied for jobs, employers told them they needed Canadian experience. This creates a vicious cycle for immigrant workers, forcing them to seek social assistance and/or assistance from Canada Employment and Immigration Centres (CEIC). (2000: 190)

One possible explanation for the differences between my findings and Vosko's is that the majority of my interviewees had adult males in the household. These adult males possibly had jobs or sought social assistance to which the women were not entitled due to their immigration status, that is, as dependents or family-class immigrants. However, the women I interviewed who were single or single parents (total: four) also did not seek government assistance. Out of all immigrant women, single women are in the most precarious situation due to meager government assistance and lack of empathy of the immigrant community in general toward single[9] women. Out of these four women, one emigrated to her country of origin temporarily (due to economic hardship), but later returned to Canada, two others left Canada after I had conducted the interview, and one decided to move to India and remain there during her old age. These immigrant women's experiences suggest that single immigrant women are on their own in terms of both job search and retirement, and the majority never have access to decommodification of labor. This lack of decommodification of labor places single immigrant women in such a precarious situation that emigrating to their country of origin is the immediate solution. As these emigrating women have Canadian citizenship and consequently, hold passports, returning to Canada again is not ruled out, as happened in the case of Farhat, who was mentioned earlier.

Flexible Work Hours and Range of Workplace

> Women from different classes, from different racial and cultural groups, from different regions, and of different ages or abilities often face different barriers and frequently have different work experiences . . . it is clear that women from economically secure households have advantage over other women in terms of preparation for and access to the labour market . . . systemic barriers disadvantage those who are not members of the dominant racial, linguistic, and cultural groups. (Armstrong and Armstrong, 1994: 45–47)

Immigrant women's narrations demonstrate that in their lives, part-time, flexible jobs are the norm, although the workplace in terms of work hours, employment standards, and work environment varies. For most immigrant women, flexibility means unpredictable schedules, the absence of employment standards, and the insecurity of jobs, as well as lack of access to social rights and entitlements. This situation results from the absence of federal government regulations and can be affected by changes made by individual provinces to their Employment Standard Acts (ESA). For instance, when the BC provincial government revised its ESA in 2002, it resulted in many adverse consequences for immigrant women. The minimum work hours declined from four to two, and the minimum wage was reduced from $8 to $6, a "training wage" that someone without documented work experience can receive for 500 work-hours. Further, BC employers are no longer required to post the ESA in the workplace, where the information it contains can be read by employees and used to safeguard their rights. The following quotation illustrates the employers' viewpoint:

> Employers need a flexible labour force and part-time work schedules allow them to maintain flexibility. The need for flexibility is acute within the service sector due to the short waves of peak activity on daily, weekly, and seasonal

bases. In this sector, not only is there a demand for part-time work, but also there is sometimes a demand for variable-hour part-time work. To cover daily peaks, part-timers may be scheduled two to four hours a day. (Duffy and Pupo 1992: 95–96)

This quotation further shows how the restructured ESA in BC has protected employers' interests at the expense of low-wage workers who generally consist of immigrants and young Canadians.

As Vosko comments, the racialized division of labor in work-hours and the workplace accelerates an exploitative work environment: "For most workers, the elusive promise of flexibility generates neither 'new' nor improved conditions of employment" (2000: 187). In her interview, Aparna described what conditions were like for her as an immigrant worker:

> There was nobody to support me and I had never taken welfare from Canada. . . . I had to be very careful to start working. As I mentioned earlier, I started working with the East Indian restaurant, which was very hard on me, and then I got the job at the Bay and I started working there. . . . At one time, I had two jobs, at the Bay and at a video store, but at that time, I had quit the East Indian restaurant. I used to work from 9 a.m. until 6 p.m. at the Bay [for 6 years], then from 6 p.m. until 1 a.m. at the video store [for 2 years]. It was almost like out of 24 hours I was out for at least 18 hours a day and it was really hard. I never took a day off for at least the first two years. . . . I used to take the bus to come back to my house [at 1 a.m.]. I was somewhat scared a lot of times because I was the only one in the bus and the bus used to stop a block from my house. Most of the time I used to ask my bus driver to wait and watch me until I go. The bus drivers were sometimes really nice, but some drivers I know, it's the end of the line at that time. At 1 a.m., their shift is over, so they are in a rush too. Sometimes they used to say sorry, which was really, really hard for me. I was so scared. For four years it was quite hard on me.

Two flexible but odd-hour jobs without any chance of decommodification of labor kept Aparna surviving financially and allowed her to keep her dignity, which she stressed even in dire financial circumstances. However, she never lost her empathy for bus drivers who worked late-night shifts. Here, class possibly transcended race and gender boundaries. Aparna was in desperate financial need as her relationship with her partner had deteriorated during the settlement period, and her partner supported her and her children very little. In spite of financial hardship, Aparna never relied on the welfare state's assistance, and this again contrasts with Vosko's (2000) findings mentioned earlier. Aparna's narration also suggests that immigrant women do not seek social assistance willingly.

Many immigrant women who enter Canada as spouses end up in jobs with flexible work hours. For example, in 1997 Anamika migrated from South Asia as the spouse of a business immigrant. Prior to her migration, Anamika had never had a paid job due to her affluent financial situation in her country of origin. She got her first job in Canada in a lottery company, which shut down after only two weeks. Later on, she worked at a resort company for two months, selling time-shares, then for a company selling long-distance telephone service. According to Anamika, the telemarketing job was not suitable for her, and she started to take a security course. Immigrants from South and South-east Asia do not value telemarketing jobs. First, such jobs receive much negative media coverage. Secondly, the job involves marketing intangible, rather than actual, products over the phone. After one month of training in security, Anamika got a part-time security job that required graveyard shifts (i.e., all night). Anamika was keen on balancing her familial obligations (she had two young children) and her flexible work-hour job. Thus, when she was interviewed for the security job, she requested a day shift. Anamika got a job in the Plaza of Nations, where she covered specific events only. Although her work-hours were short—another aspect of flexibility—Anamika enjoyed the workplace environment despite the absence of decommodification of labor, and this day-job helped her to juggle childcare/household responsibilities and paid work. Like almost all of the women interviewed, Anamika acted as the principal caregiver and performed all sorts of household chores despite the presence of an adult male, that is, husband in most cases, in the household. Rosenberg (1990) has named this extra work as "housework, wifework, motherwork." Despite lack of decommodification of her labor, Anamika seems to be quite satisfied with her flexible jobs in Canada although she had no paid jobs in her country of origin. Possibly, these flexible jobs have empowered her in spite of the juggling she had to do between childcare, household chores and paid jobs.

Among immigrant women, a "respectable" part-time job sometimes overshadows a full-time job as well as the possibilities of decommodification of labor. During the interview session, Anamika was performing two jobs: one in a storage facility and the other in a bank. Although Anamika's job in the storage facility had been full-time, she had switched to the bank's part-time, flexible-hour job. She kept five days (Tuesdays to Saturdays) available for the bank and worked just two days for the storage facility. Anamika commented about the switch to more bank hours: "As a client, I saw women are working there and the work environment is nice. People in this country say bank jobs are more respectable" (June 2002). Anamika's statement reflects her consciousness of her privileged position in her country of origin. In addition, she can financially afford to quit a full-time job to get a part-time, "respectable" job. The respectability of the workplace environment is a big issue for some immigrants, especially those who led a comfortable life in their countries of origin. Many of these immigrant women prefer to work in banks or in large, prestigious hotels although most of these jobs are not well paid. This issue reflects the consciousness of class among the so-called upper class immigrants, especially among those who migrate under the entrepreneur category. The federal government's immigration category of an entrepreneur class thus ideologically reinforces unequal social divisions and inequality among immigrants from Asia. This category in the long run defeats the very basis of social justice and equality in a welfare state.

Many immigrant women work beyond the normal average hours in their jobs. For example, Chaiti, a spouse in the family class category, had never had a paid job in her country of origin, but holds two part-time, flexible-hour jobs—one in a flower shop and the other in a food chain store. She works five to six hours maximum daily for three days a week in the flower shop. Her job in the food chain is 30 to 35 hours maximum a week, although her work-hours get shorter during the summer when students are hired. Chaiti comments on her situation: "I manage to cook for the family before going to the workplace. Some days, I go to my workplace in the morning. If I don't get a ride from either my husband or my son, I take a bus and go to another workplace. Then, I return home at night" (August 2002). Chaiti's work-hours in both workplaces together exceed the hours that make up one full-time job with possibilities of decommodification of labor; however, both jobs are considered part-time. Chaiti's "part-time" categorization denies her all benefits, and consequently, lacks the possibility of decommodification of labor.

Immigrant women's narrations demonstrate that "flexibility" means both more choices and more profits for employers, but deprives women of social benefits not given to part-time workers, such as Employment Insurance, sick leave, medical benefits, vacation, and so on. Flexible hours do allow some immigrant women to care for young children at home; however, flexibility neither provides better conditions of employment nor opens up the door to social rights and entitlements, that is, decommodification of labor. Rather, flexibility places immigrant women in a vicious cycle of juggling work-hours and familial obligations. For many of these women, familial obligations and part-time flexible jobs not only deny them social benefits, hence, decommodifcation of labor, but also make material insecurity the norm from adult years to their old age. This absence of decommodification of labor followed by material insecurity possibly forces single women to return to their country of origin, where they expect to have higher standard of living due to better exchange rate. The cases of Aparna and Chaiti explicitly illustrate this point.

Landing Jobs: Advertisements, Government-Regulated Agencies, or Personal Contacts?

Landing the first job is a big issue for most immigrants, especially for immigrant women, as it breaks through the "iron wall" that Abha, who was mentioned earlier, described. In contrast to looking at advertisements or seeking help from government-regulated agencies, the majority of interviewees from South Asia got their first jobs through personal networks or contacts. However, most domestics from the Philippines get their jobs through agencies.

Once domestics migrate to Canada, if they do quit or get fired, they frequently find new jobs through their personal networks. This may happen for several reasons: first, employed immigrants have empathy for fellow immigrants looking for work and help them find jobs. Second, government-funded agencies are not effective in finding part-time, low-wage jobs for immigrants. Consequently, immigrant women rely on personal networks for jobs and any job-related information; generally, these jobs make immigrant women's labor commodified rather than decommodified.

Munia, who migrated from South Asia as a spouse in 1985, volunteered in a daycare and baby clinic for about two years. These two places were located close to her residence. When she asked for jobs there, the agencies suggested that she take an Early Childhood Education course—a two-year program. In her country of origin, Munia had worked as a school teacher and had aspired to pursue a teaching career in Canada. When she sent her certificates to a relevant agency in Victoria, they told her to go to college for further study. Munia kept looking for a job. A family friend suggested that she apply where he was working, and Munia was eventually hired there. As Munia comments,

> I got the job through a family friend who used to work there. One day he said, "If you want to work, come to our office and give an interview." He even accompanied me to his workplace for the interview.

Munia's experience suggests that gender plays a major role in providing support for acquiring a job. Possibly, immigrant men have more information than women do about jobs because most, compared with women, interact with government agencies and organizations and perform fewer familial obligations.[10]

Relatives also extend help to immigrants looking for a job. Chinu, who had never had a paid job in her country of origin, started to look for a job out of financial necessity. Her first job was in a flower shop. A male relative recommended that she visit the shop and see the supervisor. Chinu describes her experience:

> My relative asked me to go and see the supervisor as several Indian women worked there. First, I met with the supervisor, then I applied, and later on, he interviewed me over the phone. He said, "It's very hard work. Will you be able to perform?" I said yes.

Chinu's statement suggests that racial composition in a workplace may either encourage or discourage immigrant women from applying for a job. Despite Chinu's lack of job experience, let alone Canadian job experience, she possibly got her job because of her ethnicity and her willingness to do tedious work. In addition, her relative, a well-established businessman in Greater Vancouver, may have influenced the employer to hire her. Chinu's experience is reflected in Gannage's findings, which showed that ethnicity and gender played a role in getting a job in Toronto's garment industry (1986).

Blood or marital kinship can play a major role in getting a low-wage, flexible hour, part-time job; in other words, blood or marital kinship often facilitates immigrant women's labor being commodified rather than decommodified. Hasna, a South Asian, had lived in Japan for five years. She worked sporadically in a supermarket as well as in a restaurant in Japan, then migrated to Canada as a spouse in 1997. Despite her utmost efforts, she did not find a job until 2000 and even then only when a male immediate family member mentioned a part-time job opening in the lab where he worked. Hasna finally landed the job that made her labor commodified but not decommodified (she continues to have this job).

Connections among domestic workers play a crucial role not only in finding out about jobs, but also in identifying employers who have good track records in their treatment of domestics. Cardidad, a domestic worker, migrated under the LCP and suddenly lost her job when her employer moved to the US. Through the domestic workers' informal network, Cardidad soon had the names of four prospective employers. Cardidad says:

> I worked there for fifteen months and then they moved to New Jersey, so I had to find another job. I looked in the newspaper for a new job, but I couldn't find one. . . . My friend Grace was there and I asked her to help me find a job because I had my kids in the Philippines and also I had to complete the two years. . . . I had four prospective employers. . . . I didn't know which one to choose. . . . The one I picked was the one Grace referred to me. The couple was a police officer and a nurse. I'm scared of police officers since you know how they are in the Philippines! [Laughter] They interviewed me and Grace had given me a good reference. They offered me minimum wage as a starting wage. I was lucky because they were nice.

This narration shows both that the job market for domestics in Canada is still vibrant and that Cardidad relied on her personal network to find another job. Indeed, she checked out the "credentials" of her prospective employers before pursuing the job. If they wish to find another reliable worker promptly, employers have to have a good track record with the domestics' network. Otherwise, employers have to rely on the agencies, which is a time-consuming process. The above narrations also indicate that immigrant women's labor is frequently commodified and that decommodification of labor does not occur through personal or any other networks.

Jane, another domestic, described how much the unofficial network of immigrant women could affect employers:

> They got mad at me. That's when I decided to leave. The wife talked to me and asked me to stay and told me to deal with her only and not her husband anymore. I said, "No. I already made up my mind." So I left. And after that they

could not find a nanny! It took them five nannies to find one, until the fifth one, because I was the one who referred her. They kept asking me to help them find a nanny. They kept comparing the way I work with the new nannies. "They can't stand my kids," she said.

Jane's narration shows that employers also rely on personal connections with domestic workers when seeking new workers. Volunteers at the Philippine Women Centre in Vancouver also mention that many prospective employers phone the center to find dependable workers.

Several interviewees emphasized that finding jobs, especially first jobs, was usually the result of relying on family or personal connections. It is clear that government-funded agencies neither are responsive to immigrant women's needs nor have the capacity to locate flexible work-hour jobs—likely due to these jobs' part-time, low-wage status. Incredibly, many employers find immigrant employees through "word of mouth" rather than through costly and time-consuming advertisements for commodified sectors. Hence, for new immigrants it is important to have a network, especially for part-time, flexible jobs.

Organizational Assistance: Basic Need for Immigrant Women

In desperate situations, immigrant women do seek help from immigrant organizations and some women receive assistance. Shakti, a South Asian woman who migrated to Toronto as a spouse in the 1960s, describes the nature and extent of services she received:

> There was only one organization [in Toronto] . . . this is when I had to leave my household, leave my husband with three children [in 1973]. There was an Indian organization that helped me somewhat. They helped me find a place where there were Indians and also to write a resume to look at the job market because I had never worked outside the home. . . . I received a very warm response [from Immigrant Services]. . . . Then I went to Canada Manpower and took a skill-training course. I took a course in typing because I didn't know how to type and most jobs expected me to type. I didn't get any jobs despite my education. . . . I found myself a single mother all of a sudden with three children. . . . I went to a course sponsored by Canada Manpower at a community college. . . . For this I got financial support from the government. . . . I found this information at the Indian Immigration Aid Service Society. . . . They [the government] paid for the course . . . not directly, but I was eligible for subsidized childcare, which made it possible for me to go because I had a young son who was only two years old. . . . Almost always I've had a paid job since I left my husband.

Shakti's narration demonstrates that in the 1970s, women in abusive relationships received little community or personal support. Although many immigrant women do not seek government or agency help, some do try to reach out beyond their personal network during family or conjugal crisis.

These women are more comfortable relying on impersonal government agencies and institutions and thus avoiding community "gossip,"[11] one of the greatest sources of anxiety for some immigrant women. Women in abusive marital relationships desperately need both financial help and housing if they decide to leave the relationship. Social benefits during such an unexpected event provide immigrant women with material security independent of men, and here lies the significance of the decommodification of low-wage immigrant women's labor. Despite the continuing efforts of the women's movement as well as of immigrant women's groups, immigrant women still feel shame and become isolated when they leave abusive partners. Many of these women feel fortunate to work in commodified sectors without having any chance of decommodification of labor. Any organization, governmental or non-governmental, has strong potential for providing support and services in times of personal and financial crises for immigrant women. Recent cuts by the federal government and by the BC provincial government, especially to women's shelters, women's centers, social assistance, and childcare centers, place the most needy immigrant women in vulnerable and exploitative environments. Further, absence of decommodification of labor also places the majority of immigrant women in a precarious situation throughout their lives.

Social Benefits and Immigrant Women's Entitlements: Where Do They Stand?

Due to their tenuous job situation and part-time, flexible work, very few immigrants have access to social benefits and entitlements, that is, decommodification of labor, such as Employment Insurance, extended medical coverage, full pension benefits, sick leave, vacation, and so on. Most immigrant women are employed in office work, secondary manufacturing, and service jobs, "low skills" or "unskilled" jobs characterized by low wages and unacceptable working conditions. The small number of South Asian women in professional and managerial sectors are often underpaid and work as self-employed, or on contract, because they cannot find jobs that recognize their educational and professional skills (Das Gupta 1994). Harjit's narration reflects this point:

> [B]y the time I actually migrated, things had changed. I got really frustrated that I couldn't find the job I thought I should have had.... I worked as a settlement worker in ... a neighborhood house for a couple of years. Then a similar job to what I did in England came along at ... a school district. At one place I applied, they hired somebody else, but that young woman didn't stay very long. That vacancy came up again and I applied and got that job in 1989.... It gave me a lot of satisfaction because I had a lot of knowledge that was needed for the job—for example, helping the school staff understand the background—religious, cultural everything else—about communities from South Asia. Similarly, I was

very helpful for the parents, too, because I can speak five languages [Punjabi, Hindi, Urdu, English and Gujrati]. So, I could communicate with the parents and help them understand the education system so that we could help their children better. Similarly, there were children with behavior problems, and teenagers, particularly girls caught between two cultures, who got a lot of help from me. The parents wanted them to stay Indian and their peers wanted them to be Canadian. That type of job gives me a lot of satisfaction. . . . I worked there until I retired in 2000. As far as the salary is concerned, it was nowhere near to what I would have got in England. . . . But I do get my retirement benefits.

Harjit's satisfaction came from the nature of her job, although she worked in a commodified sector, not from her salary, as she had no opportunities to be decommodified. As a spouse in the family-class category, Harjit migrated to Canada in 1979. Before her migration, she migrated from India to England in 1966 and taught in England for about thirteen years. However, her teaching skills and training in India and her job experience in England were not counted for the teaching profession in Canada. She struggled to find an alternative career where she could still interact with students and parents. In terms of salary, benefits, and pensions, Harjit never received the entitlements that she would have had from a decommodified job. In her early years of migration, she even went to a community organization to seek assistance. Harjit describes the experience:

[W]hen I was unemployed I went to a . . . neighborhood house. There, there used to be a program. . . . There was a counselor I talked with because I was so depressed emotionally and so upset. I remember going to her and she said. . . . "Don't think all the doors are closed. One day a door will open for you." But that [1980/81] was a very difficult time. . . . [T]hey said I should go to school to be a teacher. If I had gone to school and improved my education, even then the job situation for teachers in the Lower Mainland was very unfavorable for new teachers. They would have sent me to the North. I couldn't afford to go away. It was more important for me that my son should get his education rather than me. We wanted to stay around Vancouver so that he could attend the university here.

The above quote reveals that Harjit's familial obligations, the requirement to re-train to be decommodified, and the absence of guaranteed jobs in the teaching profession persuaded her to set aside her previous professional goals.

Harjit's experience is not an anomaly among professional immigrant women. As mentioned earlier, Abha had aspired to be a civil servant in India and stopped even trying to get into the labor market in Canada after a while. She describes her work-hours and current activities at home:

[A]bout twelve to thirteen hours I work everyday. . . . At a rough estimate, three or four hours go for the children—taking them to school, taking them back, feeding them. . . . At least two to three hours for housework—going for shopping and things like that. . . . I have my parents and take them to the doctor, do things for them. . . . Sometimes my dad wants me to write a letter to somebody, do his back or something. . . . Sometimes my mother-in-law wants to be taken to the doctor. . . . Sometimes she wants me to do something for her, find out something from somebody, and contact the hospital for her, so I do that for her. I take my father for massage therapy. Sometimes my mother needs to go to physiotherapy. I have to do these kinds of things and if they need anything from the store, I take them.

Abha's familial obligations, including childcare, eldercare, housework, and shopping, all indicate her life-long location in a non-commodified sector, that is, the household, without having any chances to be commodified let alone decommodified. Abha received her early education in a private English school and received a degree from a well-recognized institution in India. Abha's familial obligations have deprived her of job and job-related entitlements such as pension, Employment Insurance, sick leave, and the opportunity to contribute to a Registered Retirement Savings Plan (RRSP)—the requirements for the decommodification of labor in a liberal welfare state like Canada. The above discussion demonstrates that both Harjit and Abha are highly qualified immigrant women, but their material securities are never independent of the male members in the family. Abha's labor is used in a non-commodified sector (the household) and Harjit's labor is used in both a non-commodified sector (the household) and a commodified sector (the workplace).

Language and Job-Training Schools

As "dependents," most immigrant women are denied access to free language and employment training programs that could lead to better employment and educational opportunities (Ng 1992). The prerequisite for grade 8 English or equivalent for job-training programs frequently excludes immigrant women who are from the non-English-speaking world (Ng 1992). It is essential to mention that while the specific prerequisites for language and employment training programs may vary from time to time and from one province to another, the structural barriers of such programs remain unchanged. For instance, mentioned in chapter 3, in BC the ESL Program provides free language courses to all immigrants who serve in the low-paid, "low-skilled," non-communication[12] labor market. Immigrants who want to pursue fluency in English have to pay a hefty fee to gain access to more functional English language programs. As Ng (1992) argues, institutional discrimination against immigrant women is thus built into the statuary services for immigrants. This institutional discrimination as well as lack of funding for immigration settlement services creates a captive situation for many immigrant women. Consequently, the only option is to be commodified in the labor market without having any chance for decommodification.

Sabah, who migrated as a member of the family category, pointed out that she never received support from organizations. Sabah's mother tongue is Bangla, and she received her education in Bengali. She was too shy even to say "thank you" when she arrived in Canada. She describes her experience with language skills:

> No, we didn't receive help from any organization. When I migrated here, I thought I should learn English rather than having a paid job, because several immigrants asked me to do an ESL course. I found out the address and went to see the relevant agency. When they tested my language skills, I passed. I didn't need to take the ESL course.

Despite Sabah's desire to learn to speak fluent English, she was discouraged from taking any courses, and no free language course at a higher level was available for her. The free ESL course is quite rudimentary, and women like Sabah, who migrate from post-colonial countries such as Bangladesh, India, and Pakistan—former British colonies, generally do not require this elementary level English. To get better-paid jobs and to have opportunities to be decommodified, these women need higher levels of English courses. However, these courses are costly and not affordable for the majority of immigrant women. As a result, most immigrant women turn to low-paid, "unskilled," "non-communication" jobs without social benefits. Once they start these flexible hour jobs, these women have little time to upgrade their language skills and thus, prospects for decommodification of their labor erodes.

Institutional barriers like language programs concentrate immigrant women in low-paid, part-time, "unskilled" jobs and even hazardous commodified sectors. Because of their lack of proficiency in English and their lack of knowledge about labor rights, immigrant women are often unaware of their labor and workplace rights in commodified sectors. In any event, the BC government has eliminated the employer's obligations to post workers' rights in the workplace, as indicated earlier in this chapter. Lack of awareness about labor rights can place immigrant women in vulnerable situations, as Sabah's first job experience shows:

> I was very excited to work in this chain restaurant. I had worked less than one month when the incident happened. I was asked to get meat patties from the deep freeze. I went to get them, and the door of the freezer [it's a small room] got frozen and I was not able to open it to get out. I had the key, but I was so nervous I could not open it. Of course, the company trains workers how to press the emergency button, how to open it. I tried all different ways, but nothing worked. I cried and my eyelashes got frozen. That was at a quite busy time. When I did not come out, the manager came to find me, opened the door, and got me out. They gave me black coffee to drink and I got back to work within half an hour. They could not give me the day off. I almost passed out and I was so afraid, I cried. I did not realize I was holding the manager's hand. After that

incident, I was scared and developed a phobia about going into that room. Workers were aware of my fear and supportive of me. They themselves would go to that room rather than me if they needed anything. But one manager forced me to go there. While in the room, I kept the door open a little bit. The manager closed the door immediately even though he was aware of my presence in the room. Again, I got very scared. So, I quit the job.

To overcome her fear, Sabah needed counseling and sick leave immediately, but did not receive either of them due to the absence of decommodification of labor in her situation. Later, lack of proficiency in English and lack of knowledge of workers' rights prevented Sabah from taking necessary action against that manager. Despite her psychological trauma, Sabah, a new immigrant, did her utmost to continue her job in the commodified sector, but eventually quit rather than continue in an oppressive situation.

Getting information about language courses, even rudimentary ones, is a major issue for immigrant women. Halima, who can speak her native language as well as Japanese, got language-course information from a family friend:

I got the information from a family friend whose wife did the course. We got the address and phone number from that person. When we contacted the agency, they asked me to take a test and then I got admission. I did this language course for four months and didn't have to pay any fee. The duration of the course was three hours [9 a.m. to noon] a day, five days a week. . . . Although we read English in school [in her native home], in reality, we didn't speak English. This course helped me to speak English.

Despite her work experience in typing and in a restaurant, Halima Begum did not easily find a job even in a commodified sector. She says:

I used to take the Sky Train to go to Surrey and New Westminister to look for a job. I also took the bus to get places. After arriving here, I tried on my own. But nothing happened. In this country, nothing works out unless you know someone.

Even after her language course, Halima Begum struggled to find her first job in a commodified sector. Later on, she got a job through an immediate family member and received two weeks of training. Because of her personal experience, Halima Begum considers "knowing someone" an important factor in finding a job. Halima Begum's narration also indicates that new immigrant women might not receive information about available government services. To Halima Begum, having a job in a commodified sector is good enough and she apparently does not consider having a job in a decommodified sector.

Lack of Affordable/Subsidized Childcare and Housing

For immigrants, the family is a safe haven during the settlement period, providing support and security in the stressful process of survival (Das Gupta 1994). If we consider this statement in context, affordable housing is an important factor for immigrant women to be decommodified as most of their activities revolve around home. In her interview, Latifa told about her experience finding affordable accommodation:

> Looking for the house we faced really a very subtle un-acceptance because . . . you had to leave a message in the machine. . . . I couldn't figure out why nobody would answer. . . . When they put the ad in the newspaper, we would call up the number expecting somebody to talk to someone directly, but it never happened that way. . . . I later on found out there was a reason behind it . . . that was one of the [language] screening systems, I think. The biggest difficulty was the place we lived. We were in the basement and there were two students on top of us and . . . [my child] was very young. . . . Whenever she cried, the people from upstairs would bang on the floor and tell us to make her stop. . . . It was very hard. I didn't find it friendly here . . . not at all.

As Latifa suggests, for immigrants, renting accommodation is a huge issue as most homeowners scrutinize prospective tenants through the answering machine. Name, accent and voice easily reveal ethnicity, race, gender, and possibly even religion. This information provides enormous opportunity for homeowners to screen out "unwanted" renters. This practice also perpetuates racial and ethnic segregation in a big city like Vancouver. Achtenberg and Marcuse also found that lack of government-supported housing perpetuates multi-layer oppression, that is, gender, class and race oppression:

> [T]he housing problems faced by disadvantaged groups have broader social consequences. Housing, after all, is much more than shelter; it provides social status, access to jobs, education and other services, a framework for the conduct of household work, and a way of structuring economic, social, and political relationships. Racial segregation in housing . . . limits educational and employment opportunities for minorities. . . . Housing design and locational patterns reinforce the traditional division of labor within the male-dominant family . . . [and] restrict opportunities for female labor-force participation. . . . [T]he housing crisis today expresses and perpetuates the economic and social divisions that exist within the society as a whole. (1983: 207)

As Achtenberg and Marcuse comment, "Housing—a necessity of life—is treated not as a social good but as a commodity" (1983: 208). The majority of immigrants spend a huge portion of their income on renting or mortgage. These costs deter them from becoming decommodified as they can little afford to spend extra for upgrading or training. Having access to government-supported housing is one of the pre-conditions for decommodification of labor. Due to the shortage of housing, most immigrants do not have such access.

Childcare is a major concern for immigrant women as most immigrants from Asia, whatever their category, migrate with their children. As the Canadian population ages, immigrants with young children are the preferred group to boost up the demography and counter the declining birth rate. Even young, single, adult immigrants soon start raising a family once they migrate. Lack of affordable childcare, as well as lack of adequate government subsidy, places many women in the position of foregoing training or higher education. Lydia, who migrated from the Philippines, describes her experience:

> I sent all my credentials to Victoria to be evaluated, but it took a long time for them to answer—almost a year. They told me to take four subjects at UBC full-time. How could I go back to school full-time when I had three kids already! So I didn't pursue it. . . . I also had a fourth child on the way, so I really wasn't planning to study. . . . [T]he RN [Registered Nurse] course was only for two years. If I had someone to look after my kids, I would have taken the RN course. It was really a difficult time. It was a struggle during those years when my children were still young. My husband and I were really working together for our children. We didn't even have a social life.

Structural discrimination, that is, males as heads of households, already puts immigrant women in a subordinate situation and labels them as "second class citizens." As Lydia's narration shows, the burden of childcare responsibilities and the lack of affordable and government-subsidized daycare deteriorate the situation further. These women are thus prevented from fully participating in their educational and professional advancement and hence, from the decommodification of their labor.

AGE AND JOB-MARKET SKILLS: THE CHICKEN AND EGG DILEMMA

Most of the immigrant women I interviewed migrated to Canada as adults. Several completed their highest education (i.e., M.A. or M.Sc.) in their countries of origin and had held a paid job there. After immigration, these women's educational skills and job experience were neither accredited nor valued. Some, especially those who had experienced Western education and training before migration, either upgraded skills or wrote exams successfully in order to be decommodified. However, these women faced an ironic dilemma for the decommodification of labor—the intersection of their age, gender and race!

One woman who experienced this dilemma was Mona, who received an M.A. in Social Science from a well-recognized university in the US and migrated to Canada in 1989. Mona says,

> I have actually sat for exams [federal government job—immigration department] and passed the exam. It was entry level, about two to three hours, and I sat for it and passed. Then what happens . . . the public service commission takes your resume and puts it in and you know whenever they need people they will call. And it never happened. You have to keep on renewing it every six months. . . . You call them up and say I still want to go back into the job bank and put my resume back in. I did it for six months, then just lost interest. They never called me. In the meantime, while I'm at another job, I applied for a job in Revenue Canada. I sat for that exam too and passed in December. . . . This was about six months ago. They said they will call me by March. March ended and I called them back and they said, "Sorry, we don't need anyone now, but your name has been put in again and if we need anyone, we will call you." So, I don't know if I'm asking for too much or if I'm being too ambitious. I don't know, but I've not been able to get that job. . . . They didn't call. I'm wondering if it's my age [48]. You know, if that's going to be a problem, I don't know. But . . . first of all I'm a woman, secondly a colored woman. I think all these come into play. These jobs are still for men. It's still a men's club and I think it's very difficult to break into that.

Mona's story demonstrates strongly how some immigrant women are caught between aging and upgrading. Without doubt, it takes several years to acquire professional training and higher education in Canada, especially for a racialized woman juggling familial obligations and low-paid jobs. For most immigrant women, going to school for higher education or upgrading skills for professional jobs is a luxury. Most of these women, once they migrate, need to enter the labor market immediately out of sheer financial necessity. Consequently, they stay in commodified sectors throughout their work lives.

Mona's reference to the need to "break into" the system has some similarity with Abha's reference to breaking an "iron wall." Both these South Asian women were educated in well-recognized English schools in their countries of origin, and both became frustrated in Canada as the years passed. Their dreams and hopes about their professional career as well as the decommodification of labor were shattered due to their migration as spouses of "independent immigrants." As spouses, they were not entitled to government-sponsored job training, stipends and social assistance. Absence of such social rights keeps immigrant women like Mona and Abha from having access to social benefits and thus, prevents them from being decommodified in the future.

Farhat, who migrated to Toronto as an independent immigrant in July 1993, describes how her age, race and gender intersected in the labor market:

My first year in Toronto, I couldn't get a job, not any job at all. Lots of people said I'm overqualified because I had been an editor of a magazine and two other publications. I think I was in my 40s then. . . . In short, I couldn't get a job in print. . . . So, I just did odd jobs, cash jobs. . . . I got a very good break in July 1994. . . . I got into television. But it wasn't mainstream. It was a very low-paying job in multicultural television. . . . I would get like $200 a week, and no benefits. . . . I started an M.A. at the University of Toronto in September 1994. . . . I finished in 1996. . . . I was working and studying. . . . Then I got a part-time job . . . as an editor on one of their night shifts. . . . I used to do that Saturday and Sunday . . . from four to midnight. And then Monday, Tuesday, Wednesday, and Thursday—half I used to do my classes and some multicultural TV. . . . It wasn't that there was no gender bias against women, but there was a lot of bias against women of color because of age. You had to be young, you had to be white, and you had to be a woman—then you got a lot of breaks. But if you are a woman of color, a visible minority. I used to keep saying I'm an invisible minority. Why do they keep calling me visible minority? . . . No one sees me. . . . They just don't notice. . . . You are older, you are in your 40s, and you are not fantastic, young, and attractive in that typical sense . . .

Farhat found that her age, gender, and race made her "invisible." Despite her qualifications, that is, an M.A. in Social Science from the University of Toronto, Farhat continuously performed part-time jobs, which obviously did not permit her labor to be decommodified. As a single parent of two children, she lived in a meager financial situation in Toronto. Farhat comments, "So all these combined factors—a personal reason and a certain degree of disillusionment—made me want to go home and I did. I went back to [country of origin] in 1997." However, she returned to Canada in 2001. She explained the reasons of her return:

The first time I came, I had no capital. I was just an immigrant hoping to get a job and make the most of it. I learned that with my age and . . . the other barriers against me, getting a full-time job would not be easy. So, the second time I came with a little capital that I had saved . . . and my family gave me some support as well. . . . I felt I could come now and I don't have to struggle as much as I struggled the first time.

When she returned to Canada the second time, Farhat brought sufficient funds to support her, expecting neither social assistance nor a full-time job. Lack of decommodification of her labor as well as her personal situation forced Farhat to leave Canada the first time. She returned only when she felt she could support herself against all odds—including age, race and gender. In other words, her relatively better financial situation despite absence of decommodification of labor, that is, class, helped her to survive in a racialized and gendered labor market.

Farhat and Mona's experiences raise the chicken-egg question: Which comes first? For decommodification of labor, should immigrant women upgrade their educational skills and professional training? Otherwise, immigrant women search for jobs, their labor becomes commodified, and consequently, they lose opportunities to be decommodified. This is a daunting question when neo-liberal policies are moving social responsibilities from the state to the individual. When immigrant women do get jobs, they usually receive part-time, "low-skilled," low-waged employment. However, if immigrant women upgrade their skills and acquire enough Canadian job experience, they still run the risk that their age will work against their qualifications!

In sum, decommodification of labor is obviously an illusion for low-wage immigrant women. For most immigrant women in Canada, the prospect of decommodification of labor in terms of having access to Employment Insurance, sick leave, extended medical coverage and all other social benefits is still a dream!

NOTES

1. Immigration services are required to offer both English and French courses. BC is an English-speaking province and this chapter thus deals with English as a Second Language (ESL) courses. Several interviewees took ESL courses and, therefore, I refer to ESL.

2. Here, "legally" refers to immigrants rather than to refugees or undocumented migrants in Canada.

3. In writing the foreword of the book, Keane (1984) critically examined Offe's thesis.

4. Esping-Andersen (1990) uses this term to describe the household chores and childcare women perform, due to blood and kinship obligations.

5. Some interviewees stated that they had never worked in their countries of origin for reasons on which I will elaborate later in this chapter.

6. Scandinavian countries are considered the best, but not the ideal, welfare models as feminists in those countries have revealed.

7. South Asia in this book specifically refers to Bangladesh, India and Burma. To protect the anonymity of the interviewee, the exact country of origin in most cases has been avoided. The size of a city (for example, Vancouver) may not protect a woman's identity, especially if the woman is from a specific ethno-cultural community.

8. Abha received her elementary and high school education in English.

9. Single women here indicates unattached women; in other words, women who are currently unattached to any men, but have had previous marital relationships.

10. This comment is based on my personal observation.

11. Based on my personal observation, I consider that "gossip" is one of the strongest weapons for controlling immigrant women's mobility and may contribute to many immigrant women staying in oppressive situations.

12. Non-communication means that an immigrant woman is not required to speak with the customers.

7

Recommodification of Labor
Results of Re-Skilling

Offe discusses three different forms of contemporary resistance to the welfare state. One obviously important source of this resistance is the so-called New Right. Supported by sections of large capital and the traditional middle classes, the goal of this *laissez-faire* coalition is the recommodification of social life. It seeks to decrease the scope and importance of decommodified political and administrative power by resuscitating "market forces." (Keane 1984: 26)

We will invest $41 million over the next two years to help new Canadians to integrate quickly into our economy, whether it is second language skills, or faster recognition of foreign credentials or pilot projects to attract skilled immigrants to smaller communities. . . . [It] will be spent in partnership with provincial and territorial governments as well as regulatory bodies and employers to speed up the credential assessment process for immigrants in certain professions. (Finance Minister, quoted in Thompson 2003: A9)

RECOMMODIFICATION[1] OF LABOR

The first quote above refers to Offe's classic work *Contradictions of the Welfare State* (1984). In that book, Offe is skeptical about the viability of the New Right's *laissez-faire* strategy in recommodifying the social sectors of the welfare state and questions both the New Right's power to strengthen the state and its ideology of a lean as well as familial society (Keane 1984). Keane has correctly pointed out Offe's underestimation of the New Right's power in reviving the commodification process. For example, neo-liberal policies in Canada target only skilled,[2] that is, mostly male immigrants for accreditation; female immigrants in general are thus less likely to become re-skilled.

Due to the withdrawal of governments' gender equity[3] employment strategies, which were designed to support disadvantaged groups including women, racialized people, First Nations and people with disabilities, immigrant women's labor is commodified again even when they do their accreditations. The concept of recommodification refers to immigrant women who go to school to get accreditation for the degrees and professions they had in their countries of origin (i.e., re-skilling) and to have access to social benefits (i.e., the decommodification of labor) such as extended health care, sick leave, family vacation, retirement benefits and so on. However, many of these immigrant women's hopes and efforts are shattered due to numerous factors. As a result, these women re-enter the part-time, low-wage flexible workforce that in turn commodifies their labor again.

As the second quote above shows, the then Finance Minister in his 2003 budget speech announced the Canadian government's intention to accelerate the credential process for some immigrants. Further, in order to eliminate shortages of doctors in the Canadian health care system, a medical task force in 2004 recommended that the skills of qualified immigrants should be better utilized. The outcome of the announcement in 2003 and the medical task force's recommendation in 2004 was an allocation of federal funds in 2005:

> The federal government announced an initiative for foreign-trained workers ... launching it with a $75 million injection to get more internationally trained doctors and other medical workers into Canada's health care system. ... All the programs are aimed at overcoming obstacles facing foreign-trained workers and easing skill shortages across Canada. (Shaw and McCullough 2005: A1)

The 2003 and 2005 announcements[4] reveal that the federal government recognizes the problems inherent in the current processes for assessing foreign credentials, that is, that many immigrants are commodified or partly-commodified without having any chances to be de-commodified and are not filling jobs for which they are trained in their countries of origin. However, the government's plans focus on certain professions and categories of jobs. As a result, most government grants will benefit skilled immigrants, the majority of whom are male and already trained in the professions earmarked by the government. Further, the allocation of money from the two announcements will be distributed among ten provinces over five to six years—hence, the amount is not significant. Questions thus arise: Are there any national standards for evaluating foreign credentials? What are the processes for recognizing foreign credentials without discrepancies? How do the regulatory bodies function at the provincial, federal, and interprovincial levels? Is non-accreditation of immigrants only an "immigrant" problem in the process of becoming de-commodified? What position do immigrant women occupy when the federal government targets (knowingly or unknowingly) mostly male immigrants with certain skills? How do immigrant women have their skills recognized, in order to be decommodified and, if needed, upgraded? What happens to immigrant women who migrate to Canada either as spouses or as dependents? To what extent does the re-skilling of immigrant women recycle them in the labor market, to be recommodified or partially recommodified?

To address these questions, this chapter first presents an overview of the accreditation process in Canada. The chapter then focuses on immigrant women who tried either to re-skill through upgrading educational qualifications or re-training in a school or to explore new avenues for better jobs and working conditions so that they could be decommodified one day. Through immigrant women's narrations, the questions posed above will be further explored. Then the chapter shows that most immigrant women's credentials are either underutilized or not utilized, resulting in recommodification even after some forms of re-skilling. Briefly, the welfare of most immigrant women depends on the family rather than on the state and the combination of familial responsibilities in the non-commodified sector and employment in commodified sectors makes many immigrant women partially commodified. Finally, the chapter recommends some measures the state can adopt to alleviate many of the problems immigrant women face in becoming decommodified in Canada.

AN OVERVIEW OF THE ACCREDITATION PROCESS IN CANADA

Academic research interest in the accreditation process is quite recent; hence, published literature on the accreditation process in Canada is not readily available.[5] The identified issues involved in the accreditation process vary, ranging from skill utilization in the labor market (Reitz 2001, 2003, 2005), recognition of foreign credentials (Smith 2001), integration of immigrant skills (Alboim and the Maytree Foundation 2002; Manery and Cohen 2003), discriminatory barriers to credential recognition (Cornish, McIntyre and Pask 1999), to the integration of international physicians (The Maytree Foundation 2001). Available literature unanimously agrees on the following issues: Immigrants' skills are underutilized; immigrants are underemployed and unemployed; the assessing of immigrants' education, training and job credentials is problematic for employers due to lack of standardized systems; there is an absence of a due process of accreditation; and the list goes on. These factors together generate systemic discrimination against immigrants based on country of origin, gender, age, and class and consequently, generate barriers to becoming decommodified. Generally, most literature (Reitz 2001, 2003, 2005; The Maytree Foundation 2001) deals with immigrants as a whole and bypasses women with regard to the accreditation process, even though immigrant women's experience significantly differs from that of men. In addition to their lack of access to information and the pervasive problems pertinent to the accreditation process, immigrant women are usually preoccupied with childcare and household chores mostly overlooked in the re-skilling process.

Who Deals with the Accreditation Process?

No single provincial or federal government agency or department deals with accreditation, and no universal and harmonized system exists for evaluating "foreign"[6] credentials. In spite of the government's recent commitment to accelerating the credential process for some, no national strategy exists to assist skilled immigrants to become decommodified, let alone female migrants, in entering the Canadian labor market. Immigrants are encouraged to come to Canada according to their education, experience and job skills, but once these immigrants arrive in Canada, their skills carry no value. As a result, these skills are wasted. I agree with Reitz (2001) that current selection based on skills is insufficient, and different strategies are required to utilize immigrants' skills. More specifically, the skills of female immigrants, who mostly enter as dependents, are not adequately assessed and carry less weight in the selection of immigrants; female immigrants particularly thus face numerous barriers to being decommodified.

Lack of Knowledge about the Accreditation Process

Most overseas immigration officers lack either information or knowledge about various occupational certification regulations and consequently do not pass on accurate information about accreditation procedures and regulatory bodies to immigrants. This lack of knowledge constitutes one of the major obstacles in many immigrants' settlement process and decommodification of labor. After migration, many immigrants obtain information on accreditation procedures that incorporate language proficiency, work experience in country of origin, educational degrees, and training. Immigrants then realize that they must obtain recognition of their skills through several disjointed regulatory bodies. The wide range of professional associations (e.g., architects, doctors, engineers, lawyers, pharmacists, and so on) that evaluate immigrants' credentials often lack knowledge about educational systems and work experience in periphery countries. Indeed, no national or inter-provincial data bank exists that could shed light on these issues. Moreover, each province and territory sets different standards for recognizing degrees, training, and job experience from sending countries. For immigrant professionals, provincial requirements as well as occupation-specific regulations prevail for accreditation and licensing. Lack of uniform provincial requirements creates barriers for immigrants who migrate inter-provincially and hence, these immigrants have dual barriers to being decommodified.

Many skilled immigrants enter Canada hoping to do jobs similar to the ones they had in their countries of origin. The reality is that on arrival, many immigrants are forced into a process that is individualized, costly, and disjointed. As a result, chances of decommodification of labor are slim.

The Role of Institutions in the Accreditation Process

Several institutions are key players in recognizing educational and professional skills and determining qualifications required for professional jobs (e.g., doctors, engineers, architects, university teachers and lawyers) or for certain categories of jobs (e.g., nurses, school teachers, daycare and homecare workers, and so on). These institutions include colleges and universities, various training schools (e.g., British Columbia Institute of Technology), hospitals, daycare centers, provincial and federal governments, and professional regulatory bodies for doctors, engineers, architects, lawyers, etc. Most immigrants—except those from English-speaking countries[7]—are required to upgrade their educational skills, retrain in their professions, and get licenses from the individual professional bodies. Unless immigrants go through these procedures, they are never eligible to be decommodified. In addition to the challenges of dealing with the complexities of the procedures, immigrants, especially immigrant women, face financial constraints in pursuing re-training or upgrading in order to be decommodified. For immigrant women, returning to school in order to get back to their original professions—on top of supporting their families—creates major dilemmas in their lives. Should they upgrade their skills immediately once they migrate? Who will support the family financially while they upgrade their skills? Who will take care of the children and household chores? Chapter 6 shows that most immigrant women, to support their families, start part-time, low-paid, "unskilled" jobs on arrival and consequently become commodified throughout their lives as most of them never have opportunities to be accredited and therefore to decommodify. Due to the patriarchal ideologies embedded in families of South and South-east Asia, men after migration in most cases initiate upgrading and re-training, whereas women as spouses and dependents start low-paid, part-time, flexible-hours jobs. Patriarchal ideologies refer to the rule of men in socioeconomic-political structures in the South and South-east Asia—although women challenge these ideologies both informally and formally. To counter patriarchal ideologies, immigrant women as well as their groups organize and resist, as will be illustrated in the next chapter. Even women who migrate as domestics or independent immigrants often spend years in low-paid jobs, that is, commodified sectors, so that they can sponsor family members such as children, spouses and parents as immigrants. Despite these challenges, most immigrant women from South and South-east Asia explore ways to get through the accreditation and the re-skilling process and become decommodified.

IMMIGRANT WOMEN AND THE ACCREDITATION PROCESS: HOW DOES THE SYSTEM FUNCTION?

Immigrant women for this study can be broadly categorized in three groups: (1) full-time homemakers; (2) low-paid, flexible-hours workers who have some sort of training; and (3) those who went to school for re-skilling in order to be decommodified. In the last category, very few successfully achieved their dream[8] of working in their original profession as full-time workers in a decommodified sector. However, despite their precarious situations, most women I interviewed explored avenues that would re-skill them for the Canadian labor market and allow them to be decommodified.

Domestics and Re-Skilling

The following interviews reveal some women's experiences of the complicated and lengthy procedures involved in accreditation for decommodified sectors, such as hospitals, government-supported nursing homes and so on. These women were working in Canada as domestics while they tried to get accredited in their professions as nurses.

Cecilia (interviewer): How did you go through the accreditation process?

Pechay (interviewee): I guess it really helps a lot to have an aunt who is also a nurse, who gives you advice to pursue. I mean, it's ok even if you are working as a live-in caregiver, to go and challenge the exam and beat it. Therefore, I took the ILS last August. After a month, I filed at RNABC [Registered Nurses Association of British Columbia], and then I opened a file in September. From then on, I just did some follow-up for credentials because I already had with me the authenticated forms from the Philippines. I just sent it back to my mother and then she presented it in the school in the Philippines so they could send it back to RNABC.

Cecilia: So when you came, it was your aunt who guided you and gave you direction to go to RNABC.

Pechay: She [aunt] advised me to take the English test first, because it will take some time if you already opened your file. . . . Therefore, I opened the file, and I think a month after, I passed the ILS exam.

Cecilia: How did you get to know about the FNSG [Filipino Nurses Support Group]?

Pechay: When I took the ILS exam in Simon Fraser University, they were there, they had a table, and they gave me the form for membership. I signed the form and they called me up.

Cecilia: Did you start reviewing [exam materials]?

Pechay: When I opened my file, I was very hopeful that I would try and beat the exam, but they had some problems with my transcript from the Philippines.

They returned it. There is a part in one of the forms that the school did not fill out, so they returned it. I had to phone them and ask them to fax the papers, but still they did not make it.

Cecilia: How much did you pay RNABC for the whole accreditation process?

Pechay: $338, and then for the exam $295 . . . a total of about $633. ILS is still another $208.

Cecilia: And you shouldered all that, no government loan . . .

Pechay: No, no, I do not think you can avail of that. Everything was from my income.

As the above interview indicates, the accreditation process can be a time-consuming, costly, and complex procedure. Unlike most immigrants, Pechay was fortunate enough to have an aunt, a nurse who guided her in maneuvering through the system. Further, Pechay was single and free from financial and childcare obligations back home in the Philippines. To be acquainted with the FNSG proved advantageous as Pechay could seek assistance, such as obtaining reviewing materials and writing mock tests, without paying fees. The FNSG also linked her to other immigrants pursuing accreditation and gave her opportunities to share experiences and information.

Vivian also found the accreditation process difficult to afford:

Financially it is quite hard because I have to send back money to the Philippines. When you file your registration with the RNABC you have to pay $140 and for the English exam you pay $200 or something. It is quite expensive.

Both Vivian and Pechay were asked this question: "Is there anything that you can suggest to nurses who would like to come to Canada. How would you advise them?" Pechay responded this way:

I was able to finance [it]. . . . I would mention to them that it is difficult and it is also degrading. Most of us Filipinos, we are willing to sacrifice for some time just to go through those exams and be accredited and able to practice.

Vivian responded this way:

For the future immigrant women, they have to think a million times, especially if they have kids. It is ok if you are single. However, it's really hard professionally. If they come here as an immigrant and apply as a nurse, they face a lot of hindrances. They can't practice their profession immediately in Canada. So they have to be sure. Otherwise, they will be in trouble when they get here.

Although both Pechay and Vivian migrated to Canada as domestics, their experiences vary in the accreditation process to be decommodified. A mentor and relative who graciously supported Pechay, Pechay's own financial situation, and the FNSG's tutorials for the nursing exams facilitated her re-skilling process. "Self-help" is the key mechanism for Pechay's re-skilling in order to be decommodified. As a domestic, Pechay became commodified for a while, then after re-skilling returned to her nursing profession, which provides her with social benefits and allows her to be decommodified. However, most immigrant women from South and South-east Asia are like Vivian, that is, they have family responsibilities and financial hardship that make their accreditation and re-skilling process either longer or not sustainable. Thus, the goal of decommodification of labor is beyond most immigrant women's reach.

An Architect and Re-Skilling

As a spouse with a nine-month-old daughter, Cora migrated to Canada in 1968. She had already acquired a bachelor's degree in architecture in the Philippines. Cora described her experience with accreditation and re-skilling in order to be decommodified:

> I did not have to do the entire program. However, I had to do two main parts of the design. They gave me credit for the first half, but I had to do the second half of the design program. They made me do design work again. You had to submit projects and the university assessed them. Some volunteer professors and architects ran it. They gave you one project to design and you had to do it on your own, then submit it to them. This took forever. Even if you were ready, had everything, and asked them to look at it, they would say they were too busy to look at it. It took two months before they got back to me. Then I had to present it to these professors and some members of the architectural association and orally defend my work. After that, it took them another two to three months before they told me I had passed. I had to do four design projects. Later on, after three years or so, there were more [courses] in the RAIC [Royal Architectural Institute of Canada] syllabus and most students were immigrants. We had to meet twice a year, and we were all at different levels. Others were doing level four and I was already at design level eight. . . . I spent so much and then at the end I did not finish it. That is my only regret.

Cora's narration demonstrates the complex and often irregular processes of accreditation and re-training in certain professions that could assist these immigrants to work in decommodified sectors. First, there are no rules or time limit for assessing the submitted projects. Many months can pass before a student receives the outcome and grade of a project. Second, the expectation to do the assigned but specialized project independently or without a reasonable level of supervision is an onerous demand on immigrant women. Third, long time lapses can occur between different levels of education and between meetings with professors or evaluators—in Cora's case, she met with her evaluators only twice. Fourth, despite different levels of education, (e.g., some at level four and some at level eight), immigrant students in architecture meet as a group with their evaluators, which means that the evaluators have to judge a wide range of projects simultaneously. As a result, immigrants who seek re-skilling in order to be decommodified often receive minimal feedback on their projects and what feedback they do receive is ambiguous and general. Finally, spending money and time in the re-skilling process does not guarantee success. Despite Cora's years of education and her utmost efforts to complete the rest of the requirements for becoming decommodified, she did not obtain a degree. The whole process of re-skilling is full of impediments that may result in a waste of money and the loss of years out of immigrant women's lives. Many immigrant women like Cora and Mona (in chapter 6) give up, finding that they are either too old or too tired to obtain or compete for their targeted job in a decommodified sector.

From Resident Nurse to Community Health Worker

Gender, class, race, and age play significant roles in the acquiring of desired jobs after re-skilling. As a result, the majority of immigrant women in the study eventually became concentrated in jobs without social benefits such as Employment Insurance, extended medical benefits, vacation, sick leave, retirement benefits, and so on. Carmen, an independent immigrant, is an example of one such woman. She migrated to Toronto in 1969. Carmen said, "I received my employment through a hospital sponsorship. They provided me with a job acceptance that made my immigration possible." Carmen elaborated on her upgrading experience:

> When I was in Toronto, I upgraded according to the standard or the requirement of the College of Nurses, which was to take a three-month course at the Clarke Institute. I wrote the exam—the Canadian Nurses Association exam. . . . I passed and became a registered nurse. That is after I fought very hard to be allowed to take the board exam instead of going to school for six months for training. [I said] if I failed the exam, I would go for re-training.

Carmen acquired various job training and work experiences as an RN [Registered Nurse] in Ontario and was employed by the federal government. However, when she moved to BC, she was unable to work as an RN. She found that she lacked training in yet another skill and consequently was deprived of social entitlements, that is, retirement and other social benefits. An inter-provincial move, although in the same profession, took away Carmen's social entitlements and deterred her from being decommodified.

> I took forensic nursing when I was working with the federal government. . . . When I was working for Health Canada, I also acquired several other certificates like home visiting, peer counseling, facilitation, and parents in crisis facilitator. While I was doing my work in community health outreach, I realized that I was so not up to date with the computer world. It diminished my capacity to make reports. This resulted in me being laid off.

Carmen is now working as a community health outreach worker in a psychiatric group home in BC. Regarding her current experience in a small town in BC, Carmen comments:

> Right now, I do not know if it is my age or health care is in a crisis. I feel right now it is because of my age. In [a small town in BC], they are not as open to people who are not born here. How would you say that? They are not very open to immigrants. And immigrants need to have double the qualifications.

Due to her age and her lack of success in continuing the kind of job she did in Ontario, Carmen still feels much frustration with her situation after 34 years of living in Canada. Without naming them, Carmen points out that discrimination and racism act as additional barriers to immigrant women's entry into professional jobs and deter her from decommodification of her labor.

Lack of Finances and Frustration Are Intertwined

Frustration is also present in Dinah's narration. Dinah migrated as a domestic in 1997. When she attained permanent status in 2000, she applied for and received a student loan. Dinah said, "It is about $10,000 because my school is private. That is why it is more expensive." Dinah further elaborated:

> Even if you upgrade your education, it does not necessarily mean that you will get a job. With my computer science degree in the Philippines, I upgraded here with Canadian education, and it was still hard for me to find a job. They are really looking for that Canadian experience. Especially with the economy going down after September 11, it is really hard to find a job. I am not going to give up because I really want to develop my skills. I went to a training institute in downtown Vancouver. I took an Internet Development Program, which was eight months. It did not matter that I had a degree before; they would not have accepted me anyway.

Dinah's story reveals clearly the vicious cycle of re-skilling. All too often, the existence of the "iron wall" Abha described in chapter 6 surfaces, and the ultimate result of upgrading is difficulty in getting a job. As Dinah comments, "Even when you finish working as a nanny, you can't get a job right away. You will return to working as a nanny. You may become a housewife or go to MacDonald's." Dinah's statement illustrates why many immigrant women are concentrated in low-paid, uncharted jobs and are commodified again despite their continuous efforts to upgrade for the labor market. In the name of re-skilling, a gendered division of labor emerges between men and women and a racialized division of labor surfaces within the female labor force itself. Despite immigrant women's potential for upgrading, the female labor force in Canada reflects a class-based and racialized division of labor between those who are Canadian-born, mostly white and privileged, and those who are immigrants, that is, born in the periphery countries and disadvantaged due to complex immigration procedures and disjointed accreditation processes. Immigrant women thus become "the other" and racialized, and a division emerges. The immigration and accreditation processes recycle immigrant women into low-paid and "unskilled" jobs, that is, commodified jobs, that hinder these women's access to social benefits such as Employment Insurance, medical and extended health care benefits, sick leave, disability benefits, family leave and pensions, and thus prevent their access to decommodified sectors.

Applying for Teaching Means Joining a Long Waiting List

Another woman's story reveals the heartbreak of the accreditation process. Maria, who had been the principal of a school in South Asia, migrated with her husband and children to BC as immigrants sponsored by her brother. Maria described her experience with trying to get work in her field of expertise:

> I would go to the Employment Center. [The EC said] we can help you to find a job. We can help you return to your profession. I sent my papers, my degree, to the BC College of Teachers. They sent me a letter saying I don't qualify to become a teacher in Canada. They told me my level was under.... They suggested I go back to university. I have the experience and qualifications.

Rather than pursue a teaching career, Maria tried another strategy to enter the educational system, but it also ended in disappointment:

> After I finished my English in the college, I got other training as an assistant teacher for six months. I thought it would be a good opportunity. I applied when I finished in Kelowna and Vernon. But my name was number 200 in the application form. It indicated to me that I had to wait with 199 people before me. Nobody ever called me.

Maria's narration reminds me of when I presented a paper titled "Transnational Migration and Commodification of Immigrant Laborers in Canada" at the University of Technology, Sydney, in February 2004. One of the seminar participants angrily asked, "Why do these women migrate despite knowing the outcome [commodification and de-skilling]?" Maria's closing comment to the interview responds to this question and reveals the aspirations of many immigrant women. Maria said, "I say thanks to Canada for giving opportunity to my children, [even if] not to me." Despite never returning to their original professions and never feeling financially solvent, immigrant women hope to see their children professionally established and thus decommodified in Canada. This goal puts undue pressure on their children and produces immense intergenerational conflicts that are beyond the scope of this chapter.

Shifting Careers: From Teaching to Working in the Hotel Industry

Several immigrant women I interviewed had shifted their professional gears and adjusted to the needs of the economy, that is, worked in the commodified sectors. Marilyn, an accredited teacher in the Philippines, migrated in 1994. She did not enter the teaching profession due to the complex and lengthy qualification procedure and financial liability:

> I inquired in the schools about how I could practice my teaching, then I called ISIS [In School Integration Support] and some of the schools, like Vancouver Community College, Langara College, and Douglas College. I found out that I have to go to ISIS for my credentials to be evaluated. Finally, I did not go to ISIS because I met my former co-teacher, who went for evaluation and paid $200— it was in the year 1996. They advised her to go back to school for two years.... That is why I decided not to go back to the teaching profession, because I would have to go back for two years full-time. Who was going to support me here? Where could I get money for food, rent, and all those other things? Was I sure that I could teach after all that? That was also my fear. There were so many other people who were more qualified than I was. . . . I still miss teaching.

Marilyn shifted her interest from teaching and applied for work in a hotel. As Giles comments, "The hotel hierarchy is underpinned by the association of hotel work with a racial/ethnic and gendered categorization of the workforce" (1994: 82). Although Giles' comment is directed toward a particular ethnic group in Britain, this racialized and gendered category of the workforce is also apparent in the Canadian labor market both in the commodified and in the decommodified sectors. For Marilyn, therefore, getting a job in a hotel or other business in the commodified sectors was easier than getting a teaching position in a school, that is, a decommodified sector:

> Anyway, I also took courses in "Hotel Management" at a college here in BC. I only had one course to finish, then the school closed.... Because of illegal ... whatever it was. There was something. Then they transferred us to another college. But I did not have the time anymore because I took this job for settlement work. So, I did not manage to get that until now. I have some courses that I could apply because it is divided into nine courses for hotel management.... But I am thinking of just leaving that for now because I have so many other things. In the settlement services, we have a chance to upgrade ourselves. I have taken Basic Counseling and the Fundamentals of Counseling. Partly, I do employment counseling. Those were basic to help us prepare for our clientele needs. It was professional development. I am also taking a "Children who are abused and neglected" program, just in case we need those skills for intervention. Some of my cases are for the Ministry of Children and Families.... Without these professional funds from the organization, it would be hard to get even these qualifications. At least, this has helped. I've grabbed the opportunity to develop my skills. Whenever there are funds, I go and get the course. Some of my co-workers, they just do not want to do it.

While Marilyn switched her professional gears from teaching to hotel management to settlement services, she utilized both personal and public resources to re-skill in the labor market. The sudden closure of the college Marilyn initially attended displays the irregularities in the provincial government's monitoring of the wide range of unregulated private colleges that have been flourishing due to increasing demands from the immigrant population, especially from Asia. With recent cuts in the name of restructuring education in BC, the provincial government is further pushing immigrants to seek assistance and upgrading from private institutions rather than from government-funded, -secured and -regulated educational institutions.

A Young Female Immigrant: From Job to Job

Young female immigrants do not necessarily have better and easier lives than adult immigrants. Tara migrated to BC from Hong Kong with her parents in 1975. Tara described her experience:

> I didn't have experience working in Hong Kong.... Actually, I worked on a farm [in BC] before becoming a cashier. I started in the summer. Then I worked there full-time. My second job was as a cashier in the airport. After that I did data entry at ICBC for three months. Then after that, I worked in a Royal Bank data entry. Then I worked in the Canadian Northern Shield, filing. Then I moved up to the assembly job. Then they laid me off. Then I came here, started in filing, and moved up to the mailroom. Yep, that's about it. That's my life.

Tara also described her education in Canada: "Accounting, math at [college]. I didn't like it. I didn't make it. At that time, my father passed away. I could not take it. That is why I dropped out." According to Tara, in 1975 she could enter a college with no problem: "That year it was very easy. But not anymore. It's difficult now." The premature death of Tara's father created a sudden fluctuation in her financial situation, and she was deprived of any social benefits for surviving during this family crisis. After dropping out of college, Tara worked on a farm for a while, and then moved to numerous flexible and low-paid jobs, that is, in commodified sectors. Tara's narration dispels the myth about immigrants from Hong Kong—that they are all wealthy—especially those who migrated before the introduction of the entrepreneur category.

A Canadian Certificate: Another Name for Employment Insurance

As an alternative to accreditation, holding a certificate from a Canadian institution can prove to be effective in case of job loss for an immigrant.

Yolyn, an independent and single immigrant, migrated to Canada in 1996. She described her experience with migration and the accreditation process this way:

> I [had] graduated [in my home country] with a Bachelor of Science in Food and Technology, with good experience . . . in quality control and research and development. . . . I had some interviews when I came here. . . . I asked for accreditation for my degree. It seemed the course they were giving me was just for restaurant food inspection. I had to go back to school. . . . When I applied to the big food companies, I got interviewed. Actually, they were very impressed with my resume. But when they asked for Canadian experience or a diploma, I couldn't give anything. So, I ended up working in a factory. . . . I worked in different factories [in Ontario], packaging, shipping, and receiving. Now I work in a precision company where we produce small parts for aerospace and medical equipment. It is like a metal company. I do inspection, but it is a different type of inspection. . . . Some of the first jobs I had with factories, I wouldn't receive benefits. With this job, I get all the benefits I want. Then, I work overtime. Mostly, I work twelve hours a day from Monday to Saturday. . . . The course I took is about what I am doing right now. . . . I had to give them a certificate to show that I had studied this kind of job. I was at Seneca College in Toronto. . . . I haven't tried accreditation [in my former profession]. I would have to go back to school for sure. I don't have the money to go. I'm thinking about going for another course. . . . I want this certificate. In case they fire me, at least I will have this certificate.

Despite long hours of overtime work, Yolyn has a high level of satisfaction with her current job, which provides her benefits. However, Yolyn's job is not secure, and her busy schedule and her financial situation have kept her from pursuing accreditation in order to be decommodified. Yolyn is still faced with taking a course to acquire a certificate that could, in the end, serve as insurance should she lose her job. Her reliance on a certificate rather than on either Employment Insurance or social assistance again indicates an immigrant's reluctance to accept state assistance or to quit a job. Among immigrant women in South and South-east Asia, there exist negative attitudes toward accepting Employment Insurance in case of job loss, which sometimes causes psychological stress and community stigma. For immigrant women, having a job is one of the major sources of material security relieving them from reliance on their husbands/ fathers/brothers' financial support. Having a job also empowers immigrant women to negotiate with the adult male members in the family, resulting in a change in gender relations. Job-related benefits, such as medical, sick leave, vacation, extended health care, and so on, further provide immigrant women with material independence and social security and ultimately with decommodification.

The Physical Toll of Homecare Jobs

The jobs many immigrant women perform are tedious and repetitive, and, in certain cases, require heavy lifting. Doing these jobs often causes back pain, muscle pain, and even permanent disabilities. Sadie described her experience of working in homecare support:

> Now I realize that some people don't like it [the work] because of back problems from lifting too much. I heard it from my friends. They told me, "Before, I liked this job; now, I feel my back is very bad from lifting lots of people." So, it is a hard job, too. . . . I am planning to go to school. I am getting old now. I am a hard worker, but I need some rest. Even with working part-time every night, I come home and I just lie down—so tired.

Lifting elderly patients is a laborious job, and many immigrant women do this heavy lifting either as domestics or as home support caregivers. Josie, who migrated as an independent immigrant, worked in a hospital, that is, in a decommodified sector, as a patient care aide for almost 22 years. She now collects disability because she injured her back four years ago. She commented: "I knew my job was hard. If I [could] upgrade my education, I could find a job in the hospital as a clerk or [other] light job." Despite the nature of homecare jobs, many immigrant women persist in them because alternative options are not easily available. The pertinent issue is: If Sadie's job was part-time, temporary and for short duration and in the commodified sector, that is, household, she would never be entitled to social benefits. The market-model strategies thus drive immigrant women into commodified sectors and push them to be re-commodified despite their utmost efforts to be decommodified.

CORRELATION BETWEEN DEMAND FOR IMMIGRANT LABOR AND SUPPLY OF JOBS

Most narrations in this chapter illustrate that many immigrant women do not end up in jobs related to their original professions, that is, the professions they used to hold in their countries of origin. Nevertheless, a few women do attain their desired jobs and become decommodified, and these women's satisfaction level is naturally high. Susie, a nurse from the Philippines, migrated to Canada in the 1960s under the independent category. She described her immigration and job history:

> The director of nursing and the director of the laboratory met me at the airport [in Saskatchewan] and they put me in a hotel overnight. The following day they came to pick me up and I started working right away. . . . They gave me

an orientation right away. I [was] only trained for three months and then they sent me to a smaller hospital. I was the only one there besides the one who was in charge of the X-ray. I was in charge of the lab.

In response to the question, "Are you a registered medical tech here [in Vancouver]?" Susie replied:

> Actually, I did not register as a medical tech because from the beginning, I was working. There's no gap in my practice. It was continuous knowledge and continuous work. But they know I have units as a medical technologist. This is different with the nurses now who can't work as nurses and some of the lab technologists who work as lab assistants. You won't be allowed to be a lab technologist unless you go back to school. Otherwise you remain only an assistant. Those are the changes now, so we were lucky that they recognized our schooling. They needed us. There is a big difference between then and now. And then they were trying to restructure and wanted us to go. Well, in the first place, when they didn't have enough people to work they hired overseas.

Susie's comments clearly show a correlation between demand for immigrant labor and supply of jobs, whatever the degrees, training, and work experience from country of origin. Although Susie migrated in the 1960s, and her job was in a small town, her work experience was recognized in a certain category of job where Canadian-born labor was then unavailable. Her comments also indicate that no fixed rule or regulation existed to control the standard of professions across provinces, and this has not changed by 2005. In contrast, Cora, who also migrated in the 1960s, had a degree in architecture in her country of origin. She passed several levels of additional training/re-skilling in Canada, without ever landing a job in her profession and without ever being decommodified.

There Are a Few Success Stories

Like Susie, Emily found satisfaction in her job. Emily migrated from Malaysia in the 1990s, trained in nursing in England, and worked in England, Malaysia, and Canada as a nurse in a decommodified sector. She described her current job and the experiences leading up to it:

> I worked [in Malaysia] as a director of nursing in administration until I left. . . . [After migration] I went to "45 Plus" for women who want to get back into the job market now—how to write your resume and how to go for interviews, things like that. That was good too. Before that, I took short courses for nurses at UBC and BCIT. . . . Actually, my specialty is in public health nursing and nursing administration. But at the moment, I'm happy to work as an RN [Registered Nurse] in the clinical field.

Emily's education in England and her work experience in England and Malaysia assisted her in finding a job as a nurse in a decommodified sector.

She is highly satisfied with her current job, even though it is not in her original field or in her specialty. Emily's satisfaction mostly derives from the decommodification of her labor, which few immigrant women enjoy. Once Emily retires, her welfare will thus depend not on a male breadwinner, but on her retirement benefits.

WHAT NEEDS TO BE DONE

The narrations and case studies in this chapter present compelling evidence of the hurdles immigrant women must leap to properly establish their credentials in order to be decommodified and re-enter the labor market. There is a dire need for both federal and provincial governments to address these issues, for the sake of better utilization of human resources and enhanced productivity. According to the findings of this study, the following measures need to be undertaken to assist immigrant populations, particularly immigrant women in being decommodified:

1. Set Up a Regulatory Body

A regulatory body needs to be set up to monitor the accreditation system and minimize variations in standards required across provinces. This body could set up a comprehensive database of foreign educational and training institutions and their standards. Working with universities, colleges, training institutions, and schools in Canada, this body could then develop the database to produce comprehensive, uniform regulations across Canada.

2. Evaluate Foreign Credentials

A regulatory body could also develop mechanisms to translate foreign qualifications into Canadian terms. This could be done in terms of continents, countries and even within countries. For example, a master's degree in engineering from India or Holland could be deemed as equivalent to a master's degree in engineering in Canada. On the other hand, a master's degree in engineering from another country could be found equivalent to a bachelor's degree in engineering in Canada. A mechanism like this could help immigrants seek relevant jobs in the labor market right away, without bureaucratic hassles. Employers could easily check with the relevant agency when considering hiring immigrants with credentials from other countries.

3. Co-ordinate between/among Governments

To develop a standardized and uniform system, federal and provincial governments need to cooperate with each other. This may greatly facilitate immigrant women's decommodification. Further, co-ordination will be needed between and among provincial governments to facilitate the transfer of skills and experience across provinces.

4. Ensure Immigrants' Access to Social Entitlements

It is evident that most immigrant women enter Canada as dependents—as wives, sisters, and daughters. All too often, due to their dependent status, immigrant women do not receive the entitlements accorded to sponsored male immigrants. Unequal entitlements upon arrival not only foster the growth of gender disparity among immigrants, but also perpetuate the ideology of the "male breadwinner" that most Asian countries endorse. The very process also perpetuates a racialized, gendered and class-based labor market that deters immigrant women from being decommodified.

5. Expand Childcare Funding for Immigrant Women

Women still make up the majority of childcare providers, a role that takes them out of the labor market for certain lengths of time. Restructuring of childcare policy in two major provinces, that is, in Ontario and BC, where most immigrants have settled, has created obstacles to re-skilling for immigrant women seeking to be decommodified. As Mahon comments, however, the issue of childcare is a thorny question across Canada:

> Since the mid-1980s, a growing preoccupation with fiscal austerity, combined with a deepening crisis of federalism, have made it increasingly difficult for child care advocates to advance their case. . . . Despite a change of government, during the 1990s childcare activists operated in an environment where universally accessible care was made to seem increasingly utopian. To keep the issue alive, they joined forces with a broader coalition under the banner of fighting child poverty. (Mahon 2002:15)

It is clear that the struggle for childcare in Canada may be shifting from making childcare accessible for all women irrespective of class and race to "fighting child poverty." However, it is equally clear that child poverty among immigrants will not be eliminated without accessible childcare that provides immigrant women with opportunities to upgrade in order to be decommodified as well as to enter the labor force for the financial support of their families.

6. Evaluate the LCP

The controversial LCP (Live-in Caregiver Program) needs to be carefully evaluated so that migrant workers/domestics enter Canada as permanent residents. Entry as permanent residents would provide these workers with the opportunity to do re-training or to upgrade skills without going through immigration hassles and hence, increase their chances of being decommodified. Domestics under the LCP can apply for permanent status only after they work for two years within a three-year period. Until they acquire permanent status, they can neither live in their own residences nor upgrade skills (including taking language training) without an immigrant officer's approval. For each training or course taken, a domestic is required to pay an immigration fee. These and other constraints of the LCP create huge—often-insurmountable—barriers for domestics even when they become permanent residents of Canada. Consequently, their labor becomes re-commodified. The interviews in this chapter demonstrate clearly that most domestics, even after achieving resident status, continue to work as live-in nannies—or, if fortunate enough, as live-out domestics—all in commodified sectors.

The Filipino Canadian community is divided in opinion about the LCP. One group recommends the scrapping of the LCP; another group supports it as the LCP is one of the most popular mechanisms in the Philippines, especially for women, to get away from that country's unemployment, poverty, and political uncertainties. The latter argument suggests that the LCP is facilitating Canada's hiring Filipino women driven out of the Philippines by poverty and chronic unemployment, thus solidifying a gendered, racialized and class-based market in Canada.

NOTES

1. Although the concept of recommodification is rarely used, I find it a useful term in analyzing what happens to immigrant women who are re-skilled. My analysis has been influenced by Offe (1984) as well as by Keane's (1984) incisive comments on Offe's interpretation.

2. In chapter 3, it was shown that 75 percent of skilled immigrants are male, and thus women migrants are at a disadvantage when it comes to acquiring government-selection and accredited credentials.

3. For example, Ontario introduced employment equity (in concurrence with the federal government's employment equity) when the NDP (New Democratic Party), a left-leaning party, was in power. When the Conservatives came to power in Ontario about ten years ago, they scrapped the employment equity program, a move that adversely affected women, racialized people, First Nations, and people with disabilities.

4. Critics have said that the 2005 announcement was an effort to appeal to immigrant voters in a time when the minority federal government faced an election if the government was defeated on certain motions and bills put forth in the House.

5. The resources available are mostly on websites and in unpublished materials. Some are reports prepared by organizations that deal with immigrants' issues.

6. In common use, the term "foreign" as it pertains to immigrants generally refers to people from or in non-English-speaking countries.

7. Immigrants from English-speaking countries face fewer constraints. For example, a Ph.D. in a British university is considered equivalent to a Ph.D. in a Canadian university.

8. Most immigrants aspire to get back to their original professions, but very few racialized women achieve this goal; hence, I consider it a "dream."

8

Immigrant Women as Agents of Change
The Role of Networks and Associations

The previous chapters have investigated how immigrant women's labor become commodified and re-commodified and face both structural and systemic constraints to become decommodified. Despite their utmost efforts, immigrant women, the majority of whom are concentrated in low-paid, flexible and non-secure jobs, are commodified and subordinated in the labor market. Most of the immigrant women whose narrations appear in this book are conscious of their commodification, their low chances of attaining decommodification of their labor, and their oppressive work environments; consequently, their individual resistance strategies toward unjust situations in the workplace are numerous. It is clear that immigrant women act as agents of change and improve their situations, especially their work conditions, and at the same time challenge the pervasive sexism and racism in the wider society. Immigrant women act through formal as well as informal organizations, sociocultural-political associations, and advocacy groups, with affiliations primarily based on country of origin or regional affinity.

In this chapter, I will examine two immigrant women's organizations—the India *Mahila* (Women's) Association (IMA) and the Philippine Women Center (PWC)—as most of the women interviewed, except the Bangladeshis, are members of these organizations. Indeed, the interviews for this study were conducted by the PWC. The South Asian Women's Centre (SAWC) referred to in this chapter is a government-funded organization that generally operates as a referral agency. This chapter examines the SAWC's role within the context of individual women's narration.

Like many immigrant women's organizations, the IMA and the SAWC function as autonomous groups at the local level, although they build up connections with various women's and grassroots organizations pertinent to various issues, such as violence against women at home and in the workplace, low-cost housing, and so on. Only one organization—the Philippine Women Centre—has links at the national as well as the global level.

Among immigrant women in this study, Bangladeshis do not have their own women's organization although some women attend the meetings of the Bangladesh Association, a Greater Vancouver-based organization comprised of men, women and their families. The absence of a Bangladeshi immigrant women's organization may be due to the fact that Bangladeshis are very recent immigrants—the majority migrated to Vancouver in the 1990s and afterwards. In fact, a vast number of Bangladeshis in Greater Vancouver arrived in Canada in the late 1990s and at the beginning of the 21st century. This incremental migration trend indicates that 9/11 has not negatively affected Bangladeshis' migration[1] to Canada. The interviews and my personal experience suggest that there were fewer than ten Bangladeshi families in Vancouver in the 1970s. In the 1980s, most Bangladeshis in Greater Vancouver were acquainted with each other. This pattern had changed by the late 1990s.[2]

In comparison to Bangladeshis, Filipinos have had a history of migration to Canada since the 1960s. Chapter 5 has affirmed that the acceleration of Filipino labor migration happened due to the Philippine's aggressive LEP and Canada's LCP. Since the beginning of the twentieth century, Canada has received many immigrants from India, many of whom worked as farm laborers. Chapter 4 has pointed out that racist immigration legislation, which deterred South Asians from entering Canada in the beginning of the twentieth century, triggered the organizing of South Asians in British Columbia. Thus, it can be argued that the history of women's migration, in conjunction with overt racism and sexism in the workplace and in the wider society, has provided fertile ground for the establishment of the IMA, the SAWC and the PWC.

The active role of these organizations in immigrant women's lives as well as the agency of individual immigrant women in the workplace[3] is examined in four sections. The first section sheds light on the advocacy role of the IMA and the PWC, which organize to challenge local, national and global forces for transforming immigrant women's lives. Through women's voices, the second section demonstrates the devices individual immigrant women use to counter and improve unfair conditions in the workplace. The next section illustrates the network building through which immigrant women negotiate and develop strategies to change their work conditions. The final section analyses the active role of the organizations for both structural and systemic change so that the labor of these immigrant women can be decommodified.

THE IMA AND THE PWC: ADVANCING IMMIGRANT WOMEN'S RIGHTS WHILE FIGHTING RACISM AND SEXISM

The IMA, which originated in 1973, is a Vancouver-based immigrant women's organization. IMA members mostly come from India, although a few come from Bangladesh, Fiji, Sri Lanka, Pakistan, Africa, and Europe. The IMA's membership is open to anyone from South Asian ancestry—a fluid category that incorporates women from Africa, Europe, Fiji, and other countries. The secular and comprehensive principle of the IMA reflects its membership across religions and ages, including seniors and youth. The IMA is solely dependent on its volunteers, runs its office through a member's residence, and even uses the member's phone line for its activities. This is a grassroots immigrant women's organization that has aimed at fighting racism and sexism in society and has also raised public awareness about the commodification of South Asian women's labor and the absence of decommodification of their labor. About the history and growth of the IMA, Singh (1993) writes:

> It was the rigours of the immigrant experience, the burdens of their lives as women and exclusion from male-dominated community organizations and a white dominated women's movement which first brought Raminder Dosanjh, Harjit Dhillon and Premchit Sripawa together in 1972. . . . After many discussions, Dosanj, Dhillon and Sripawa created the India Mahila Association—the first South Asian women's organization in North America. (10)

Since the non-discriminatory immigration legislation in the 1960s, Vancouver has become the second largest city for immigrants from Asia, especially from India. It is no wonder that the IMA as the first Indo-Canadian women's organization in Canada originated in Vancouver. Since the birth of the IMA in Vancouver, many South Asian immigrant women's organizations have formed across Canada—for example, the South Asian Women's Group in Toronto, the South Asian Women's Community Centre in Montreal, and the South Asian Women's Group in Alberta.

At the early stage of its growth, the IMA assisted new immigrant women by arranging field trips around the city, transporting women to language training classes, showing them how to get around in shopping centres, and so on. Since its inception, the IMA has also addressed the issue of violence against immigrant women in the community. In 1994, the IMA published a report titled *Spousal Abuse: Experience of 15 Canadian South Asian Women* funded by the Feminist Research, Education, Development and Action (FREDA) Centre. This report against chauvinism was a bold step taken by the IMA against its own male members. As a result of the IMA's efforts, various programs were set up that would work on eradicating violence against South Asian immigrant women. The IMA set up a support group to provide immigrant women with advocacy and emotional support, especially needed because many immigrant women live in alienated and isolated situations. In 1991, the IMA organized demonstrations and protests against a doctor in Blaine, located on the border of Greater Vancouver and Washington state. This doctor targeted the South Asian community, promoting a test for detecting the sex of a fetus (the test ultimately could lead to the abortion of female fetuses). In collaboration with other organizations, the IMA arranged demonstrations in South Asian markets in Vancouver and criticized the community newspapers for publishing advertisements for female-fetus abortion clinics. The act of this particular doctor was denounced by the larger community, and consequently, the doctor stopped targeting this specific community.

The IMA frequently protests against the media portrayal of South Asian women. Indeed, the organization has assigned a position titled "Spokesperson" to someone who can handle media questions. To raise awareness of violence against women and of racism and sexism in the workplace and in the wider society, including media portrayal of South Asian women, several women of IMA have appeared on television and radio and published columns in the Vancouver-based South Asian community newspapers, The Link and The Indo-Canadian Times. To have access to services for South Asian women, the IMA has also forged links with service agencies and transition houses across BC. This was a daunting task because until the 1980s, most services used English as a medium of language. These alliances have assisted several South Asian women who are in desperate need of these services.

To raise the consciousness of South Asian immigrant women with regard to workplace sexism and racism, the IMA organizes a number of events throughout the year. In addition to celebrating International Women's Day[4] in a befitting manner, the IMA organizes a *Mahila Mela* (Women's Exhibition) and annual picnic regularly, and these have always been well attended. In 2000, the IMA-organized *Mahila Mela* had stage performances, *Bhangra* (a Punjabi folk dance), folk songs, *Dholak Geet* (a song that is sang with a special drum called *Dholki*), and so on. In addition, through stage performances and showing films, the IMA raises consciousness of its members and of the general immigrant community in Greater Vancouver.

In essence, the IMA was established in response to male domination of a community organization and a white-dominated women's movement. To challenge male authority within the community, the IMA takes a strong stand against all kinds of violence. Fighting against violence ranging from "wife" killing to aborting female fetuses, the IMA members empower one another to work for social change.

The inception of the PWC, on the other hand, is essentially engrained in the mass migration of Filipino women to Canada. The formation of the PWC dates back to 1986 when a group of Filipino-Canadian women realized that Filipino women's mass migration and domestic laborers' working conditions in Canada were intricately linked to the global restructuring process. To improve the conditions of Filipino women working in Canada, who face sexism, racism and classism as immigrants, the group realized the urgent need for an organization. At a fund-raising dinner dance attended by over 200 people, the PWC was formally launched in 1990 and registered as a non-profit society by the BC provincial government in 1991 (Zaman and Tubajon 2001).

Upholding the principles of global human rights and workers' rights, the PWC illustrates its objectives in various brochures and reports: (1) to foster feminist views and to link with various immigrant communities to exchange information; (2) to raise awareness among Filipino women in Canada about their common interests and the hurdles they face as a minority group; (3) to disseminate information about the Filipino community in Canada; (4) to connect with other groups having common interests; and (5) to empower Filipino women in Canada through various community-based projects and programs. The membership of the PWC is restricted to women of Filipino descent, although a non-Filipino woman is eligible to be an honorary member provided the board of directors approves. The PWC has its own office, which is located in the Downtown Eastside—a poverty-stricken area known for pan handlers, sex workers, and immigrants—a marginalized population in a city of affluence. To run its office, the PWC has one paid worker and several volunteers.

The PWC's activities operate at three levels: global, national and local. In contrast to mainstream women's groups in Canada, the PWC works directly at advancing and restoring Filipino women workers' rights across countries and disseminates information about the historical and transnational contexts of Filipino women's mass exodus from the Philippines. To promote individual worker's rights and expose transnational predatory forces, and to empower its members, especially domestic workers, the PWC organizes various events—such as arts and crafts displays, annual fund-raising dances, consciousness-raising workshops, petition-signing and participatory action-research projects. Out of one of its participatory workshops, SIKLAB (*Sulong, Itaguyod and Karapatan ng mga Manggagawang Pilipino sa Labas sa Bansa*, literally meaning "Advance the Rights of Filipino Workers Overseas") was established. In 1996, SIKLAB joined in MIGRANTE International, an organization formed to protect rights for transnational contract workers. MIGRANTE International fought successfully for the release of Sarah Balagan, who was sentenced to death by the United Arab Emirates' court for killing her employer while defending herself against an attempted rape. Due to transnational protests by migrant workers' organizations and mounting pressure across nations, Sarah Balagan escaped the death sentence. Instead, the court sentenced her to one year in prison. She also had to pay CDN $55,000 to the deceased employer's family and was forced to submit to 100 lashes. Through protests, demonstrations and workshops, the PWC itself also works to achieve freedom and justice for migrant workers who are wrongfully detained in foreign prisons. In sum, the PWC focuses all its efforts on protecting the rights and dignity of Filipino immigrants and on decommodifying these women in Canada. No wonder domestic workers' rights are a widely publicized issue across Canada. The PWC, along with other migrant workers rights' organizations, deserve much credit for this publicity.

To protect transnational Filipino workers' rights, the PWC was also involved with the "NO! to APEC" campaign of 1996 and 1997. APEC, an economic group of eighteen countries including Canada, advocates both intensified economic liberalism and free trade. In November 1997, APEC convened its yearly meeting in Vancouver—the largest summit meeting ever held in Vancouver. Through newsletters, workshops and protest meetings, the PWC revealed that the globalization process through APEC, NAFTA and the WTO ultimately intensified the commodification of women's bodies and labor and turned women workers into "modern-day slaves" torn away from their indigenous culture and roots.

In addition its transnational activism, the PWC is involved in protecting its members from exploitation and harassment at local and national levels. For example, in 2000, to protest the Immigration Department's deportation of Ms. Cables, a domestic worker who lived in Edmonton and took on extra jobs without the Department's authorization, the PWC circulated flyers describing the deportation as "unjust." The PWC made statements to the media and organized a demonstration at the Vancouver airport the day Ms. Cables flew from Edmonton to Manila via Vancouver. On July 5, 2000, the Immigration Department allowed Ms. Cables to return to Canada as a domestic worker (Matas 2000). Cables' case illustrates the strong organizing abilities of the PWC and various other immigrant/migrant groups, which persuaded the Immigration Department to allow Cables to return to Canada only four months after her deportation on February 29, 2000. This case further illustrates how the Canadian state unwittingly creates social inequality and injustice, as chapter 5 has argued. Due to her violation of immigration rules, Cables was deported by the Immigration Department immediately; in contrast, her employers were not charged for hiring a domestic worker without proper work authorization.

The PWC conducted a participatory action research in 1996 to address the needs of domestic workers who reside in their employers' houses as part of the LCP requirements. For example, in case of a dispute between the employer and the domestic worker, the latter had no place to stay. The PWC's study, titled *Housing Needs Assessment of Filipino Domestic Workers* (1996), demonstrated that the live-in requirement under the LCP creates conditions unique to domestic workers, although their needs are comparable to those of other low-income groups in Canada. Due to this study's findings, the PWC in collaboration with SIKLAB arranged affordable co-op housing for domestic workers. Although it was a challenging living experience for some, it also provided an alternative and desperately needed arrangement for other domestic workers. Another positive outcome of this study was that, while assessing housing needs for domestic workers, the PWC made alliances with similar groups such as the Tenants' Rights Action Coalition (TRAC), the

Downtown Eastside Residents Association (DERA), Four Sisters' Co-op, and the Co-operative Housing Federation of BC.

In 1997, in collaboration with FREDA (Feminist Research, Education, Development and Action Centre), the PWC conducted a major study entitled *Trapped: "Holding on to the Knife's Edge": Economic Violence against Filipino Migrant/Immigrant Women*. Exposing the systemic de-skilling of domestic workers who had been nurses, teachers and midwives in the Philippines, the study described de-skilling as pervasive "social and economic violence." One of the recommendations of the study was that both provincial and federal governments recognize immigrant women's country-of-origin credentials, including education and training, a step that would alleviate the de-skilling process and its consequences. The study further proposed accreditation as something that would facilitate immigrant women's integration and settlement in Canada.

To build solidarity with women against globalization, the PWC since its inception has built and strengthened its links with both local and transnational groups. Thus, it has forged a link with Gabriela, the national alliance of militant women's organizations in the Philippines. To end the trafficking of the Filipino women, the PWC in collaboration with Gabriela initiated the Purple Rose Campaign around the world in September 1999. Initially, representatives from the PWC, Gabriela Philippines, the Gabriela Network in the US, and Filipino women from Europe met in Vancouver at the Filipino-Canadian Women's National Consultative Forum organized by the PWC. To celebrate International Women's Day in March 2000, the Purple Rose Campaign reached new heights as the PWC hosted a gala performance by singers, cultural dancers, poets, and actors in a large theatre in Vancouver. The PWC further conducted a community-based action-oriented study titled *Canada: The New Frontier for Filipino Mail-Order Brides* (2000). Through this research, the PWC reiterates how Filipino women as "mail-order brides" become commodified and how this innovative migration process has accelerated due to the global predatory forces. "Commodification" is a term widely used in the PWC's newsletters; many women who are members of the PWC are thus aware of this term and the underlying assumptions.

In October 2001, the PWC co-organized the North American Consultation for Women of Filipino ancestry in Seattle, Washington. The theme was "Migration, Labor Export and Traffic of Women," and about 200 women of Filipino ancestry from the US, Canada, Europe, and the Philippines attended (Labrador 2001). The participants at the Consultation Forum declared a statement of unity that condemned forced migration, labor export and the trafficking in women. Thus, the PWC struggles against local and transnational exploitative forces while establishing immigrant women workers' rights through various consultation forums, demonstrations, and participatory action-research projects. While the origin of the PWC was connected to the unregulated work environment of domestic workers and the commodification and decommodification of their labor, the PWC, over the years, has been able to build alliances that cut across ethnic and racial boundaries.

EVERYDAY RESISTANCE AND PERSONAL STRATEGIES: THREE DOMESTIC WORKERS

As mentioned in chapter 5, domestic workers who migrate under the LCP live in a commodified sector that was previously non- or under-commodified. The relationship between the employer and the domestic is commodified and feudalized, and this relationship intensifies due to the private nature of the workplace. The domestic workers I interviewed were aware of their commodified situations, but individual resistance strategies toward their exploitative situations varied. The following narrations illustrate the diverse strategies three domestic workers adopted.

The first narration belongs to Jane:

> After a year, they [the employers] asked me if I wanted to buy the car since I was always driving it. So I did. . . . When I already bought the car, they were only giving me $25 for the gas. I said, "No. You have to give me more." They said, "No." I said, "Well, then I won't use the car. We will just take the bus. Give me money for bus fare for the kids and myself. It will be more than $25." They got mad at me. That's when I decided to leave.

Jane was sincere when she purchased the car from the employers, while her employers were not. They sold the car to Jane, and then expected her to use her car for transporting their children to school. As mentioned in chapter 5, the contract between employers and the domestics is often ambiguous and ranges from "no-name" activities to use (albeit abuse) of domestic worker's belongings. The only way for Jane to resist this unacceptable demand was to quit her job. Despite Jane's precarious situation, she was reluctant to stay in a job that treated her unjustly.

The second narration belongs to Marlyn:

> There are three kids [five, two, and six-months] with me. I had to push a double stroller. And the eldest boy was walking beside me. The walk is half an hour and the place was very remote. . . . After five months, my employer, who was a teacher, told me she couldn't afford to pay me for July and August because there's no school and she would not be receiving a salary. She couldn't pay me for that two-month period, but she doesn't want to let me go. I quit. I decided to go because I have a family back home. I have a son. I spent too much [equivalent to CDN. $5,000] to come here.

Realizing she would not be paid for July and August because of her employers' financial constraints, Marlyn neither complained to an authority nor forced her employer to pay her salary. Instead, Marlyn decided to quit. This kind of case is rarely publicized due to the worker's commodification in an unregulated workplace. The employer can thus get away with not paying salaries. Quitting her job was a temporary solution for Marlyn. She sacrificed two months' salary to be commodified again in another employer's place.

The third narration belongs to Helen:

> One time my employer asked me to mow the lawn. . . . So I did it the first time they asked me, but the second time they asked me, I burst out and said, "Excuse me! Mowing the lawn is out of my job!" Then my employer got mad. I explained the work I was supposed to do: things inside the house. . . . One time they asked me to clean their cars. I didn't clean them, and I told them that if they want me to clean their cars, they would have to pay me extra. They asked me how much. And I said my friend was being paid $100 per month from her employer. My employer was really demanding after a while. . . . Then one night I talked to my employer seriously, and I said, "If you're not contented with my work and services with you, then I better leave. You better find another nanny to work with you."

Helen's narration illustrates clear agency: she on her own bargained with the employer, she resisted the employer's undue demands for lawn mowing and car cleaning, and she demanded extra money for additional chores. As a domestic worker, Helen knew clearly the nature of the tasks the employer should expect from her. Thus, when Helen was asked to perform beyond her assigned tasks, she refused. Moreover, Helen challenged her employer by quitting the job and telling them to search for another domestic worker. This courageous step was possible because Helen had links with her fellow workers and sufficient information about the domestic worker's expected tasks. Connection with fellow workers thus provides information, empowers women, and creates avenues of resistance in an alienated workplace.

CHALLENGING RACISM AND DISCRIMINATION IN THE WORKPLACE: INDIVIDUAL WOMEN'S AGENCY

Cecilia provides this narration:

> Other head nurses that I worked with [in Montreal], some were very English with a very old school attitude and she didn't really care if she said something nasty. She would just say it! She couldn't care less about whether you were hurt! So I had to fight with her. I said, "I don't like the way you talk to me!" At that time I started to be assertive already because if you are working with these people you have to survive. Some patients—perhaps because it's the first time they have seen many women of colour in that place—also acted that way.

Cecilia's narration supports Calliste's findings (1996a) that the labor force in nursing has been racialized and gendered and that racism continues today. Cecilia's experience with patients and co-workers took place in the 1970s when not many women of color were working in the nursing profession in Montreal,[5] let alone in other small towns. To rectify the situation and to fight against the negative attitudes of patients, co-workers, and employers, Cecilia became assertive and got her points across. Clearly the increasing number of racialized workers in the workplace now would raise workers' morale and raise the consciousness of others about diversity in terms of ethnicity, country of origin and religion.

Susie provides this narration:

> I again decided to go back to my hospital job, so I started looking in the newspaper. I went straight to St. Paul's Laboratory to apply and submitted my application form. The director of the lab said, "There are five more applicants to be interviewed, so I'll let you know after three days." After three days, she phoned me. So I decided to work in the hospital rather than in research. In research I was always asking for a salary increase, but they never gave me one. If I'm working in the hospital, I'll automatically be a member of the union. Luckily they hired me so I gave my resignation at . . . research.

Susie was quite aware of the effectiveness and role of the union. Thus, when she was dissatisfied with her salary in the research job, she first asked for a salary hike. After being refused a raise for years, Susie decided to move from research to hospital work. Because Susie did this on her own initiative, she had prospects for being decommodified. Susie's action reflects both her courage to change a job in an adverse situation and her knowledge about the role of the labor union to protect workers' rights, including benefits and entitlements.

Linda provides this narration:

> That's why we moved here to Vancouver, because I gave up in Winnipeg. I passed the interview, I passed the exam, but they have a way of stopping you from being promoted if they don't like you. We passed it to the union but nothing happened. It's hard because you're competing against the number one on the list. . . . We are unionized, but sometimes some of the members are lazy. Like the one who handled my case, is a very old man who didn't really listen to me, and he didn't want to fight my case. Nothing happened with my case.

Linda's experience contradicts Susie's statement about the union. In Linda's case, it was not the union, but the ineffectiveness of the union members, that caused her to move from Winnipeg to Vancouver. Although Linda did not mention racism as a factor for not being promoted, her statement indicates subtle racism existed in the workplace. Her strategy involved moving to a more ethno-culturally diverse city.

Nesta provides this narration:

> Once when I was sick in Winnipeg, they called me back to work. My doctor said that I could return to work, but I had just had an operation and with the cold I didn't feel well and I couldn't force myself to go back to work. The UI asked me why I stopped working and I told them that it was really cold and I had had an operation. The guy said to me in English, "You know already that the weather in this country is cold, what are you complaining about?" I wasn't complaining about the weather, I was making the point that I was sick and recently had an operation. Why should I complain about the weather? Why should I force myself to work? I told him that they could stop my UI claims rather than me killing myself from work!

Despite her operation and post-operation sickness, Nesta was expected by Employment Insurance (EI; formerly UI) personnel to go back to work. The EI worker's comments about the weather indicate implicit racism. Nesta showed her agency by challenging the EI worker to stop her EI claims. Nesta was firm in her position as she was convinced that returning to work would deteriorate her health. By refusing EI—an entitlement of being decommodified—Linda was determined to take care of her own health.

Liza provides this narration:

> One time I had an argument with the manager because my manager left a message saying that I have to sweep the floor. When he returned he asked me if I really swept the floor. I told him, "Why should I? No I didn't. I'm not a cleaner." He got mad at me. . . . Then he told me that if I'm going to quit he has the form ready. But I said, "No, but if you're going to fire me, then let me know." I think they don't want to fire anyone, and they don't want you to claim Employment Insurance.

Liza's narration shows that she was aware of her rights. She knew that sweeping was not part of her job. Liza also knew that if she resigned, she would not be entitled to claim EI. On the other hand, if the manager fired her, she would have access to EI. Such knowledge placed Liza in an advantageous situation that challenged the manager's authority—more precisely, male authority in the workplace.

Beth provides this narration:

> We get our contract [for special needs children] from the School Board. It is a ten-month contract. So every summertime, for the two months we go to claim our EI and we're covered. This has been a long struggle with EI and the School Board because every end of the term, in the month of June, we just get our ROE [Release Order from Employment] and go to EI. This is also a struggle because teachers are given ten-month contracts, but their salary is distributed over twelve months, so they don't have to apply for EI. But for us. . . . One time I received a call from EI and they suggested I take other training instead

of working with special needs. They said I could get a secretarial or an accounting job. I said, "Are you telling me what to do? This is a vocation. It's my right to choose what vocation I want to pursue in life, and for me, this is my career and I am trained to do this. I'm specialized to do this and you can't tell me to look for another job in the summertime!" She said, "This is just a suggestion." I said, "Thank you for your suggestion, but I'm telling you that I am trained and I have a lot of experience."

Beth's narration illustrates how she rejected the EI worker's suggestion and stood up for her own entitlements. Beth was proud of her profession and developed strategies to overcome EI's requirements. Being an informed immigrant about the entitlements of decommodification, Beth made analogies between her job and a schoolteacher's job and succinctly described the injustice for all of the employees in her position.

Farhat provides this narration:

[T]hat place I was put was the worst shift of all. . . . I often used to go home and cry. I often would go to the bathroom and cry there. . . . He would look at me and say. . . . "What about the Algerian story? Haven't you got it ready?" I said, "But I asked you ten times. Would you want the story now?" "O sure!—in five minutes!" The news has started and I'm running up three flights of stairs, cutting the tape, bringing it down, shooting it in, and if I don't get it on time they will say, "Oh, you know immigrants! . . . These women!" . . . Anyway eventually I got so frustrated I had to leave and I joined radio. . . . That was much easier.

To cope with a hostile racist and sexist work environment, Farhat tried her utmost to adjust and to retain a job that she desperately needed. Although Farhat was commodified again due to her flexible-hours and non-secure work in radio, at least she did not experience racism and sexism in her new workplace.

Challenging racism and sexism in the workplace is a frightening task for any women, let alone immigrant women, and often results in dismissal and harassment. To avoid racism and sexism, most women try to move to another workplace even though they will be commodified again. It is not surprising that both the IMA and the PWC are vocal about racism and sexism in the wider society.

NETWORKING WITH OTHER IMMIGRANT WOMEN

Knowing other immigrant women, including immigrant co-workers, is one of the best adaptive strategies for immigrant women to survive in a new country and workplace. The following narrations illustrate how networking serves immigrant women even in a workplace where women's labor is commodified.

Cardidad gives this narration:

I had to find another job. . . . I got the newsletter of the Domestic Workers' Association (DWA) and I read that they had meetings, so I went to their office. . . . I talked to the lawyer there and she wanted me to be a member of the Board of Directors right away! I didn't want to because I was just new.

Chapter 6 mentions that many women get jobs through informal networking. The above narration also shows that newsletters like the one of the Domestic Workers' Association are a great source of information as well as a networking medium for domestic workers. When Cardidad was approached to be a member of the Board of Directors, she declined, giving as her reason that she had not been in Canada long. This reason contradicts most women's statements in this study. When immigrant women were asked why they were not involved in community organizations, many cited lack of time. Cardidad's narration also demonstrates that she never lost her willingness to have control over her own work life even while she was commodified.

Ana gives this narration:

At first we were hesitant about getting involved because we were just new in this country and we didn't know our way around. In the month of September [of 1995], we were having a hard time sleeping over wherever we could, so [Jennifer] told us we could stay at the centre for a small donation. It happened that one bedroom at the centre was vacated. We were twelve women in our group. Out of the twelve of us, six decided to rent and would go back and forth between their employer's place, but most of the twelve of us stayed together in that one bedroom!

Ana describes how six domestic workers got together to rent one room so that they had liberties unavailable in their employers' residence. Surprisingly, although six paid the rent, all twelve used that one room off and on. This unusual and crowded living arrangement reflects how domestic workers' strong networking fosters collective strength. Sleeping together in one room also facilitates an exchange of information about commodification that is impossible for domestic workers who work in private homes. This networking among domestic workers who are commodified also provides opportunities for developing strategies to become decommodified.

Dina and Cora give these narrations:

When I became a member of SIKLAB [Migrant Workers' Organization], I learned a lot. I learned my basic rights as a live-in caregiver. I also learned how to depend on myself. . . . Before, I can't even open my mouth and say something to defend myself, but now I can say, "No!" or I can insist on what I want.

Since SIKLAB was formed, we have been invited three times to women's studies at UBC, and even at the YWCA to present our issues and situations as domestic workers here in Canada. . . . Our resistance and empowerment became stronger. We have organizations across Canada in Winnipeg, Montreal, Ottawa, and in the US in Oregon, Seattle and many more.

Membership in SIKLAB made both Dina and Cora aware of their rights. Not only did they exert their rights in their own lives as domestic workers, but Cora with other domestic workers delivered lectures at UBC and the YWCA to inform the public about the processes of commodification. This consciousness as well as advocacy for migrant workers has clearly fostered the inception of several sister organizations across Canada and beyond.

Pinky gives this narration:

> When I first came to Kalayaan [PWC], I was hesitant. . . . [Then] I realized that the Centre's objectives are really ideological and sensible. That they really want to change society. . . . After that, I attended the BC Human Rights and then on and on and on until I even tried catering. I became active. I used to live in Surrey, but I just moved downtown. Before I felt so homesick, but at the Kalayaan Centre it's as if this is my family. I did a lot of growing up.

Living far away from the Philippines, Pinky missed her family. The Kalayaan Centre (the PWC) became for Pinky the symbol of her family. Pinky's active involvement in the Centre eventually motivated her to move from outlying Surrey to downtown Vancouver. Her involvement with BC Human Rights activities as well as with the catering services of the PWC indicates Pinky's strong commitment and networking around immigrant women workers' entitlements and rights.

Harjit gives this narration:

> I've been one of the founding members of . . . neighborhood house, which has been there for six years now. . . . I've been on many other boards like BC Multicultural Education Society—I've been on their board. And I've been on many other boards like BC Multicultural Society and . . . and India Mahila Association—in many positions since 1980. I'm still continuing to work with them and I initiated two senior groups in Burnaby. . . . South Asian senior programs . . . with the help of other people around later. I'm an active member of Surrey Delta Senior Indo-Canadian group and still very busy with the neighborhood house.

Through various organizations, Harjit, an advocate for the IMA, participates in an enormous amount of networking across Vancouver. Due to her commitment, Harjit established two senior groups in Burnaby that are vital for the elderly Indo-Canadian population whose labor was historically commodified and who consequently were never decommodified. Harjit is an active member of Surrey Delta Senior Indo-Canadian group in an area where the majority of elderly Indo-Canadians reside. Aging and old age is not an issue much discussed publicly by immigrants; consequently, the IMA and the PWC do not address these issues.

The wide range of networking through formal and informal ways fosters an awareness of commodification and creates collectivity among immigrant women. Indeed, several immigrant women work as advocates for their organization and in the process change lives. This has been manifested in numerous ways, such as renting a single room for sleeping, delivering lectures to educational institutions/public forums, catering for a non-profit organization, establishing much-needed senior groups and so on.

COLLECTIVE EFFORTS: CHALLENGING LOCAL, NATIONAL, AND GLOBAL FORCES

By July 1995 we were encouraged to form a group for migrant workers. The Philippine Women Centre is limited in its scope since it's only focusing on women's issues. In SIKLAB we deal with all the issues facing migrant workers outside the Philippines. Our issues were also triggered by Flor Contemplacion's death. We really saw the urgent need to form a group to assert our rights. By October we officially launched SIKLAB. . . . Through SIKLAB we do a lot of networking, so I've attended events with the Guatemalan and Chilean communities, International Women's Day events, and in 1997 during the APEC conference, we formed a NO! to APEC coalition and I was involved. . . . We integrate also with the Filipino-Canadian youth. At the Kalayaan Center the Filipino-Canadian youth are also studying their own identity issues and at the same we integrate with them to understand the root causes of their situation. (Ana)

Ana's narration points out that the PWC deals with issues beyond those of migrant workers, including working with Filipino-Canadian youth and discussing issues like racism and sexism in the wider society. Ana adds another piece of background information about the formation of SIKLAB. Flor Contemplacion, a Filipina domestic worker, was executed by the Government of Singapore on March 17, 1994, for the alleged murder in May 1991 of another Filipino domestic worker, Delia Maga, and her four-year-old ward, Nicholas Huang (Ordinario 1995). As mentioned earlier, many Filipina migrant workers came to Canada via Singapore and Hong Kong. This execution made them aware that women migrant workers are vulnerable to coercion and exploitation that might strip them even of their right to be alive. To protest against the execution order of Flor Contemplacion, the PWC at first held demonstrations at the Philippine and Singapore consulates in Vancouver and at the Vancouver Art Gallery. Outraged by the actual execution, the PWC then organized a two-day training workshop to deal with the specific needs of Filipino migrant workers. Out of this workshop emerged the action-oriented group called SIKLAB (Zaman and Tubajon 2001). According to Ana,

SIKLAB makes connections with various community groups such as Guatemalan and Chilean groups, as well as with the global community:

> SIKLAB was formed in 1995, and since then, we have really put a lot of hard work into it. We started a campaign to end double taxation. [W]e were required to pay to the government of the Philippines and Canada. . . . The campaign to end double taxation was successful. As long as you register at the Consulate, you don't have to pay. This is one of the campaigns that succeeded through our determination and hard work. We really went out to the malls and other public places to gain support from other Filipinos. (Ana)

The above narration describes how SIKLAB in collaboration with the PWC changed a double taxation policy by collecting signatures and convincing the government of the Philippines that this policy was unjust and created a double burden for the Filipino population in Canada. Thus, SIKLAB goes beyond domestic workers' issues and embraces general issues that involve men and women of Filipino ancestry. This narration also justifies the use of the concept of transnational migration—where immigrants play active roles and maintain ties to their countries of origin—over either international or global migration, as this book has argued.

An interview session between Cecilia and Dina reveals another collective effort:

> **Dina:** I found out about the FNSG [Filipino Nurses Support Group] through my cousin's sister-in-law. When I heard about it, I came with her to attend one of the meetings and became a member. From then on most of the time, I am attending some of the meetings. If I can't, I'll just phone one of the volunteers here at the Centre for an update. The only thing that I can help is to go with them for some meetings or rallies.
>
> **Cecilia:** Have you attended rallies of FNSG?
>
> **Dina:** Yes, I did. The issue was the privatization of health care. I attended that in the Vancouver Art Gallery on Robson, downtown.
>
> **Cecilia:** How did you feel?
>
> **Dina:** Oh, excited! It was a really good feeling because you were really voicing out what you believed in. Then, I was helping FNSG by relaying information or messages to my friends and encouraging them to be a member. I encouraged both of them to be a member. But then they were still not active because they work mostly on the weekend since they are still fulltime live-in caregivers.

The PWC has another umbrella group called the Filipino Nurses Support Group (FNSG) that actively organizes Filipinos who have degrees in nursing from the Philippines. In addition to achieving these goals, the FNSG raises consciousness among Filipino nurses about the processes of accreditation as well as the prospects of being decommodified. To achieve its goal, the FNSG offers "nursing classes" at the PWC on weekends. The interview session between Dina and Cecilia illustrate that this collaborative research has made efforts to make immigrant women aware of effective re-skilling processes and decommodification. The FNSG's alliance with the PWC to organize a protest march against the privatization of health care indicates that the FNSG serves both to protect the interests of Filipino nurses and to empower them.

Another interview Cecilia conducted, this time with Beth, concerns Beth's involvement in a PWC campaign against trafficking:

> **Cecilia:** How about collectively with other women at the Center, what are some of the concrete examples of your experience in terms of exploitation and oppression as an individual? Have you participated in the work of the Centre in organizing?
>
> **Beth:** For example, the mail-order bride project is one of the concrete works of the Centre in terms of being a collective effort of the women at the Centre. When we launched the Purple Rose Campaign, this became the concrete example of how women are being exported and commodified. We are not exporting copra and bananas, but women are a number one export in the Philippines. Realizing this and learning from this, it is right to collectively voice that we are not just instruments, we are people, and we are human beings. We are being commodified as women. This is a reality I realized after being involved in the project.

The above interview session refers to the Purple Rose Campaign to stop trafficking in Filipino women. The campaign was initiated by the PWC in September 1999. The PWC uses the concept "trafficking in women" in a comprehensive way that includes sex workers, domestic workers, mail-order brides, entertainers, and so on. The Philippines is a classic example of trafficking as thousands of women depart the country to become either mail-order brides or entertainers for the US, Japan and Singapore.

One interview shows that some immigrant women demonstrate agency in choosing between working conditions on two kinds of jobs:

> **Cecilia:** Could you compare your working conditions as a nanny to being a seamstress?
>
> **Mila:** As a seamstress and a nanny, it is really different. As a nanny, you are really tied ten hours a day. How much time you can take a break? While you are working as a seamstress, you have your regular work time, break time, and overtime. As a Live-In Caregiver, you don't have overtime. When you are required to work overtime, you get good pay in a company. As a nanny, I was always working more than the hours required. But, I never get paid with that. Sometimes, you don't go anywhere because you are new in this country. You don't go anywhere. So, it benefits the employer too. I would just stay and help, but not get paid. There is a big difference.

Mila not only distinguishes between various forms of commodification, but also describes her awareness of commodification. The nature and intensity of commodification of domestic workers differ distinctly from that of seamstresses. The move from domestic work to a seamstress job did not allow Mila to be decommodified, but having overtime and regular work hours took her to a different level of commodification.

Harjit's interview gives a first-person account of issues an immigrant woman can be involved with through the IMA:

> We [IMA] had a visiting professor here from Baroda University. She talked about the situation of seniors in India and how old-people homes are emerging there and that was new to us. . . . We had a woman from Afghanistan who came and talked about the lives of women in Afghanistan before the Americans went there. This way we raise awareness about the lives of women in South Asia. In the mid-'90s [we saw] in the local papers [community] about the fetuses [female] being aborted. Across the border [Seattle] there is a doctor. . . . We are the ones who led a march. We went to the various organizations and through the Indian Bazaar and Punjabi market. We had a rally on that issue and talked a lot in the media about that and on television, radio, etc. We are always looking at the points of advocacy for women's rights. We participate in International Women's Day and for the last three years, we have been showing a film, which will raise more awareness about women around International Women's Day in the Indian community.

One of the goals of the IMA is to revive and promote positive aspects of Indian culture. The IMA achieves this objective in numerous ways. The IMA invites speakers from South Asia who have feminist views. The IMA works with women in South Asia irrespective of class, caste, religion, and so on. Through speakers, published reports, demonstrations and rallies, the IMA has raised awareness about various issues, such as racism and sexism, that are pervasive in immigrant women's lives across generations and create barriers to recognition of foreign credentials.

Shibani describes her work with the SAWC (South Asian Women's Centre):

> I'm a . . . for South Asian Women's Centre. It's mainly an information and referral centre. So you know, we help women with any issues that they have, any problems, anything that they need to know, in person as well as over the phone. We also do outreach in the community to let them know about the kind of work we do. We also do community education on issues of violence against women and other issues that come up and do coalition work with other women's organizations on various issues.

Besides offering education on issues such as violence against women, the SAWC refers South Asian women to transition houses and crisis centres. In addition to combating sexism and racism, the SAWC also provides information on job training and educational opportunities.

Shakti adds more detail about the SAWC:

[T]his has a very interesting history. . . . This place was started by a spectrum of women from different backgrounds, you know, from southern India, from northern India, from Africa, from Fiji. When I came to one of the earliest meetings, I was totally amazed. It was truly a South Asian Women's group, not an Indian, not a Punjabi, not a Tamil, not a Fijian, and these women were activists in the community. They were doing, they were watching. One of the things was there was sometimes racist portrayal of the community in the media, so these women kept watch over the media . . . also on the right for women working in farming—the bulk of women, Punjabi women at that time. They also came together around sex selection in the South Asian community where female fetuses were aborted after going through ultrasound or some kind of testing. So, we have a very proud beginning, something very inclusive of various segments of South Asian community as well as wanting no less than, you know, social change in the community. (Shakti)

Shakti's narrative upholds Shibani's view that the origins of SAWC are rooted in the needs of the South Asian community in Greater Vancouver. In addition to working with immigrant women on their particular issues, the Centre also addresses the media's racist portrayal of the community. The SAWC embraces all women of South Asian ancestry and consequently crosses boundaries of religion, class, nation and ethnicity.

The inception of the PWC, the IMA, and the SAWC, and other immigrant women's organizations is inextricably linked to sexism, racism and exploitation in the workplace as well as in the wider Canadian society. These organizations are derived from and shaped by immigrant women actively as agents of change. In turn, these organizations not only empower their own members, but also act toward the liberation of all marginalized women from commodification of their labor. While these organizations began for specific reasons, their very existence continues to spawn new forms of consciousness and alliances that crosscut individual, local, and transnational boundaries.

NOTES

1. In Bangladesh, approximately 86 percent of the population are Muslims, and the majority of the migrants in Greater Vancouver are Muslims. The relaxation of immigration may be due to Bangladesh's secular sociopolitical context where the majority of Muslims do not practice Islam in their daily lives.

2. I was an assistant professor at the University of Victoria from 1992–1993. The General Secretary of the Bangladesh Association phoned and invited me to attend cultural events. Although I did not know him, he invited me to join the event so that it would be well attended. Recently, I attended another potluck/drama event (selected invited participants, which was organized by seven women). About 300 men, women and children attended, although the numbers of expected guests were 200. One of the organizers described a dilemma: their anxiety now was not about the attendance, but about how to limit the numbers without offending people.

3. I have examined immigrant women's agency pertinent to their paid labor, which is the book's central thesis.

4. I attended one International Women's Day dinner at Fraser View Hall in Burnaby in 2000. Both women and men attended and the hall was full (it had an approximate capacity of 300 people).

5. Of Canadian cities, Montreal now has the third largest immigrant population.

9

Summary and Conclusions

In this study, I have examined various facets of commodified sectors, including the household, while looking at the links between globalization, neo-liberal globalism and transnational migration. Special attention has been paid to immigrant women in relation to semi-periphery and periphery countries. The core objective of my work was to look at immigrant women's labor and the processes of commodification and decommodification in Canada. Most researchers who study immigrants in Canada rely on numbers, statistics, and demographic profiles. This book provides a human dimension, with immigrant women narrating various layers of commodification and lack of decommodification of labor in their own words, describing their individual and collective responses. The study results, therefore, should be valuable to assist researchers and policy planners to comprehend the complex processes and bureaucratic hurdles through which immigrant women's labor becomes commodified in the national economy.

This book has investigated the processes of commodification of immigrant women's labor in Canada, a liberal welfare state. The book has further investigated how a non- or under-commodified sector, that is, the household, has increasingly shifted to a commodified sector. The key findings of this study include a number of issues with regard to the concepts of commodification and decommodification—the latter a concept so far rarely used—pertinent to analyzing immigrant women's labor as well as various sectors like hospitals, households, schools, and so on. The study findings presented lead to the conclusion that the welfare state through immigration policies creates structural barriers for immigrants from periphery countries to attain equal opportunities irrespective of race, gender and class and to become decommodified. These structural barriers generate a racialized, gendered and class-based labor market and solidify the commodified sectors while changing the non- and under-commodified sectors.

Distinguishing between the frequently used term "globalization" and the infrequently used term "globalism," in chapter 2 I have demonstrated the interconnection between globalization, neo-liberal globalism and migration and argued for using the concept "transnational migration" instead of "international" and "global" migration, pointing out the utility of transnational fields and current trends. Exploring the numerical significance of gendered and racialized migration and the causes of women's migration, I have shown where migrant women's labor is needed and how it is being used in commodified sectors of a receiving country like Canada. Further, because most of these lower-echelon jobs in the commodified sectors are perceived as feminine, immigrant women are considered suitable for cheap and disposable labor only. This study has shown that gender, class and race have intertwined in racialized immigrant women's lives. I have touched on the issues of sexism, classism and racism, but these issues deserve further and thorough exploration in future research pertinent to decommodification of immigrant women's labor.

Another key finding, discussed in chapter 3, is that the historical discriminatory race-based immigration act in Canada has been replaced by a class-biased act, with upper- and upper-middle class immigrants from Asia as a preferred category. In order to be competitive in a "knowledge"-based and service-oriented global economy, Canada now recruits skilled immigrants, a significant change from Canada's previous emphasis on "family category" and the use of "unskilled" labor from Asia. Through tables and graphs, I have pointed out that seven of the top ten source countries of immigrants in the beginning of the 21st century are in Asia and almost 50 percent of recent immigrants to Canada originate from Asia. Yet, even when women have entered Canada as part of a preferred category, the gendered nature of immigration in terms of recognizing women's credentials and skills has created an environment where racialized women enter as "secondary," "dependent," and thus "unequal," whatever their qualifications. Consequently, compared with immigrant men and Canadian-born women and men, racialized immigrant women have performed the least in the labor market and have concentrated in commodified sectors. Under whatever category they enter Canada, immigrant women and men generally face numerous obstacles in the labor market because efforts of various agencies, licensing bodies and professional associations to recognize immigrants' credentials and skills remain disjointed. It is almost impossible for most immigrant women's labor to be decommodified at this time. Unless Canada develops strategies to recognize international credentials, I argue that many skilled immigrants will emigrate to be decommodified. As a result, the infinite flow of skilled immigrants to Canada may be jeopardized.

In chapter 4, I have suggested that the Canadian state through the LCP has contradicted the very nature of the welfare state's equal opportunity policy. The LCP has demonstrated that Canada as a welfare state continues to enact its legacy of the pre-welfare state's racialized, gendered and class-based policies. Through the LCP, the Canadian state has gradually transformed a non- or under-commodified sector, that is, the family, into a commodified sector, where domestic workers' labor, due to their contractual obligations, has become commodified. In the past, most of the literature that focused on the LCP and its consequences for domestic workers emphasized racism, sexism and classism. This study's findings have greatly enhanced the existing literature, revealing the dynamics of commodification of racialized women's labor and the contradictions and conflicts within the welfare state. To solve childcare and eldercare crises, the state has adopted a market-driven, neo-liberal strategy that has transformed a non-commodified or under-commodified sector into a commodified or partially commodified sector where immigrant women's labor has been bought through state-sanctioned immigration policy. The very process of immigration policy defeats the notion of equal opportunity for all immigrants and citizens irrespective of gender, race and class in a liberal welfare state like Canada.

A key finding in chapter 5 is the multiple layers of commodification experienced by immigrant women in Canada. Although widely used in the case of labor, albeit male labor, the concept of commodification of labor has been rarely used in analysis of immigrant female labor. Perhaps this is my contribution to the established literature. I have analyzed different layers of commodification, such as "non-commodification," "under-commodification," "partial commodification," and "full commodification" with regard to immigrant women's labor in the introduction. I have elaborated on the concepts through women's narrations in chapter 5 and also examined these concepts while analysing women's labor under the LCP. I have clarified (and declined to use) the commonly used concept of "pre-commodification." I have shown that the Canadian government through the LCP has liberated many upper- and middle-class, privileged, and educated women in Canada from the non- and under-commodified sector, that is, the family, indicating "defamilialization" of these privileged women. Defamilialization is one of the pre-conditions of decommodification of labor; thus, privileged women's labor has the potential to be decommodified. Immigrant women's narrations presented in this book have shown that the Canadian welfare state has created structural and systemic barriers for domestics under the LCP to become decommodified. The state has also unduly denied the educational qualifications of professionals from their country of origin, effectively commodifying their labor again in the post-immigration process. The LCP has rejuvenated a feudal relationship that I have identified as "refeudalization," meaning the employer-employee relationship is contractual in a commodified but hidden sector endorsed by the state. Finally, I have pointed out that domestics' labor, even after domestics achieve permanent status, becomes fully or partially commodified because most domestics shift from childcare to eldercare while performing work in their own households—that is, the non-commodified sector. This shift has been described as "stroller to wheelchair," and as "cradle to grave," another indication of how immigrant women's labor becomes commodified and then re-commodified despite utmost efforts to become decommodified.

In chapter 6, I have pointed out that the concept of decommodification, an under-developed concept, has been used in Sweden, the US and Germany. The latter two countries have similarities with Canada, especially the nature of the welfare state. However, no researcher to my knowledge has so far used the concept of decommodification within the context of sectors as well as of immigrants' labor in Canada. Through immigrant women's narrations, I have illustrated the barriers that prevent racialized immigrant women's labor from being decommodified, with very few women seeking assistance from government agencies. Women's narrations have poignantly demonstrated that part-time, "flexible" jobs in commodified sectors feature prominently in immigrant women's lives, although their workplace in terms of work-hours, employment standards, and work environment varies. "Flexibility," for most immigrant women, means unpredictable schedules, the absence of employment standards, and insecurity in jobs, as well as lack of access to social rights and entitlements. Due to the tenuous job situations of immigrant women, very few have access to social benefits, sick leave, vacation, Registered Retirement Savings Plan, and so on—in other words, the entitlements and benefits of decommodification. Some immigrant women have become caught between aging and upgrading and have rightfully compared the whole experience of finding a job with breaking an "iron wall" to succeed. I believe that I have successfully illustrated that for the majority of immigrant women, the potential of decommodification of labor in terms of having access to social benefits is still a dream that shows no signs of being realized even in the distant future!

Chapter 7 has revealed another key finding: even after some forms of re-skilling, most immigrant women's credentials and training are either under-utilized or not utilized, resulting in the recommodification of their labor. This study has suggested that responsibility for the welfare of most immigrants rests with the family instead of the state. In addition, the combination of familial responsibilities and employment has transformed many immigrant women's labor into partially commodified labor. Immigrant women's narrations have revealed that most have not ended up in jobs pertinent to their original professions, that is, the professions they used to hold in their countries of origin and in decommodified sectors. Whenever immigrant women's labor has been decommodified, satisfaction levels seem to be unusually high. Future research may compare the labor of immigrant and

Canadian-born professional women, various decommodified sectors, and the forces behind the decommodification of immigrant women's labor. One cautionary comment is that interviewing only immigrant women whose labor have been decommodified or who work in decommodified sectors may send out an incorrect message (i.e., all immigrants are professionals and work in the decommodified sectors, etc.) to the wider society.

Chapter 8 illustrates that racialized immigrant women are conscious of the commodification of their labor and barriers to decommodification of their labor; consequently, their individual and collective resistance strategies are varied. Examining the two immigrant women's organizations—the IMA and the PWC—in which most of the interviewee women are members, the chapter points out the IMA as an autonomous group functions at the local level, although it does have links with various women's and grassroots organizations, whereas the PWC has links with various local, national and transnational groups. Due to the PWC's transnational connections and its active role in challenging the commodified sector, that is, the household, and commodification of immigrant women's labor, the chapter has focused more on the PWC than on the IMA. However, both organizations have one commonality: empowerment of women in the fight against racism and sexism in the wider society. The PWC in particular also assists immigrant women with information and training toward the decommodification of their labor.

Women's narrations in this book have shown that although periods of migration differ, women's efforts and the potential for the decommodification of their labor have not changed. Although immigrant women from South Asia and South-east Asia have entered Canada under various categories ranging from domestic to skilled category to dependents, these women's labor has been utilized in various commodified sectors without a chance of being decommodified. Despite their utmost efforts to be decommodified, most immigrant women's labor eventually becomes re-commodified. The success of very few immigrant women in decommodifying their labor does not raise hopes for dramatic change without commitment and change at government levels.

Revisiting the findings with regard to the existing literature on immigrants, especially immigrant women from South Asia and South-east Asia, this book has minimized gaps in first-hand knowledge about immigrant women's labor in the commodified and decommodified sectors as well as about the processes and prospects of commodification and decommodification of labor. The rarely used concepts of commodification and decommodification in various sectors and in the case of immigrant women's labor in particular have provided valuable frameworks by which future academics can pursue research not only with immigrants, but with any disadvantaged groups such as single parents, aboriginal population, people with disabilities, women, and so on. Indeed, there exists room to improve and refine both these concepts in the case of labor. Here lies the utility of these two conceptual categories. Future researchers may compare the differences in the labor market, as well as commodification and decommodification processes, between immigrant women's labor and immigrant men's labor. A comparative study of semi-periphery (but immigrant-receiving) countries such as Canada and Australia may also provide insightful information on how immigrant women's labor becomes commodified, the potential of decommodification processes, and immigrant women's participation in various commodified and decommodified sectors.

This study has indicated constraints that immigrant women encounter in terms of commodified sectors. To alleviate some of these constraints, I am making the following recommendations:

First, both the federal government and the provincial governments should provide full funds supporting ESL classes so that free advanced-level English is offered. ESL courses must be offered beyond rudimentary levels as the desire to learn English is immense among immigrant women. Further, despite a women's movement in place for several decades, childcare remains a woman's responsibility, and free child-care services need to be provided when immigrant women take ESL courses. Ideally, providing childcare to all irrespective of gender, race and class paves the way for the decommodification of labor.

Second, to monitor the accreditation system and minimize variations in standards across provinces, a regulatory body must be established. Working with universities, community colleges, training institutions, and other schools in Canada, this regulatory body could compile a nation-wide database to generate comprehensive, uniform regulations across Canada. Recognition of degrees and diplomas of immigrants will go a long way toward providing them with equal opportunities for attaining decommodification of their labor.

Third, the controversial LCP needs to be carefully evaluated so that migrant workers and domestics enter Canada as permanent residents. The federal government's Annual Immigration Plan clearly recognizes this group as prospective immigrants and acknowledges the need for this group's labor. The temporary migrant worker status transforms a non- or under-commodified sector to a commodified sector. Entry as permanent residents would allow these domestics to do re-training or to upgrade skills immediately without going through unnecessary expense and bureaucratic hassles and this too may facilitate the decommodification of their labor.

Finally, the federal government needs to develop an immigration system where both adult women and men, irrespective of race and class, enter Canada on an equal footing rather than the present situation where women are labeled as "dependents." Such a process will truly reflect equal opportunity for all immigrants, whatever their gender, race and class, in a liberal welfare state like Canada.

Appendix

Demographic Profiles of the Interviewees

The interviewee sample presented in this book represents a specific demographic profile of immigrant women in Canadian society and does not represent a homogenous group. As the book has shown, gender, class and race interact as oppressive factors in these women's lives in unique ways, creating complex and nuanced issues. However, as argued, these oppressions are systemic, fostered by structural barriers and socioeconomic inequalities.

Sixty-four women from various countries of South and South-east Asia—racialized immigrants—comprise the sample. Though their diversity in terms of age, class in country of origin, educational background, religion, and work experience seems to defy classification, what unites them is a common experience of marginalization in an increasingly globalized era.

INTERVIEW CONTEXT

The interviews are contextualized by two interview situations: focus groups and individual interviews. In total, 28 interviewees participated in focus groups, and 36 in individual interviews.

The tone and flow of the focus group interviews were quite different from the individual ones, as they tended to foster consciousness-raising among participants. Often, participants would be reminded of similar experiences while listening to others speak. The sense of commonality underscores and provides a basis for undertaking a critical analysis of the broader context. In contrast, the individual interviews tended to follow a question-and-answer style, and the integrating and connecting of issues that arose from interview to interview fell to the researcher.

COUNTRIES OF ORIGIN

All of the women interviewed are women from Asia. The distribution of countries of origin is shown below:

Table A.1. Country of Origin

Country of Origin	Interviewees
Philippines	47
Bangladesh	10
India	3
Malaysia	1
Fiji	1
Hong Kong, China	1
Not reported	1
Total	64

The Filipinos are heavily represented among this group because immigrants from the Philippines are particularly relevant in terms of globalization and various forms of commodification of labor. As this book has noted, the aggressive labor export policy of the Philippines and Canada's immigration and labor import policy have made these women's experiences of neo-liberal globalism particularly poignant—but such trends prevail when considering other countries of origin as well, such as Bangladesh.

YEAR OF ARRIVAL

The year of arrival in Canada is shown in table A.2 below.

Table A.2. Year of Arrival

Year of Arrival	Interviewees
Before 1980	14
1981–1990	8
1991–2000	35
2000 onward	6
Not reported	1
Total	64

Interestingly, few interviewees immigrated in the 1980s, which is reflective of the link between Canada's economy and its immigration policy. This finding illustrates the tightening of immigration during times of recession, that is, the 1980s.

CITIZENSHIP

Comparing the status of the Filipina with the Bangladeshi and Indian women (the majority of whom migrated as spouses and family-sponsored immigrants) shows that all of the women from Bangladesh and India are now Canadian citizens, while 25 of the Filipinas reported having Canadian citizenship. Of the other Filipinas, 21 had obtained landed status, and four had not yet obtained landed status. One reason for the difference in citizenship status may be that Filipinas as a Canadian ethnic group have increased in numbers relatively recently and represent a more recent part of the sample.

Other barriers exist for Filipinas for obtaining citizenship—the LCP requirements probably being one such barrier. As the book has noted, live-in caregivers who immigrate via the LCP are considered temporary workers until they receive landed status, which is permissible after more than 24 months of employment as a caregiver within three years. Bangladeshis and Indians who immigrated via the other categories obtain landed status right away. It is thus more common for immigrant women in the various categories other than the LCP to be Canadian citizens, since it takes less time for them to obtain it.

AGE GROUP

Table A.3 shows that the sample is very diverse in terms of age. As the book has noted in chapter 6, common experiences exist across age brackets, due to the "chicken and egg" dilemma, where women of all ages are marginalized in a demand for an impossible balance of youth and education.

Table A.3. Age Group

Age Group	Interviewees
20–25	3
26–30	13
31–40	16
41–50	12
51–60	12
61 and above	4
Not reported	4
Total	64

The age distribution of the interviewees illustrates that many are in the 31–61 bracket, reflecting Citizenship and Immigration data showing that working-age immigrants are favored. Indeed, the points system of the Immigration

Department supports the working-age group—with the implicit expectations of contribution to the economy and labor force participation that has ensured this distribution.

PLACE OF LANDING

Vancouver was the most common place of landing, as well as the most common current place of residence. This suggests that there is not a great deal of geographical mobility among immigrant women, although several women had undertaken at least one move. Other landing places included Saskatoon, Winnipeg, Toronto, and Montreal. Most commonly, a move occurred after the completion of the LCP 24-month requirement. These moves were characterized by a move from a small city to a larger one, or from a less ethnically diverse city to a more diverse one. For example, one woman arrived in Saskatoon, but now lives in Surrey. Another arrived in Winnipeg, and now lives in Vancouver. Interestingly, very few women arrived in rural areas.

CURRENT PLACE OF RESIDENCE

All women reside in British Columbia. The "snowball" research technique indicates that women are geographically concentrated in areas roughly mirroring their social networks. Consequently, the Lower Mainland, from Vancouver to Surrey, is a common place of residence, as is the Kelowna area. These cities are roughly 400 km apart, representing a diverse geographic cross-section.

OTHER COUNTRIES OF RESIDENCE

Twenty women had resided in countries other than their countries of origin and Canada. The most common were Hong Kong and Singapore, attributable to the large representation of live-in caregivers in the sample, although not all of the twenty were LCP immigrants.

Having such a large portion of women who had resided in other countries is an interesting characteristic of this sample. This also confirms my argument in the book that most trans-migrants become immigrants. Many women, after going through the selection process that emphasizes skills and training, were surprised to find their skills and credentials of little value in Canada. A few women expressed feelings of betrayal and regret about coming to Canada, especially since their skills were in demand elsewhere.

SOCIAL CLASS IN COUNTRY OF ORIGIN

Women were asked to identify their social/economic class in their countries of origin and most reported middle and upper-middle class. This suggests poverty was not the main reason that these women immigrated. Certainly, they are a highly educated group, which would presumably lead to professional success in the labor market of their countries of origin. However, numerous forces are at play in the identification of social and economic class, and the issue is not as simple as this interpretation takes it to be.

EDUCATION IN COUNTRY OF ORIGIN

Only ten women obtained no more than a high school level of study or did not report any post-secondary education in their countries of origin.[1] Thirty-three women obtained at least an undergraduate degree from their countries of origin, with a few having undertaken post-graduate work. Nursing and health-related fields are the most common degrees; degrees in education and experience in teaching are also common. This distribution reflects the selection processes for immigrants, which favor skills that fill skills shortages or labor market needs. This is especially true for caregivers, since those trained in nursing and teaching are certainly highly skilled as caregivers, and there is a shortage of caregivers. Lack of recognition of skills acquired elsewhere than in Canada is a problem and leads to immigrants becoming unemployed, underemployed and de-skilled.

EDUCATION/TRAINING IN CANADA

Most respondents undertook some form of training or upgrading, but very few seemed to find that their experiences were positive or that training or upgrading resulted in the desired outcome, that is, the decommodification of their labor. The most common undertaking was attempting to acquire accreditation, since a large portion of the interviewees already had degrees and training from their countries of origin. Many found the accreditation process lengthy and confusing, as noted in the book. Interestingly, those who tried to obtain accreditation and encountered major barriers for the decommodification of labor often turned to re-skilling in a field related to their previous employment. For example, several respondents are certified nurses in their country of origin and after failing to obtain accreditation in Canada, re-skilled as nurses' aides or became long-term care aides. Most chose community and private colleges rather than universities for upgrading and re-skilling.

The majority of women did not report taking English (or French) classes. Many of the women who did take such classes considered the government-funded English course too easy and remedial. Despite many immigrants expressing a strong desire for training in advanced English in order to compete in the job market, there seem to be no such government-funded services available.

A few respondents expressed a desire or described plans for upgrading and training, but noted that finances and time constraints did not currently permit pursuing such goals. Many expressed a concern for their children and their ability to support their children in terms of time and money.

CURRENT AND PAST JOBS IN CANADA

Caregiving is the most common job held by the interviewees, as are occupations in the health sector. In fact, 30 women reported undertaking paid employment at some point or other as a caregiver in Canada. This includes childcare, eldercare, and care for people who are ill or who have disabilities. Twenty-one women reported having worked in the health sector as home support workers, dietary aides, nurses and the like, and many of these women had also been caregivers in the past.

Other common workplaces were fast-food restaurants, retail stores, factories, hotel industries, and warehouses. Common jobs were data entry, clerical services, nursing aides, and cleaning. While very few women worked as professionals outside of the health or low-wage service sectors, the sample did include a doctor, an adjudicator[2] and an architect.

Interestingly, a few respondents had undertaken work in the non-profit sector with community groups and activist organizations. This reflects not only the way the interviewee sample was procured, that is, through contacts with the Philippine Women Centre in Vancouver, but also that there is a consciousness of social issues in the sample. A non-profit group is a place where women's country of origin, class and gender are an advantage and not a hindrance in competing for a job.

UPWARD SOCIOECONOMIC MOBILITY

Gauging upward mobility is difficult. For one thing, it is a relatively subjective undertaking on the part of the researcher. For example, a woman migrated to Canada as a live-in caregiver, and now holds a job as a resident care aide. While the care aide position generally requires some formal training, the nature and difficulty of work, compared with live-in caregiving, is quite similar, apart from the live-in requirement. Yet, generally, the care aide would earn more than the live-in caregiver would. To further complicate things, it seems that care aide positions are frequently part-time or on-call; something live-in caregiving does not generally permit. A possible way to remedy the problematic interpretation of social mobility would be to ask the women themselves whether they consider themselves to have moved upward in the labor market.

If the women's level of satisfaction is used as a guide, this does not take into consideration that many respondents expressed dreams of practicing their profession, which they had given up, or another profession. Workers frequently accept lower standards of satisfaction, often being extremely satisfied with finding a full-time job and thus, decommodification of labor. Other workers accept jobs based on social perceptions, as noted in the book—for example, working at a bank for lower pay than can be obtained elsewhere because banks are seen as more respectable.

Despite these problems, it appears that most of the women interviewed experienced some social mobility. However, the mobility was generally quite limited and multidimensional. The caregiver-to-care-aide scenario outlined above is an example. One reason for the absence of substantive mobility is that many women reported not receiving on-the-job training. The reason is that the kinds of jobs in which these women are concentrated provide very little opportunity for socioeconomic advancement. A live-in caregiver has no infrastructure or institution from which to obtain training or advancement. Similarly, low-wage service-sector jobs offer little training and consequently little opportunities for upward mobility. Furthermore, some women who had experienced mobility in the low-wage service sector found that their working conditions deteriorated, as they were expected to do more work and work longer hours without complaining.

WAGES

Live-in caregivers generally make minimum wage or below minimum wage, so the interviewees often reported receiving minimum wage. Positions in the health sector (not including nursing but including resident-care aide, long-term-care aide and support worker) generally received $12–$16 per hour, though many of these positions are part-time.

Long hours and low wages are common occurrences, especially among the live-in caregivers who are often forced to work long hours without pay or overtime pay, or who receive less than minimum wage.

RELIGION

Most respondents, when asked, identified a religion that they practice or identify with. Not surprisingly, the identifications mostly coincided with their country of origin: Filipinos reporting Catholic or Christian, women from Bangladesh reporting Islam, and women from India reporting Hinduism or Sikhism.

COMMUNITY WORK

Many respondents reported feeling a deep sense of community within their ethnic group. This is particularly true of the Filipina, who often mentioned churches as places of support and interaction. In terms of community work, there seems to be a divide between those women who are hesitant to be involved in progressive activism and those who are politicized and conscious of women's and disadvantaged groups' issues. Often, the hesitation seemed to originate in a lack of time, particularly if the respondents had children. A few women were worried that political activity would harm their LCP contract positions or applications for landed status. For example, Marlyn admitted: "I was still hesitant at that time because I didn't know that many people and I was scared that if I got involved, it might affect my application for landed status." However, since the "snowball technique" was used and because the study was undertaken with the PWC, most women had some contact and involvement with the Vancouver Filipino community that centers around the Kalayaan Centre where the PWC is housed. Interviewees reported attending rallies, participating in campaigns and attending workshops. The Filipino Nurses Support Group (FNSG) was also an often-mentioned organization.

Filipino organizations exist in Winnipeg as well, as mentioned by some women. These include the Filipino Association of Manitoba and ATOM (August 21 Movement—the day Ninoy, a popular one-time presidential candidate and political prisoner of Marcos, was assassinated). There were also movements to get Filipino co-operative housing in both Vancouver and Winnipeg.

Interestingly, women often noted a difference between themselves and their children—their children being more willing to get involved in the community and in progressive activism. Immigrants' experiences with oppression often lead to the politicization of the next generation.

The study was also a means of politicization. The interviews were utilized as a means to inform women briefly about community activities they might want to attend and groups they may want to join. Thus, the collaborative research project itself fostered some community growth.

NOTES

1. One of the interviewees became a lawyer and one a doctor at Canadian institutions. Five had done at least some other form of post-secondary education in Canada.

2. The doctor and the adjudicator obtained their educations in Canada.

Bibliography

Abu-Laban, Yasmeen, and Christina Gabriel. *Selling Diversity: Immigration, Multiculturalism, Employment Equity, and Globalization.* Peterborough: Broadview Press, 2002.

Achtenberg, Emily Paradise, and Peter Marcuse. "Toward the Decommodification of Housing: A Political Analysis and a Progressive Program." Pp. 202–31 in *American Housing Crisis: What Is To Be Done?* edited by Chester Hartman. Boston: Routledge and Kegan Paul, 1983.

Adilman, T. "A Preliminary Sketch of Chinese Women and Work in British Columbia: 1858–1950." Pp. 53–78 in *Not Just Pin Money: Selected Essays on the History of Women's Work in British Columbia*, edited by B. Latham and R. Pazdro. Victoria: Camosun College, 1984.

Agnew, Vijay. *Resisting Discrimination: Women from Asia, Africa, and the Caribbean and the Women's Movement in Canada.* Toronto: University of Toronto Press, 1996.

Akbari, Ather H. "Immigrant 'Quality' in Canada: More Direct Evidence of Human Capital Content, 1956–1994." *International Migration Review* 33, no. 1 (1999): 156–75.

Alarcon-Gonzalez, Diana, and Terry McKinley. "The Adverse Effects of Structural Adjustment on Working Women in Mexico." *Latin American Perspectives* 26, no. 3 (1999): 103–7.

Alboim, Naomi, and the Maytree Foundation. "Fulfilling the Promise: Integrating Immigrant Skills into the Canadian Economy." 2002. <www.maytree.com/pdf-files/fulfillingpromise.pdg> (retrieved 24 Feb. 2005).

Amin, Samir. *Unequal Development: An Essay on the Social Formation of Peripheral Capitalism.* New York: Monthly Review Press, 1976.

Anderson, Bridget. *Doing the Dirty Work: The Global Politics of Domestic Labour.* London: Zed Books, 2000.

Anderson, Erin. "Immigration Shifts Population Kaleidoscope." *Globe and Mail*, 22 Jan. 2003, A6.

Arat-Koc, Sedef. "In the Privacy of Our Own Home: Foreign Domestic Workers as the Solution to the Crisis in the Domestic Sphere in Canada." *Studies in Political Economy* 28 (1989): 33–58.

———. "Importing Housewives: Non-Citizen Domestic Workers and the Crisis of the Domestic Sphere in Canada." Pp. 81–103 in *Through the Kitchen Window: The Politics of Home and Family* (2nd edition), edited by Meg Luxton, Harriet Rosenberg, and Sedef Arat-Koc. Toronto: Garamond Press, 1990.

———. "Neo-liberalism, State Restructuring and Immigration: Changes in Canadian Policies in the 1990s." *Journal of Canadian Studies* 34, no. 2 (1999/2000): 31–56.

Bibliography

Armstrong, Pat, and Hugh Armstrong. *Double Ghetto: Canadian Women and Their Segregated Work.* Toronto: McClelland and Stewart Inc., 1994.

Arrighi, Giovanni. *Semiperipheral Development.* Beverly Hills: Sage Publications, 1985.

Arrighi, Giovanni, and Jessica Drangel. "Stratification of the World Economy: An Explanation of the Semiperipheral Zone." *Review* 10, no. 1 (Summer 1986): 9–74.

Asis, Maruja M. B. "Asian Women Migrants: Going the Distance, But Not Far Enough." 2003. *Migration Resource Centre.* <www.migrationinformation.org> (retrieved 5 Apr. 2005).

Australian Department of Immigration and Multicultural Affairs. "DIMA Fact Sheet 2: Key Facts in Immigration." <www.immi.gov.au/facts/02key> (retrieved 1 October 2000).

Badets, Jane, and Linda Howatson-Leo. "Recent Immigration in the Workforce." *Canadian Social Trends* Spring (1999): 16–23.

Bakan, Abigail B., and Daiva Stasiulis. "Foreign Domestic Worker Policy in Canada and the Social Boundaries of Modern Citizenship." *Science & Society* 58, no. 1 (1994): 7–33.

———. "Making the Match: Domestic Placement Agencies and the Racialization of Women's Household World." *Signs* 20, no. 2 (1995): 303–35.

———. "Introduction." Pp. 3–27 in *Not One of the Family: Foreign Domestic Workers in Canada,* edited by Abigail Bakan and Daiva Stasiulis. Toronto: University of Toronto Press, 1997.

Baldwin, P. *The Politics of Social Solidarity.* Cambridge: Cambridge University Press, 1990.

Basok, Tanya. "Free to be Unfree: Mexican Guest Workers in Canada." *Labour, Capital and Society* 32, no. 2 (1999): 192–221.

Basran, G. S. "Canadian Immigration Policies and Theories of Racism." Pp. 86–96 in *Racial Minorities in Canada,* edited by P. S. Li and B. S. Bolaria. Toronto: Garamond Press, 1983.

Bishop, Anne. *Becoming an Ally: Breaking the Cycle of Oppression.* Halifax: Fernwood Publishing, 1994.

Bolaria, B. S., and P. S. Li. *Racial Oppression in Canada.* Toronto: Garamond Press, 1988.

Boreham, P. R., et al. "Semi-Peripheries or Particular Pathways: The Case of Australia, New Zealand and Canada as Class Formations." *International Sociology* 4, no. 1 (1989): 67–90.

Bottomore, Tom. *A Dictionary of Marxist Thought.* Oxford: Basil Blackwell, 1983.

Boyd, Monica. "Family Personal Networks in International Migration: Recent Developments and New Agenda." *International Migration Review* 23, no. 3 (1984): 638–70.

———. "Immigrant Women in Canada." Pp. 45–61 in *International Migration: The Female Experience,* edited by Rita Simon and Caroline Brettel. New Jersey: Rowman and Allanheld, 1986.

———. "Immigrant Women: Language, Socioeconomic Inequalities and Policy Issues." Pp. 275–95 in *Ethnic Demography: Canadian Immigrant, Racial and Cultural Variations,* edited by Shiva Halli, Frank Trovato, and Leo Driedger. Ottawa: Carleton University Press, 1990.

Boyle, Paul. "Population Geography: Transnational Women on the Move." *Progress in Human Geography* 26, no. 4 (2002): 531–43.

Braidotti, Rosi. "The Exile, the Nomad, and the Migrant: Reflections on International Feminism." *Women's Studies International Forum* 15, no. 1 (1992): 7–10.

Brennan, Frank. *Tampering with Asylum: A Universal Humanitarian Problem.* Queensland: Queensland University Press, 2003.

Brodie, Janine. "Introduction: Globalization and Citizenship Beyond the Nation State." *Citizenship Studies* 8, no. 4 (2004): 323–32.

Bronson, Diana, and Stephaine Rousseau. "Globalization and Women's Human Rights in the APEC Region." Paper drafted for participants attending the experts' meetings on Globalizations and Workers' Rights in the APEC Region, Kyoto, Japan, November 1995.

Burke, Mike. "Efficiency and the Erosion of Health Care in Canada." Pp. 178–93 in *Restructuring and Resistance: Canadian Public Policy in an Age of Global Capitalism,* edited by Mike Burke, Colin Mooers and John Shields. Halifax: Fernwood Publishing, 2000.

The Calgary Herald. "Immigration Program Eases Hiring." February 7, 2005.

Calliste, Agnes. "Canada's Immigration Policy and Domestics from the Caribbean: The Second Domestic Scheme." Pp. 133–65 in *Race, Class, Gender: Bonds and Barriers,* edited by Jesse Vorst et al. Toronto: Garamond Press, 1991.

———. "Race, Gender and Canadian Immigration Policy: Blacks from the Caribbean, 1900–1932." Pp. 70–87 in *Gender and History in Canada*, edited by Joy Parr and Mark Rosenfield. Toronto: Coop Clarke Ltd, 1996a.

———. "Antiracism Organizing and Resistance in Nursing: African Canadian Women." *The Canadian Review of Sociology and Anthropology* 33 (Aug. 1996b): 361–90.

Carr, Marilyn, and Martha Chen. "Globalization, Social Exclusion and Gender." *International Labour Organization* 143, nos. 1–2 (2004): 129–60.

Castles, Stephen. "Globalization and Migration: Some Pressing Contradictions." *International Social Science Journal* 50, no. 156 (1998): 179–86.

Castles, Stephen, Robyn Iredale and Ellie Vasta. "Australian Immigration Between Globalization and Recession: A Report on the Proceedings of the Immigration Outlook Conference held November 11–13, 1992, Sydney, Australia." *International Migration Review* 28, no. 3 (1994): 370–83.

Castles, S., and M. Miller. *The Age of Migration: International Population Movements in the Modern World*. London: Macmillan Press, 1993.

The Centre Update. "Towards the 21st Century: Heighten the Resistance." 6, no. 3 (1996): 1–2.

Chase-Dunn, Christopher. "Resistance to Imperialism: Semiperipheral Actors." *Review* 12, no. 1 (1990): 1–31.

Cheng, Lucie. "Globalization and Women's Paid Labour in Asia." *International Social Science Journal*, no. 160 (June 1999): 217–28.

The Chinese Women's Collective. *Jin Guo: Voices of Chinese Canadian Women*. Toronto: Women's Press, 1992.

Citizenship and Immigration Canada. *The Monitor*. Spring 2004a. <www.cic.gc.ca> (retrieved 11 Jan. 2005).

———. *The Monitor*. Fall 2004b. <www.cic.gc.ca> (retrieved 10 Feb. 2005).

———. "Recent Immigrant Trends, 1980–2000." *Immigration Occupations: Recent Trends and Issues*. 2004. <www.cic.gc.ca/english/research> (retrieved 9 Dec. 2004).

———. "Facts and Figures 2002: Immigration Overview." (2002): 92–93.

———. "Minister Tables Immigration Levels." 2001. <www.cic.gc.ca/english> (retrieved 21 Jan. 2002).

———. "Canada's Recent Immigrants: A Comparative Report Based on the 1996 Census." 2001.

———. "Annual Immigration Plan for the Year 2000." 1999. <http://cicnet.ci.gc.ca/english/pub/anrep00e.html> (retrieval undated).

———. "Building on a Strong Foundation for the 21st Century: New Directions for Immigration and Refugee Policy and Legislation." Undated. <http://cicnet.ci.gc.ca/english/about/policy/lr/e_lr08.html> (retrieval undated).

The City of Vancouver, Canadian Heritage and MOSAIC. *Building Community: A Framework for Services for the Filipino Community in the Lower Mainland Region of British Columbia*. Vancouver, 2000.

Clark, Tom. "Migrant Workers in Canada." <www.december18.net/paper4Canada.htm> (retrieved 22 Oct. 2000).

Cohen, Marjorie Griffin, and Stephen Clarkson, eds. *Governing Under Stress: Middle Powers and the Challenge of Globalization*. London: Zed Press, 2004.

Cohen, Rina. "The Work Conditions of Immigrant Women Live-in Domestics: Racism, Sexual Abuse and Invisibility." *Resources for Feminist Research* 16, no. 1 (1987): 36–38.

Cohen, Robin. *Global Diasporas: An Introduction*. London: UCL Press Ltd, 1997.

Cornish, Mary, Elizabeth McIntyre and Amanda Pask. "Strategies for Challenging Discriminating Barriers to Foreign Credential Recognition." 1999. <www.cavalluzzo.com/publications/newsletters/access-website> (retrieved 24 Feb. 2005).

Counting on Diversity. "Migration—The Global Context." 1998. Issue 5, February.

Cox, Robert W. "Global Perestroika." Pp. 26–43 in *Socialist Registrar*, edited by Ralph Miliband and Leo Panitch. London: The Merlin Press, 1992.

Culhane, Dara. "Domesticated Time and Restricted Space: University and Community Women in Downtown Eastside Vancouver." Pp. 91–108 in *BC Studies: The British Columbia Quarterly*, edited by Kathy Mezei. Vancouver: The University of British Columbia, 2004.

Cyr, Reiko. "Few Rights for Women Domestic Workers." 2004. <http//ursu.uregina.ca/> (retrieved 23 Oct. 2004).

Dalla Costa, M., and S. James. *The Power of Women and the Subversion of the Community*. Bristol: Falling Wall Press, 1975.

Das Gupta, Tania. "Looking Under the Mosaic: South Asian Immigrant Women." *Polyphony* 8, no. 1/2 (1986): 67–69.

———. "Political Economy of Gender, Race, and Class: Looking at South Asian Women in Canada." *Canadian Ethnic Studies* 26, no. 1 (1994): 59–73.

Dei, George. *Anti-Racism Education: Theory and Practice*. Halifax: Fernwood Publishing, 1996.

Department of Economic and Social Affairs. *2004 World Survey on the Role of Women in Development*. United Nations: New York, 2005.

DeVoretz, Don. *Asian Skilled-Immigration Flows to Canada*. Vancouver: Asia Pacific Vancouver Foundation, 2003.

Driedger, Leo. *Multi-Ethnic Canada: Identities and Inequalities*. Toronto: Oxford University Press, 1996.

Dryburgh, Heather, and Jason Hamel. "Immigrants in Demand: Staying or Leaving?" *Canadian Social Trends* (Autumn 2004): 12–17.

Duffy, Ann, and Norene Pupo. *Part-Time Paradox: Connecting Gender, Work and Family*. Toronto: McClelland and Stewart Inc., 1992.

Dumenil, G., and D. Levy. "The Nature and Contradictions of Neoliberalism." Pp. 244–74 in *The Globalization Decade: A Critical Reader*, edited by L. Panitch, C. Leys, A. Zuege and M. Konings. London: The Merlin Press, 2002.

Eisenstein, Z. *Capitalist Patriarchy and the Case for Socialist Feminism*. New York: Monthly Review Press, 1979.

England, K., and B. Stiell. "'They think you're stupid as your English is': Constructing Foreign Domestic Workers in Toronto." *Environment and Planning* 29 (1997): 195–215.

Esping-Andersen, Gosta. *Politics against Markets*. Princeton: Princeton University Press, 1985.

———. *The Three Worlds of Welfare Capitalism*. Cambridge: Polity Press, 1990.

———. *The Social Transformations of Postindustrial Economies*. New York: Oxford University Press, 1999.

Evans, M. D. R. "Immigrant Women in Australia: Resources, Family and Work." *International Migration Review* 18, no. 4 (1984): 1063–90.

Fincher, R. "Gender, Age and Ethnicity in Immigration for an Australian Nation." *Environment and Planning* 29 (1997): 217–36.

Frank, Andre Guder. *Latin America: Underdevelopment or Revolution*. New York: Monthly Review Press, 1969.

———. *Dependent Accumulation and Underdevelopment or Revolution*. New York: Monthly Review Press, 1979.

Friesen, Wardlow. "APEC and Labour Migration." *Labour, Capital and Society* 31, nos. 1–2 (1998): 44–71.

Gannage, Charlene. *Double Day, Double Bind: Women Garment Workers*. Toronto: The Women's Press, 1986.

Garton, S. and M. McCallum. "Workers' Welfare: Labour and the Welfare State in 20th Century Australia and Canada." *Labour/Le Travail* 38 (November 1996): 116–41.

Gereffi, Gary, and Peter Evans. "Transnational Corporations, Dependent Development, and State Policy in the Semiperiphery: A Comparison of Brazil and Mexico." *Latin American Research Review* 16, no. 3 (1981): 31–64.

Giddings, Lisa, Irene Dingeldey, and Susan Ulbricht. "The Commodification of Lone Mothers' Labor: A Comparison of US and German Policies." *Feminist Economics* 10, no. 2 (2004): 115–42.

Bibliography

Giles, Wenona. "It's the Foreigners Who Do the Laundry." Pp. 80–95 in *Maid in the Market: Women's Paid Domestic Labour*, edited by Wenona Giles and Sedef Arat-Koc. Halifax: Fernwood, 1994.

Gindin, Sam. "The Terrain of Social Justice." *Canadian Dimension* 35, no. 4 (2001): 33–38.

The Global Assembly Line. Prod. Lorraine Gray, Anne Bohlen, and Maria Patricia Fernendez Kelly and dir. Lorraine Gray, 58 min., Educational TV and Film Center, 1986, videocassette.

Globe and Mail. "Volpe Unveils Plan to Approve Immigrants Job Credentials." 26 April 2005, A11.

———. "Settlement of Lawsuit Applies Old, Softer Rules to Would-Be Immigrants." 20 Novermber, 2004, A5.

———. "Bureaucratic Sea Stands Nannies." 16 September 2000, A3.

Goodman, James, ed. *Protests and Globalisation: Prospects for Transnational Solidarity*. Australia: Pluto Press, 2002.

Goldring, Luin. "The Power of Status in Transnational Social Fields." Pp. 165–95 in *Transnationalism from Below: Comparative Urban and Community Research*, edited by Michael Peter Smith and Luis Eduardo Guarnizo. London: Transaction Publishers, 1998.

———. "The Gender and Geography of Citizenship in Mexico-U.S. Transnational Spaces." *Identities* 7, no. 4 (2001): 501–37.

Gorz, Andre. *Critique of Economic Reason*. New York: Verso, 1989.

Gould, A. *Capitalist Welfare States: A Comparison of Japan, Britain and Sweden*. Sweden: Harlow, 1993.

Grandea, Nona. *Uneven Gains: Filipino Domestic Workers in Canada*. Ottawa: The North-South Institute, 1996.

Greenway, Norma. "Newcomers Put Stress on City Services." *Vancouver Sun*, 19 August 2004, A5.

Guarnizo, Luis Eduardo. "The Economics of Transnational Living." *International Migration Review* 37, no. 3 (Fall 2003): 666–99.

Guendelman, Sylvia, and Auristela Perez-Itriago. "Double Lives: The Changing Role of Women in Seasonal Migration." *Women's Studies* 13 (1987): 249–71.

Gulati, Leela. "Asian Women in International Migration: With Special Reference to Domestic Work and Entertainment." *Economic and Political Weekly* 32, no. 47 (1997): 3029–35.

Habib, Sanzida Z. *Gender, Race and Class Biases in Canadian Immigration Policies: The Impact on Women of Color*. Unpublished MA extended essay, Simon Fraser University, 2003.

Halli, Shiva, and Leo Driedger. "The Immigrant Challenge 2000." Pp. 3–17 in *Immigrant Canada: Demographic, Economic, and Social Challenges*, edited by H. Halli and L. Driedger. Toronto: University of Toronto Press, 1999.

Harding, Katherine. "A Leap of Faith." *Globe and Mail*, 8 January 2003, C1.

Harding, Sandra. "Is There a Feminist Method?" Pp. 1–14 in *Feminism and Methodology: Social Science Issues*, edited by Sandra Harding. Bloomington: Indiana University Press, 1987.

Hartmann, Heidi. "The Family as a Locus of Gender, Class, and Political Struggle: The Example of Housework." *Signs* 6: 366–94.

Hefti, Anna Misti Babaylan. "Globalization and Migration." In *European Solidarity Conference on the Philippines: Responding to Globalization*. Zurich: Boldern House, 1997.

Held, Virginia. "Care and the Extension of Markets." *Hypatia* 17, no. 2 (2002): 19–33.

Henry, F., C. Tatar, W. Mattis, and T. Rees. *The Colour of Democracy: Racism in Canadian Society*. Toronto: Harcourt Brace, 1995.

Heyzer, Noeleen. "Introduction: Creating Responsive Policies for Migrant Women Domestic Workers." Pp. xv–xxx in *The Trade in Domestic Workers: Causes, Mechanisms and Consequences of International Migration*, edited by Noeleen Heyzer et al. London: Zed Press, 1994.

Holton, R. J. *Globalization and the Nation-State*. New York: St. Martin's Press, 1998.

Hondagneu-Sotelo, Pierrette. "Regulating the Unregulated: Domestic Workers' Social Networks." *Social Problems* 41, no. 1 (February 1994): 50–64.

Hoogvelt, Ankie. *Globalisation and the Postcolonial World: The New Political Economy of Development*, 2nd edition. Hampshire: Palgrave, 2001.

India Mahila Association. *Spousal Abuse: Experience of 15 Canadian South Asian Women*. Vancouver: India Mahila Association, 1994.

International Labour Organization. "Female Asian Migrants: A Growing but Increasingly Vulnerable Workforce." *International Labour Organization Press Release*, 5 February 1996, 1–3.

———. "As Migrant Ranks Swell, Temporary Guest Workers Increasingly Replacing Immigrants." *International Labour Organization Press Release*, 18 April 1997, 1.

International Organization of Migration. *Overview of International Migration*. Geneva: IOM, 1995.

Jacobson, D. *Rights Across Borders: Immigration and the Decline of Citizenship*. Baltimore: Johns Hopkins University Press, 1996.

Jakubowski, Lisa Marie. *Immigration and the Legalization of Racism*. Halifax: Fernwood Publishing, 1997.

Jang, Brent. "Birth Decline Again; Poor are Living Longer." *Globe and Mail*, 27 September 2002: A1.

Janigan, Mary. "Immigrants: How Many Is Too Many? Who Should Get In?" *Macleans*, 16 December 2002, 20–25.

Jayasuriya, L., and K. Pookong. *The Asianisation of Australia? Some Facts about the Myths*. Melbourne: Melbourne University Press, 1999.

Kagarlitsky, Boris. "The Agony of Neo-Liberalism or the End of Civilization?" *Monthly Review* (June 1996): 36–39.

———. "The Challenge for the Left: Reclaiming the State." *Socialist Registrar* (1999): 294–313.

Keane, John. "Introduction" in *Contradictions of the Welfare State*, edited by Claus Offe. Cambridge, Mass.: The MIT Press, 1984.

Kearney, Michael. "Borders and Boundaries of State and Self at the End of Empire." *Journal of Historical Sociology* 5, no. 1 (1991): 52–74.

Knowles, Caroline. "The Symbolic Empire and the History of Racial Inequality." *Ethnic and Racial Studies* 19, no. 4 (1996): 899–911.

Kofman, Eleonore. "Female 'Birds of Passage' a Decade Later: Gender and Immigration in the European Union." *International Migration Review* 33, no. 2 (1999): 269–99.

Labrador, L. "SIKLAB Takes Part in Breakthrough North American Women's Consultation." *Balitang* [Newsletter of SIKLAB] 4, no. 2 (2001): 9.

Lange, Peter. "Semiperiphery and Core in the European Context: Reflections on the Postwar Italian Experience." Pp. 179–214 in *Semiperipheral Development*, edited by Giovanni Arrighi. Beverly Hills: Sage Publishing, 1985.

Larner, Wendy. "Policy, Ideology, Governmentality." *Studies in Political Economy* 63 (Autumn 2000): 5–25.

Lazarus, Neil. "Charting Globalisation." *Race and Class* 40, nos. 2–3 (1998/1999): 91–109.

Leah, Ronnie. "Anti-Racism Studies: An Integrative Perspective." *Race, Gender and Class* 2, no. 3 (1995): 105–22.

Leira, A. *Welfare States and Working Mothers: The Scandinavian Experience*. Cambridge: Cambridge University Press, 1992.

Levitt, Peggy. "Transnational Migrants: When Home Means More Than One Country." *Migration Policy Institute*. 2004. <www.migrationinformation.org> (retrieved 5 Apr. 2005).

Lutz, Helma. "At Your Service Madam! The Globalization of Domestic Service." *Feminist Review* 70 (2002): 89–104.

Macklin, Audrey. "Foreign Domestic Worker: Surrogate Housewife or Mail Order Servant?" *McGill Law Journal* 37, no. 3 (1992): 681–760.

———. "On the Inside Looking In: Foreign Domestic Workers in Canada." Pp. 13–39 in *Maid in the Market: Women's Paid Domestic Labour*, edited by Wenona Giles and Sedef Arat-Koc. Halifax: Fernwood Publishing, 1994.

Mahler, Sarah. "Engendering Transnational Migration: A Case Study of Salvadorans." *American Behavioral Scientist* 42, no. 4 (1999): 690–719.

Mahon, Rianne. "Gender and Welfare State Restructuring: Through the Lens of Child Care." Pp. 1–30 in *Child Care Policy at the Crossroads: Gender and Welfare State Restructuring*, edited by Sonya Michel and Rianne Mahon. New York: Routledge, 2002.

Mahon, Rianne, and Susan Phillips. "Dual Earner Families Caught in a Liberal Welfare Regime: The Politics of Child Care Policy in Canada." Pp. 191–218 in *Child Care Policy at the Crossroads: Gender and Welfare State Restructuring*, edited by Sonya Michel and Rianne Mahon. New York: Routledge, 2002.

Manery, Margaret, and Marjorie Griffin Cohen. "Community Skills Training by and for Immigrant Women." Pp. 145–60 in *Training the Excluded for Work*, edited by Marjorie Griffin Cohen. Vancouver: UBC Press, 2003.

Massey, Douglas et al. "Theories of International Migration: A Review and Appraisal." *Population and Development Review* 19, no. 1 (1993): 431–66.

Matas, R. "Nanny Gets Back to Work Carrying New Visa Papers." *Globe and Mail*, 6 July 2000, A3.

Maytree Foundation. "Doctor Shortages and the Integration of International Physicians: Opportunities and Solutions." 2001. <www.maytree.com/html.siles/doctorshortageshtm> (retrieved 24 Feb. 2005).

McBride, Stephen. *Paradigm Shift: Globalization and the Canadian State*. Halifax: Fernwood Publishing, 2001.

McKay, Deirdre Christian. *Imaging Igorots: Performing Ethnic and Gender Identities on the Philippine Cordillera Central*. Unpublished Ph.D. dissertation. Department of Geography, The University of British Columbia, 1999.

McMurty, John-Justin. "The Commodity Cul-de-sac." *Socialist Studies Bulletin* 65 (July–December 2001): 5–21.

Mellgren, Doug. "Rich Norway Can't Find Takers for Low-Pay Jobs." *Nation and World*, 19 October 1999.

Meyers, Eytan. "Theories of International Immigration Policy—A Comparative Analysis." *International Migration Review* 34, no. 4 (2000): 1245–82.

Michel, Sonya, and Rianne Mahon, eds. *Child Care Policy at the Crossroads: Gender and Welfare State Restructuring*. New York: Routledge, 2002.

Mies, Maria. *Patriarchy and Accumulation on a World Scale: Women in the International Division of Labour*. London: Zed Press, 1986.

Miliband, Ralph. *Socialism for a Sceptical Age*. Cambridge: Polity Press, 1994.

Morokvasic, M. "Birds of Passage Are Also Women." *International Migration Review* 18, no. 4 (1984): 886–907.

NAID Center. "The Extent, Pattern, and Contribution of Migrant Labor in the NAFTA Countries: An Overview." NAID Center, UCLA. 2001. <http://naid.sppsr.ucla.edu/pubs.news/public/wp-008-00/wr00800intro.1> (retrieval undated).

National Film Board of Canada. *When Strangers Reunite*, prod. Malcom Guy and Michelle Smith and dir. Marie Boti and Florchita Bautista, 51 min., 1999, videocassette.

———. *Who Gets In?* 52 min., National Film Board of Canada, 1989, videocassette.

Nemeth, Roger J., and David. A. Smith. "International Trade and World System Structure: A Multiple Network Analysis." *Review* 8, no. 4 (Spring 1985): 517–60.

Ng, Roxana. "Immigrant Women: The Construction of a Labour Market Category." *Canadian Journal of Women and Law* 4 (1990): 96–112.

———. "Sexism, Racism, and Canadian Nationalism." Pp. 12–26 in *Race, Class, Gender: Bonds and Barriers*, edited by Jesse Vorst et al. Winnipeg: Society for Socialist Studies, 1991.

———. "Managing Female Immigration: A Case of Institutional Sexism and Racism." *Canadian Woman Studies* 12, no. 3 (1992): 20–23.

———. "Racism, Sexism, and Immigrant Women." Pp. 243–77 in *Changing Patterns: Women in Canada*, edited by S. Burt, L. Code, and L. Dorney. Toronto: McClelland and Stewart Inc., 1993.

Ng, Roxana, and Tania Das Gupta. "Nation Builders? The Captive Labour Force of Non-English-Speaking Immigrant Women." *Canadian Woman Studies* 3, no. 1 (1990): 83–85.

Nyberg, Anita. "Gender, (De)commodification, Economic (In)dependence and Autonomous Households: The Case of Sweden." *Critical Social Policy* 22, no. 1 (2002): 63–95.

O'Connor, J., A. Orloff and S. Shaver. *States, Markets, Families: Gender, Liberalism and Social Policy in Australia, Canada, Great Britain and the United States*. Cambridge: Cambridge University Press, 1999.

OECD (Organization for Economic Co-Operation and Development). *Trends in International Migration*. Annual Report, 2000.

Offe, Claus. *Contradictions of the Welfare State* (John Keane, ed.). Cambridge, Mass.: The MIT Press, 1984.

Ohmae, Kenichi. *The Borderless World: Power and Strategy in the Interlinked World Economy*. New York: Harper Business, 1990.

Ordinario, Jane. "Women Form Group to Organize OCWS." *The Centre Update* 5 (1995): 2.

Panitch, Leo. "Globalisation and the State." Pp. 60–93 in *Socialist Registrar*, edited by Ralph Miliband and Leo Panitch. London: The Merlin Press, 1994.

———. "Reflections on Strategy for Labour." Pp. 367–92 in *Socialist Registrar 2001*, edited by Leo Panitch and Colin Leys. London: The Merlin Press, 2001.

Parrenas, Rachel Salazar. "Mothering from a Distance: Emotions, Gender, and Intergenerational Relations in Filipino Transnational Families." *Feminist Studies* 2 (Summer 2001): 361–90.

Pecoud, Antoine, and Paul de Guchteneire. *Migration Without Borders: An Investigation Into the Free Movement of People*. Geneva: Global Commission on International Migration, 2005.

Petras, James, and Todd Cavaluzzi. "Latin American Liberalisation and US Global Strategy." *Economic and Political Weekly*, 7 January 1995, 26–29.

Petras, James, and Henry Veltmeyer. *Globalization Unmasked: Imperialism in the 21st Century*. London: Zed Books, 2001.

The Philippine Times. "Scrap the LCP." Vol. 5, no. 9 (2000): 1–14.

The Philippine Women Centre. *Housing Needs Assessment of Filipino Domestic Workers*. Vancouver: The Philippine Women Centre, 1996.

———. *Trapped: 'Holding on the Knife's Edge.'* Vancouver: The Philippine Women Centre, 1997.

———. *The New Frontier for Filipino Mail-Order Brides*. Policy Research, Ottawa: Status of Women Canada, 2000.

Piper, Nicola, and Rochelle Ball. "Globalisation of Asian Migrant Labour: The Philippine-Japan Connection." *Journal of Contemporary Asia* 31, no. 4 (2001): 533–54.

Polanyi, Karl. *The Great Transformation*. Boston: Beacon Press, 1957.

Portes, A., and J. Walton. *Labor, Class, and the International System*. New York: Academic Press, 1981.

Powell, M., and M. Hewitt. *Welfare State and Welfare Change*. Buckingham: Open University Press, 2002.

Pratt, Geraldine. "Is This Really Canada? Domestic Workers' Experiences in Vancouver, BC." Pp. 1–48 in *Gender, Migration and Domestic Service*, edited by Janet Henshall Momsen. London and New York: Routledge, 1999a.

———. "From Registered Nurse to Registered Nanny: Discursive Geographies of Filipina Domestic Workers in Vancouver BC." *Economic Geography* 75, no. 3 (1999b): 215–36.

Quadagno, J. *How Racism Undermines the War on Poverty: The Color of Welfare*. Oxford: Oxford University Press, 1994.

R. B. Global. "Immigrant Trends." 29 Oct. 2004. <www3.telus.net> (retrieval undated).

Read, Nicholas. "Immigrants Misinformed about Jobs, Martin Says." *Vancouver Sun*, 13 May 2003, A1–2.

Reinharz, Shulamit. *Feminist Methods in Social Research*. Oxford: Oxford University Press, 1992.

Reitz, Jeffery G. "Tapping Immigrants' Skills: New Directions for Canadian Immigration Policy in the Knowledge Economy." *IRPP Choices* 11, no. 1 (February 2005): 2–18.

——. "Occupational Dimensions of Immigrant Credential Assessment: Trends in Professional Managerial and Other Occupations, 1970–1996." 2003. <www.utoronto.ca/ethnicstudies/reitz.html> (retrieved 24 Feb. 2005).
——. "Immigrant Skill Utilization in the Canadian Labour Market: Implications of Human Capital Research." *Journal of International Migration and Integration* 2, no. 3 (2001): 347–78.
Resnick, Philip. "From Semiperiphery to Perimeter of the Core: Canada's Place in the Capitalist World-Economy." *Review* 12, no. 2 (1989): 263–97.
Rosenberg, Harriet. "The Home is the Workplace: Hazards, Stress and Pollutants in the Household." Pp. 57–80 in *Through the Kitchen Window: The Politics of Home and Family* (2nd edition), edited by Meg Luxton, Harriet Rosenberg and Sedef Arat-Koc. Toronto: Garamond Press, 1990.
Samuel, T. John. "Third World Immigration and Multiculturalism." Pp. 383–98 in *Ethnic Demography Canadian Immigrant, Racial and Cultural Variations*, edited by Shiva Halli, Frank Trovato and Leo Driedger. Ottawa: Carleton University Press, 1990.
Sassen, Saskia. "Women's Burden: Counter-geographies of Globalization and the Feminization of Survival." *Journal of International Affairs* 53, no. 2 (2000): 503–24.
——. *The Mobility of Labor and Capital: A Study in International Investment and Labor Flow*. Cambridge: Cambridge University Press, 1998.
——. *Losing Control: Sovereignty in an Age of Globalization*. New York: Columbia University Press, 1996.
——. "Beyond Sovereignty: Immigration Policy Making Today." *Social Justice* 23, no. 3 (1996a): 9–20.
——. *The Global City: New York, London, Tokyo*. Princeton: New Jersey, 1991.
Satzewich, Vic. *Racism and the Incorporation of Foreign Labour: Farm Labour Migration to Canada since 1945*. New York: Routledge, 1991.
Schiller, Nina Glick, and Linda Basch. "From Immigrant to Transmigrant: Theorizing Transnational Migration." *Anthropological Quarterly* 68, no. 1 (1995): 48–64.
Seacomb, Wally. "The Housewife and Her Labour Under Capitalism." *New Left Review* 83, (1974): 3–24.
Sen, Amartya. *Poverty and Famines: An Essay on Entitlement and Deprivation*. Oxford: Oxford University Press, 1981.
Sharma, Nandita. "On Being Not Canadian: The Social Organization of Migrant Workers in Canada." *The Canadian Review of Sociology and Anthropology* 38, no. 4 (2001): 415–39.
Shaw, Gillian, and Michael McCullough. "Ottawa to Help Foreign Doctors and Nurses in the Workforce." *Vancouver Sun*, 26 April 2005, A1.
Silvera, Makeda. *Silenced: Talks with Working Class Caribbean Women about Their Lives and Struggles as Domestic Workers in Canada* (2nd edition). Toronto: Sister Vision, 1989.
Singh, Manisha. "A 19-Year-Old Herstory: India Mahila Association." *Kinesis*, March (1993): 10–11.
Sivanandan, A. "Globalism and the Left." *Race and Class* 40, nos. 2–3 (1998/1999): 5–19.
Skeldon, Ronald. "Migration in Asia after the Economic Crisis: Patterns and Issues." *Asia Pacific Population Journal* 14, no. 3 (1999): 3–24.
Smith, Ekuwa, and Andrew Jackson. "Does Rising Tide Lift All Boats? The Labour Market Experience and Incomes of Recent Immigrants, 1995–1998." Canadian Council on Social Development, Ottawa. 2002. <www.ccsd.ca/pubs/2002> (retrieved 24 Feb. 2005).
Smith, Linda Tuhiwai. *Decolonizing Methodologies: Research and Indigenous Peoples*. London: Zed Books, 1999.
Smith, Marilyn. "Recognition of Foreign Credentials: A Survey of Recent Community-Based and Research Projects (1995–2001)." 2001. <www.pch.gc.ca/progs/multi/pubs/ras/sra-ras-e.pdf> (retrieved 24 Feb. 2005).
SOPEMI Norway. *Trends of Migration to and from Norway and the Situation of Immigrants in Norway*. Norway: The Directorate of Immigration, 2001.

Stalker, Peter. *International Migration*. Oxford: New Internationalist Publications Ltd., 2001.
Stanley, Liz. *Feminist Praxis: Research, Theory and Epistemology in Feminist Sociology*. New York: Routledge, 1990.
Statistics Canada. "Earnings of Immigrant Workers and Canadian-born Workers 1980–2000." *The Daily*. 8 Oct. 2003 <www.statcan.ca/daily> (retrieved 13 Sept. 2004).
———. "Employment Rates, By Selected Countries." *The Canadian Labour Market at a Glance*. 2004. <www.statcan.ca/english/freepub/71-222-XIE/2004000/chart-p87.htm> (retrieval undated).
———. *The Canadian Labour Market at a Glance*. 2004. <www.statcan.ca/english/freepub/71-222-XIE/2004000/chart-p85.htm> (retrieval undated).
Stein, Janice Gross. "The Global Context of Immigrants." Pp. 27–45 in *Canadian Immigration Policy for the 21st Century*, edited by Charles M. Beach, Alan G. Green and Jeffrey G. Reitz. Montreal and Kingston: McGill-Queen's University Press, 2003.
Stephen, Lynn. "Globalization, the State, and the Creation of Flexible Indigenous Workers: Mixtec Farmworkers in Oregon." *Urban Anthropology* 30, nos. 2–3 (2001): 189–214.
Strange, S. *The Retreat of the State: The Diffusion of Power in the World Economy*. Cambridge: Cambridge University Press, 1996.
Tacoli, Cecilia. "International Migration and the Restructuring of Gender Asymmetries: Continuity and Change among Filipino Labor Migrants in Rome." *International Migration Review* 33, no. 3 (Fall 1999): 658–82.
Taran, Patrick. "Seven Causes of Migration in the Age of Globalization." Paper for International Migration Policy and Law Course for Asia-Pacific, Bangkok, Thailand, November 1999.
———. "Migration and Migrants Rights: International Dimensions." Paper presented at the Symposium on Migration in the Americas, San Jose, Costa Rica, September 2000.
Taylor, K. W. "Racism in Canadian Immigration Policy." *Canadian Ethnic Studies* 23, no. 1 (1991): 1–19.
Teeple, Gary. *Globalization and the Decline of Social Reform*. Toronto: Garamond Press, 1995.
———. "What is Globalization?" Pp. 9–23 in *Globalization and Its Discontents*, edited by S. McBride and J. Wiseman. New York: Macmillan Press, 2000.
Terlouw, C. P. "The Elusive Semiperiphery: A Critical Examination of the Concept Semiperiphery." *International Journal of Comparative Sociology* 34, nos. 1–2 (1993): 87–102.
Third World Network. "Asian Female Migrant Workers Require Protection." 2001. <www.twnside.org.sg/title/ilo1.cn.htm> (retrieval undated).
Thobani, Sunera. *Globalization and Racialization of Citizenship in Late 20th Century Canada*. Unpublished Ph.D. dissertation, 1998.
Thompson, Allan. *Toronto Star*. 19 February, A9, 2003.
Thompson, Eden. *Immigrants and the Canadian Labour Market: An Overview*. Human Resources Development Canada, 2002.
Toronto Star. "Immigration: Funding Does Not Add Up." 8 April 2005, A21.
———. "A Mess Martin Could Clean Up." 7 February 2005, A14.
———. "Editorial: Easing Immigrants' Way." 27 April 2005, A24.
Tyner, James. "The Global Context of Gendered Labour Migration from the Philippines to the United States." *American Behavioral Scientist* 42, no. 4 (1999): 671–89.
———. "The Globalization of Transnational Labor Migration and the Filipino Family: A Narrative." *Asia and Pacific Migration Journal* 11, no. 1 (2002): 95–116.
UNESCO. "The Migration Boom." *UNESCO SOURCES* (Magazine) January (1998).
Ungerleider, Charles. "Immigration, Multiculturalism, and Citizenship: The Development of The Canadian Social Justice Infrastructure." *Canadian Ethnic Studies* 26, no. 3 (1992): 7–21.
United Nations. *2004 World Survey on the Role of Women in Development. Women and International Migration*. New York: Department of Economic and Social Affairs, UN, 2005.
Vancouver Sun. "B. C. Gets Failing Grade in Services from Immigrants." Vancouver Sun, 22 February 2005, A1.

Vosko, Leah. *Temporary Work: The Gendered Rise of a Precarious Employment Relationship.* Toronto: University of Toronto Press, 2000.

Wallerstein, Immanuel. *The Modern World System, Capitalist Agriculture and the Origins of the European World Economy in the Sixteenth Century.* New York: Academic Press, 1974.

———. "The Rise and Future Demise of the World System: Concepts for Comparative Analysis." *Comparative Studies in Society and History* 16 (1974): 387–415.

———. *The Capitalist World Economy.* Cambridge: Cambridge University Press, 1979.

———. "The Relevance of the Concept of Semiperiphery to Southern Europe." Pp. 31–39 in *Semiperipheral Development*, edited by Giovanni Arrighi. Beverly Hills: Sage Publications, 1985.

Waring, Marilyn. *If Women Counted: A New Feminist Economics.* San Francisco: Harper, 1988.

Weiss, Linda. "Globalization and the Myth of the Powerless State." *New Left Review* 225 (Sept./Oct. 1997): 3–27.

Wichterich, Christa. *The Globalized Woman: Reports from a Future of Inequality.* Trans. Patrick Camiller. London: Zed Books, 2000.

Wiest, Raymond E. "External Dependency and the Perpetuation of Temporary Migrants to the United States." Pp. 110–35 in *Patterns of Undocumented Migration: Mexico and the United States*, edited by Richard C. Jones. Totowa, N.J.: Rowman and Allanheld, 1984.

Williams, Allan, and Vladimir Balaz. "From Private to Public Sphere, the Commodification of the au pair Experience? Return Migrants from Slovakia to the UK." *Environment and Planning* 36 (2004): 1813–33.

Williams, Colin C. "A Critical Evaluation of the Commodification Thesis." *The Editorial Board of the Sociological Review* (2002): 525–42.

Williams, Colin C., and Jan Windebank. "The Slow Advance and Uneven Penetration of Commodification." *International Journal of Urban and Regional Research* (2003): 250–64.

Wilson, Tamar Diana. "Weak Ties, Strong Ties: Network Principles in Mexican Migration." *Human Organization* 57, no. 4 (1998): 394–403.

The Windsor Star. "Immigration: Ontario's Valid Argument." 18 March 2005: A8.

Women's Book Committee and Chinese Canadian National Council. *Jin Guo: Voices of Chinese-Canadian Women.* Toronto: Women's Press, 1992.

Zaman, Habiba. *Women and Work in a Bangladesh Village.* Dhaka: Narigrantha Prabartana/Feminist Bookstore, 1996.

Zaman, Habiba, and Gina Tubajon. "'Globalization from Below': Feminization of Migration, Resistance and Empowerment—A Case Study." *Canadian Journal of Development Studies* 22 (2001): 1109–29.

Zlotnik, Hania. "Trends of International Migration since 1965: What Existing Data Reveal." *International Migration* 37, no. 1 (1999): 21–61.

Index

Index note: page references in *italics* indicate a figure on the designated page

accreditation: Canadian certificate as alternative to, 127–28; costs of, 79, 121; gender factor in, 119; interviews on the process of, 120–28; overview, 117–19; role of institutions in, 119; time requirements for, 122. *See also* recommodification

accreditation system: national standardization of requirements, 118, 122, 123, 131–32; recommendations for improving, 129–31, 141, 160

Alberta, immigrant recruitment rights, 56

Asia: economic benefits of immigrant labor to, 33, 70; immigration industry in, 33–34, 47; policies affecting immigration from, 42, 46–47, 51, 53, 62–64, 66; recruitment of labor from, 30, 63–64; societal role of women in, 31, 34, 51, 62, 95–96, 119, 132; source-country standing, 1, *43–44*, 44–46, *45*; transnational migration in, 31–32, 33; women working abroad, statistics on, 30, 33. *See also specific countries in Asia*

Asian immigrants: attitudes toward state assistance, 128; job placement of, 101–2; racist myths regarding, 15; settlement patterns, 55, 137

Australia, politics of immigration, 18n1, 28–30, 36

Balagan, Sarah, 139

Bangladeshi immigrants, 28, 32, 135–36

British Columbia: accreditation process, 122, 127; commodification of health care, 92; daycare costs vs. domestic help, 72n14; eldercare demand growth, 82–83; federal funding for new immigrant services, 57, 105, 107; Filipina domestic worker statistics, 77; labor regulation and monitoring, 73, 86, 87, 98–99, 108; language training courses, 57, 107; political activism of South Asians, 64; settlement statistics, 55. *See also* Vancouver, British Columbia

Cables, Ms., 140

Canada: childcare accessibility in, 132; costs of non-recognition of credentials to, 57; costs of underutilization of skills to, 58; domestic care crisis in, 88; economic benefits of immigrant labor to, 28; eldercare demand growth in, 82–83; emigration of skilled worker entrants from, 48–49; native vs. immigrant participation in the labor market, 53–54, 66; semi-periphery status of, 5–6

Canada, federal government: funding for new immigrant programs, 56–57, 64;

gender equity employment strategies, 65, 116; initiative for foreign-trained workers, 116; minimum wage and work hours in, 98; new immigrant program funding, 56–57, 64, 105; politics of immigration, 29–30; settlement programs, 55–58. *See also* immigration policies

Canada, federal government, neo-liberal policies and: commodification, 64–67, 76–77, 115; immigration planning, 39–40; labor migration, 70–71; new immigrant program funding, 56–57, 64; social benefits, 82–83, 94–95

Canada, provincial governments: accreditation in, 118; childcare/eldercare funding, 69, 75, 76; new immigrant program funding, 56; reliance on global market for domestic labor, 48, 76

Canada Employment and Immigration Centres (CEIC), 97

Caribbean countries, recruitment of labor from, 67, 77

Caribbean Domestic Scheme, 77

childcare: daycare costs vs. domestic help, 69, 72n14; deregulation and privatization of, 69, 75; duties of domestic workers, 80–81, 84, 87, 106–7, 142; for immigrant women, 111, 132, 160

China, 42–46, 43–44, 63

Chinese Immigration Acts, 63

citizenship, domestic workers' eligibility for, 3, 46, 53, 67–69, 84–87, 163

commodification: concept, 74–76; LCP perpetuation of, 8, 17, 73–74, 80–83, 88–89; of lone mothers, 75, 95; neo-liberalism and, 64–67, 76–77, 115, 157; non-, 9; pre-, 8–9; psychological, 85–87; in study framework, 7–11; of temporary workers, 88–89, 160; under-, 8–9, 74–77, 155–57, 160; welfare state and, 74–76, 78, 82–83, 86–88, 92–94. *See also* decommodification; recommodification

commodification, partial: commodification vs., 9; concept, 9, 69; erosion of skills and, 77–79; familial obligations and, 100, 101, 106–7, 117, 158; immigration processes and, 81; neo-liberalism and, 157; working conditions supporting, 85, 88

commodification layers, 3, 157

Contemplacion, Flor, 149

contract labor, 2, 30–31, 63–64, 70. *See also* temporary workers

Contradictions of the Welfare State (Offe), 115

decommodification: conservative vs. social democrat positions on, 94–95; defamilialization and, 68, 81, 87–89, 157; in study framework, 7–11

decommodification barriers: accreditation process, 120–28; accurate skills assessment on entry, 118; affordable housing, 110–11, 140; childcare, lack of subsidized, 111, 132, 160; dependency classification of entrants, 34, 47–53, 61–62, 64–67, 93, 97, 107, 112, 132, 134; familial obligations, 106–7, 111; financial need, 97, 99; government programs, access to, 57, 64, 66–67; labor regulation and monitoring, 82–84, 86–89, 98–99, 108; non-recognition of credentials, 54, 57, 62, 66, 82–83, 96, 102, 105–6, 131, 141; organizational assistance lacking, 104–5; range of workplace, 98–101; re-skilling costs, 79, 107; skills erosion, 42, 77–84, 141; skills underutilization, 117–19, 158; social benefits and entitlements access, 92–94, 98–99, 101, 105–12, 132, 145–46; social safety net erosion, 82–83, 105; summary, 158, 160; training program access, 57, 107–9, 160. *See also* Live-in Caregiver Program (LCP)

decommodification barriers, employment-related: Canadian work experience, 95–98, 124, 128; discrimination, 66, 96, 102–3, 111–14, 123–25, 143–46; flexible work hours, 98–101, 158; lack of opportunities, 102–4, 111–14; methods of obtaining jobs, 86–87, 101–4

decommodified sectors, 7–11

defamilialization and decommodification, 68, 81, 87–89, 157

de-skilling process, 42, 77–84, 141

discrimination, employment-related: age/ethnicity/gender intersection, 111–14, 123–24; Canadian work experience requirement as, 95–98, 124, 128; gender-based, 65, 102–3, 116; race-based, 66, 102–3, 124–25, 143–46

discrimination, in immigration policies: by class, 3, 73; by gender, 11–12, 31–32, 40, 47–53, 64–67; history of, 62–63; by job skills, 39–40, 48; by race, 11, 39–40

Domestic Scheme, 8, 62, 67–69, 77

domestic workers: accreditation process, 120–28; Canadian-born women as, 67; citizenship opportunities, 3, 53, 67–69, 84–87, 163; demand for, 1–2, 48, 76, 103–4,

129–31; duties of, 80–84, 87, 128–29, 142; educational backgrounds of, 78; employment outside the LCP, 86–87, 101–3; execution of Flor Contemplacion, 149; housing needs, 140; labor regulation and monitoring, 76, 78, 80, 82–84, 86–89; live-out, 69; living conditions of, 85; mothering from a distance, 88–89; networking by, 102, 103–4, 143; physical demands on, 80–81, 82, 128, 129; power of, 103–4; primary countries of origin, 67, 70, 77; on quitting work, 85, 103–4, 109, 142–43; recruitment of, historically, 67–69; resistance strategies, 142–43; skills erosion in, 77–83, 141; social benefits and entitlements access, 92–94; wages, 72n14, 80–81, 85, 86, 87, 142–43, 151, 167; working conditions, 69, 80–81, 82, 85, 87, 151. *See also* immigrant labor; Live-in Caregiver Program (LCP)

domestic workers, commodification of: historically, 76–77; partial, 9, 69, 77–79, 81, 85, 100, 101, 106–7, 157, 158; psychological, 85–87

Domestic Workers' Association (DWA), 147

eldercare: deregulation and privatization of, 69, 75, 82–83; by domestic caregivers, 81–83, 128–29

El Salvador, 27–28

emigration, causal factors, 45–46

Employment Standard Acts (ESA), 98–99

family: commodification of the, 62, 74–75, 77, 79–84, 85–86; immigrant obligations to, 100, 101, 106–7, 111, 117, 158

family class entrants: classified as dependents, 34, 47–53, 61–62, 64–67, 93, 97, 107, 112, 132, 134; entrant statistics (2000–2002), 47; gender/education distribution, 51, 52; preference for, 39–40, 46–49, 47; social rights and entitlements of, 48, 64–65, 93, 97, 107

Filipinas: barriers to citizenship, 163; immigrant worker statistics, 55, 71, 77; LCP and LEP link to migration of, 69–71, 133, 136, 138; remittances to families, 33, 81; settlement patterns, 56; trafficking of, 56, 141, 151. *See also* Philippine Women Centre (PWC); SIKLAB

Filipino Nurses Support Group (FNSG), 120–21, 150–51, 168

Foreign Domestic Movement program (FDM), 68

Gabriela Network, 141
Germany, 75, 94
Global Commission on International Migration, United Nations, 29
global economy, labor in the, 33–34, 48–49
globalism: globalization vs., 4–5, 22–23
globalism, neo-liberal: commodification resulting from, 2; ideology of, 4; migration and, 2, 22–24, 30, 45, 46, 62, 70–71
globalization, 4–5, 21–26, 140–41, 149

Haiti, remittances from women migrants, 33

immigrant categories: business class, 51, 53; economic class, 65; entrepreneur class, 51, 100–101; family class, 39–40, 46–49, 47, 51, 52, 65; independent class, 65; refugee, 40, 41, 46; skilled class, 39–40, 46–49, 47, 48–49, 51, 53

immigrant labor: importing countries, 28–31, 36; labor market participation, 53–55, 66; primary source countries, 1, 32–33, 42–46, 43–44, 45; recruitment of, historically, 2, 62–64, 67–69. *See also* domestic workers

immigrant labor, female: accreditation process, 79, 120–28; as agents of change, 135–36; class consciousness in, 100–101; conclusions, 155–60; demographic profiles of study interviewees, 161–68; discrimination against (*see* discrimination); educational qualifications of, 34, 51–53, 52, 66, 78, 111–13; employment opportunities, 1–2, 112, 113, 129–31; employment rates for vs. native-born, 53, 66; in health care, 120–31, 150–51, 168; hotel workers, 125–26; introduction, 1–11; methods of obtaining jobs, 96–97, 101–4, 109; networking, formal and informal, 34, 101–4, 146–49; organizational assistance, 104–6, 108; resistance strategies, 142–53, 159; single, difficulties of, 97–98; social rights and entitlements, 93, 96, 97–99, 101, 105–12, 132, 145–46; study framework, 12–18, 35–37; trafficking of, 56, 141, 151; wages, 144; working conditions, 99, 106, 108–9, 144, 151. *See also* domestic workers

immigrant labor, female, resistance strategies: collective, 149–53, 159; individual, 142–46
immigrants: costs of immigrating, 53, 56, 63, 79, 107; defined, 3–4; discrimination against (*see* discrimination); integration of, 55–58; national identity duality in, 28; primary countries of origin, 42–45, *43–44, 45*; selection criteria, 165; settlement patterns, 55–58. *See also by specific nationality*; migrants
immigrants, statistics: by age, 50, 55; by category, 47; demographic composition (1967–2003), 42–46; by educational levels, 52, 66; employment rates vs. native-born, 53, 66; Filipinos, percentage female, 55; by gender, 51; number of entrants, 3, 6, 39, 55; primary-source countries, *43–44*; professional-level, by gender, 51; skilled category, by gender, 51; technical-level, by gender, 51
Immigration Acts, 11, 39–40, 44–45, 47–49, 62–66
immigration policies: affecting Asian immigration, 42, 46–47, 51, 53, 62–64, 66; Annual Immigration Plan, 39–42, *41*, 46–47, 69; influences on, 29–30, 36; liberalization of, 39–40; points system, 44, 47–48, 49, 62, 64; recommendations for improving, 160; for refugees, 40, *41*, 46; selection criteria, shifts in, 39–40, 44, 46–49. *See also* Canada, federal government
immigration policies, discrimination in: by class, 3, 53, 73; by gender, 11–12, 31–32, 40, 47–53, 64–67; history of, 62–63; by job skills, 39–40, 46–49, *47*; by race, 11, 39–40
immigration theory, 35–37
India: female emigration restrictions, 32; history of recruitment from, 63–64; source-country standing, 42, *43–44*, 46
India *Mahila* Association (IMA), 64, 135–38, 152, 159
International Monetary Fund (IMF): Structural Adjustment Policies (SAP) of, 24
International Mother Language Day, 28
International Organization of Migration, 1

job training programs, 57, 107–9, 160

Kalayaan Centre. *See* Philippine Women Centre (PWC)

Labor Export Policy, Philippines' (LEP), 16, 62, 69–71, 136
landed immigrant status, 3, 53, 68–69, 163. *See also* citizenship, domestic workers' eligibility for
language training programs, 57, 107
Live-in Caregiver Program (LCP): citizenship opportunities with, 3, 68, 69, 163; commodification perpetuated by, 8, 17, 62, 73–74, 76–77, 80–83, 88–89; domestic workers on, 80, 83, 86; LEP and, 69–71; live-in requirement of, 9, 69–70, 78, 82, 88, 133, 140; neo-liberal globalism and the, 62; recommendations for improving, 132–33, 160; relocation of social reproduction with, 69–71, 75; statistics, 77; two-tier immigration perpetuated by, 3, 73. *See also* temporary workers
lone mothers' commodification, 75, 95

Maga, Delia, 149
methodology vs. method, 12
MIGRANTE International, 28, 139
migrants: defined, 3; economic, 46; environmental, 24; female, statistics on, 2, 31–35; international, statistics on, 2, 26, 29; primary countries of origin, 1, 31–32. *See also* immigrants; transmigrants
migration: causal factors, 24, 32–33, 69; feminization of, 31–35; globalization and, 1, 24–26; neo-liberalism and, 70–71; post-9/11, 30–31; transnational, 4–5, 26–34
Montreal, Quebec, 55
mothering from a distance, 33, 88–89

national identity, 28–29, 36
9/11: effect on immigration, 46, 136
non-commodification, 9. *See also* commodification
NO! to APEC campaign, 140, 149

Ontario, 55, 57, 82–83

Pakistan, 32, *44*, 44, 46
People's Republic of China (PRC) *See* China
permanent residents, 46, 67, 84–87. *See also* citizenship, domestic workers' eligibility for
Philippines: contract workers, statistics, 70, 71; economics of labor export, 32, 70–71; Gabriela Network, 141; Labor Export

Policy (LEP), 16, 62, 69–71, 136; settlement patterns of immigrants, 55–56; source-country standing, 43–44, 45–46; transmigrants' political power, 28. *See also* Filipinas; Philippine Women Centre (PWC)
Philippines 2000 plan, 70
Philippine Women Centre (PWC): membership restrictions, 139; political advocacy role, 28, 138–42, 146, 148–53, 159; in study framework, 12–14, 135, 168; summary, 159. *See also* Filipinas
pre-commodification, 8–9. *See also* commodification

Quebec: immigrant settlement in, 55–56

recommodification, 115–17, 158, 159. *See also* accreditation system; commodification
refugee immigrants, 40, 41, 46
re-skilling. *See* accreditation system; recommodification

Scandinavia, welfare state in, 6–7, 93, 94
Second Domestic Scheme, 67, 77
semi-periphery countries, 4–5, 28
SIKLAB, 139–40, 147–50
skilled class entrants: emigration from Canada, 48–49; gender distribution, 51; number of entrants (2000–2002), 47; preference for, 39–40, 46–49, 47, 51, 53
skills erosion, 77–84, 141
South Asian Women's Centre (SAWC), 64, 135–36, 152–53

technological change, link to migration, 24
Temporary Employment Authorization Program, 67, 76–77

temporary workers: commodification of, 88–89, 160; LCP immigrants' classification as, 3, 163; liberalized trade policies and, 24; receiving countries' preference for, 36. *See also* contract labor; Live-in Caregiver Program (LCP)
Toronto, Ontario: immigrant settlement in, 55
trade liberalization, 2, 24
transmigrants, 3, 27–29, 31–33. *See also* migrants
transnational migration theory, 35–37

under-commodification, 8–9, 74–77, 155–57, 160. *See also* commodification
United States, 7, 27–28, 70, 75, 94

Vancouver, British Columbia: Bangladeshi immigrant settlement, 136; domestic worker statistics, 77; ESL classes available, 57; immigrant activism in, 136–38, 140–41, 148–50, 153; immigrant settlement statistics, 55

wealth gap, 29, 34
welfare state: commodification and the, 74–76, 78, 82–83, 86–88, 92–94; neo-liberalism and the, 23; overview, 6–8; in Scandinavia, 6–7, 93, 94
welfare state regime types: conservative, 6, 10, 94–95; liberal, 6, 7, 10, 55, 74, 94–95; social democratic, 6, 10, 74, 93, 94–95
When Strangers Unite (film), 89
women, Canadian-born: class-based labor force, 124–25; commodification of, 65; defamilialization and decommodification in, 68, 81, 87–89, 157; as domestic laborers, 67; employment rates for vs. immigrants, 53, 66; racialized division of labor, 124–25

About the Author

Habiba Zaman is an associate professor in the Department of Women's Studies at Simon Fraser University, British Columbia, Canada, where she teaches women in the economy, feminist research methods, gender and international development and women in cross-cultural perspectives. Zaman is the author of *Women and Work in a Bangladesh Village* (Narigrantha Prabartana/Feminist Bookstore, Dhaka, Bangladesh, 1996) and *Patriarchy and Purdah: Structural and Systemic Violence against Women in Bangladesh* (Life and Peace Institute, Uppsala, Sweden, 1998). She has published in such journals as *Women's Studies International Forum*, *International Journal of Canadian Studies*, *Atlantis*, *Journal of Contemporary Asia*, *Canadian Journal of Development Studies*, *Asian Profile* and *Journal of Developing Areas*.